Sugar and the Making of International Trade Law

This book traces the changing meanings of free trade over the past century through three sugar treaties and their concomitant institutions. The 1902 Brussels Convention is an example of how free trade buttressed the British Empire. The 1937 International Sugar Agreement is a story of how a group of Cubans renegotiated their state's colonial relationship with the US through free trade doctrine and the League of Nations. And the study of the 1977 International Sugar Agreement maps the world of international trade law through a plethora of institutions such as the ITO, UNCTAD, the GATT, and international commodity agreements – all against the backdrop of competing Third World agendas. Through a legal study of free trade ideas, interests, and institutions, this book highlights how the line between the state and market, domestic and international, and public and private is always a matter of contest.

Michael Fakhri is an assistant professor at the University of Oregon School of Law, where he teaches courses in international economic law, food law, and agricultural law.

CAMBRIDGE STUDIES IN INTERNATIONAL AND COMPARATIVE LAW

Established in 1946, this series produces high quality scholarship in the fields of public and private international law and comparative law. Although these are distinct legal sub-disciplines, developments since 1946 confirm their interrelations.

Comparative law is increasingly used as a tool in the making of law at national, regional, and international levels. Private international law is now often affected by international conventions, and the issues faced by classical conflicts rules are frequently dealt with by substantive harmonization of law under international auspices. Mixed international arbitrations, especially those involving state economic activity, raise mixed questions of public and private international law, while in many fields (such as the protection of human rights and democratic standards, investment guarantees and international criminal law) international and national systems interact. National constitutional arrangements relating to "foreign affairs," and to the implementation of international norms, are a focus of attention.

The series welcomes works of a theoretical or interdisciplinary character, and those focusing on the new approaches to international or comparative law or conflicts of law. Studies of particular institutions or problems are equally welcome, as are translations of the best work published in other languages.

A list of books in the series can be found at the end of this volume.

Sugar and the Making of International Trade Law

Michael Fakhri

CAMBRIDGE
UNIVERSITY PRESS

CAMBRIDGE
UNIVERSITY PRESS

University Printing House, Cambridge CB2 8BS, United Kingdom

Cambridge University Press is part of the University of Cambridge.

It furthers the University's mission by disseminating knowledge in the pursuit of education, learning and research at the highest international levels of excellence.

www.cambridge.org
Information on this title: www.cambridge.org/9781107040526

First published 2014

A catalogue record for this publication is available from the British Library

Library of Congress Cataloguing in Publication data
Fakhri, Michael, author.
Sugar and the making of international trade law / Michael Fakhri.
pages cm. – (Cambridge studies in international and comparative law; 114)
ISBN 978-1-107-04052-6 (hardback)
1. Sugar laws and legislation. 2. Sugar trade. 3. Commercial law. 4. Foreign trade regulation. 5. Law – International unification. I. Title.
K3947.S93F35 2014
382′.456641–dc23

2014014343

ISBN 978-1-107-04052-6 Hardback

Contents

Acknowledgements

This book was made possible through the support and friendship of numerous people. I cannot list everyone and I am bound to miss a few names, so it is best to list the networks and institutes through which I have had the most helpful conversations. Over the years I have benefited from people affiliated with the African International Economic Law Network, Annual Junior Faculty Forum for International Law, European Society of International Law, Society of International Economic Law, Toronto Group for the Study of International, Transnational and Comparative Law. I have most benefited from Third World Approaches to International Law (TWAIL) and hope I have been able to give back to this movement. I am extremely grateful for grants from the Wayne Morse Center for Law and Politics, and the Institute for Global Law and Policy at Harvard Law School; each one also provided me with the opportunity to be part of their wonderful communities. I am grateful to the University of Oregon School of Law, under the leadership of Michael Moffitt and Adell Amos, for providing me with the resources and time I needed to finish the book. I was also lucky to have two comrades-in-arms, Ibrahim Gassama and Michelle McKinley, who gave me the moral support I needed on a daily basis.

A number of individuals were incredibly kind with their time in regard to specific parts of this book: Antony Anghie, Lorand Bartels, Lara Bovilsky, Ruth Buchanan, Steve Charnovitz, B. S. Chimni, Patricia Clavin, Matt Craven, Andrew Green, Michael Hames-García, Hendrik Hartog, Susan Karamanian, David Kennedy, Benedict Kingsbury, Karen Knop, Dino Kritsiotis, Andrew Lang, Doreen Lustig, Risham Majeed, Erez Manela, Manivelle, Mark Mazower, Usha Natarajan, Liliana Obregón, Anne Orford, Sundhya Pahuja, Rose Parfitt, Kal Raustiala, Guy Sinclair, Thomas Skouteris, Fleur Johns and Joseph H. H. Weiler.

Kerry Rittich has read the largest number of versions of this book. I am indebted to her generosity, keen eye, and pressing questions. Many thanks also to Professor James Crawford, Kim Hughes, Finola O'Sullivan, and Richard Woodham at Cambridge University Press.

Some of the treaties that I examine in this book, I have studied in a narrower context in "The 1937 International Sugar Agreement: Neo-Colonial Cuba and Economic Aspects of the League of Nations" (2011), 24 *Leiden Journal of International Law* 89, and "The Institutionalisation of Free Trade and Empire: A Study of the 1902 Brussels Convention" (2014), 2 *London Review of International Law* 1.

This book would not have been possible without the dedication and kindness of librarians and archivists from Cornell University, League of Nations Archives at the UN Office in Geneva, Redpath Sugar Museum in Toronto (which is excellently curated by Richard Feltoe), Virginia Kelly Karnes Archives and Special Collections Research Center at Purdue University, University of Oregon (especially Kelly Reynolds), and University of Toronto. My thanks to Jason Tashea for his skills in the German language, Sara van Dijck for her skills in the French language, and to Elizabeth Brown and Will Johnson for their editorial assistance.

Finally, I owe the greatest debt to Joe Fakhri, Ragheda Fakhri, Mark Fakhri, Omar Naim, Lina Mounzer, the fdz, Domenico Romano, Marianne Romano, and (especially) Lisa Romano, for their love, support, and patience.

Abbreviations

BET	basic export tonnage
BISD	Basic Instruments and Selected Documents
ECLA	United Nations Economic Commission for Latin America
EEC	European Economic Community
EFO	Economic and Financial Organization
FAO	Food and Agriculture Organization
GATT	General Agreement on Tariffs and Trade
ICA	International Commodity Agreement
ICCICA	Interim Coordinating Committee for International Commodity Arrangements
ILO	International Labour Organization
ISA	International Sugar Agreement
ISI	import substitution industrialization
ISO	International Sugar Organization
ITO	International Trade Organization
LNTS	League of Nations Treaty Series
LON	Archives of the League of Nations, Library of the League of Nations, Geneva, Switzerland
MFN	most favored nation
NIEO	New International Economic Order
SCM	WTO Agreement on Subsidies and Countervailing Measures
UNCTAD	United Nations Conference on Trade and Development
UNTS	United Nations Treaty Series
WTO	World Trade Organization

Table of cases

Lochner v. *New York*, 198 US 45 (1905) 28n84

Uruguay – Recourse to Article XXIII, Panel Report, adopted November 16, 1962, BISD 11S/95 170n691

EC – Sugar Exports (Australia), Panel Report, *European Communities – Refunds on Exports of Sugar*, L/4833, adopted November 6, 1979, BISD 26S/290 188n765

EC – Sugar Exports (Brazil), Panel Report, *European Communities – Refunds on Exports of Sugar – Complaint by Brazil*, L/5011, adopted November 10, 1980, BISD 27S/69 188n765

US – Gasoline, Appellate Body Report, *United States – Standards for Reformulated and Conventional Gasoline*, WT/DS2/AB/R, adopted May 20, 1996 141n562

US – Shrimp, Panel Report, *United States – Import Prohibition of Certain Shrimp and Shrimp Products*, WT/DS58/R and Corr.1, adopted November 6, 1998, as modified by Appellate Body Report WT/DS58/AB/R 141n561

US – Gambling, Panel Report, *United States – Measures Affecting the Cross-Border Supply of Gambling and Betting Services*, WT/DS285/R, adopted April 20, 2005, as modified by Appellate Body Report WT/DS285/AB/R 141n561

Mexico – Taxes on Soft Drinks, Panel Report, *Mexico – Tax Measures on Soft Drinks and Other Beverages*, WT/DS308/R, adopted March 24, 2006, as modified by Appellate Body Report WT/DS308/AB/R 149n592

Mexico – Taxes on Soft Drinks, Appellate Body Report, *Mexico – Tax Measures on Soft Drinks and Other Beverages*, WT/DS308/AB/R, adopted March 24, 2006 149n592

Table of agreements and resolutions

PART I

Prologue

The power of the book . . . lies in its ability to make the familiar strange – so that the reader sees it in a new light.

Cayley, "Ideas: Markets and Society. Part Three – Socialism and Freedom"

1 International institutions as part of the history of agriculture

One cannot discuss international trade law and policy without some reference to the World Trade Organization (WTO). Even with the proliferation of bilateral and regional trade agreements, the multilateral institution remains a principal component of international trade law. How is it, then, that the idea of multilateral institutions came about and became an important practice and arrangement?

The answer lies in an account of agriculture. The history of agriculture begins approximately 12,000 years ago in the Neolithic era. Agriculture has been central to many moments of human social transformation, playing a role (though not always one of causation) during profound innovations in law, social relations, political economy, and religion.[1] Against the backdrop of the long history of agriculture, we can examine international institutions, which are first created in the late nineteenth century, as a relatively novel phenomenon.

Around 1400 CE, people around the world developed a number of modes of (mainly agricultural) production.[2] Some places were organized through a tributary mode in which a famer or herdsman was granted access to land and resources, and in return they paid a tribute to a political or military ruler. Others were kin-based, in which the social organization of working and producing was structured around different ideas of consanguinity, marriage, and affinity. Other people organized themselves through capitalism, which was a mode in which

[1] Toynbee, *Industrial Revolution*; Weber, *Roman Agrarian History*; Friedmann and McMichael, "Agriculture and the State System"; Cauvin, *Birth of the Gods*; Mazoyer and Roudart, *History of World Agriculture*.

[2] Wolf provides an elucidating definition of modes of production: "a specific, historically occurring set of social relations through which labor is deployed to wrest energy from nature by means of tools, skills, organization, and knowledge." Wolf, *Europe*, p. 75.

one group – capitalists – controlled and restricted the means and tools of production. Those people who produced goods through work – laborers – had to sell their time for money in order to gain access to the very goods that they produced and all their other needs.[3] Capitalism's principal goal was to indefinitely accumulate and employ labor, land, and money – capital – in order to accumulate and generate more capital.

By 1760, the invention of the steam engine sped up transportation and mechanized production of agricultural products. Legal innovations in agricultural land expanded industry's geographic scope and compressed rates of production. Due to new enclosure laws, wealthy men (property transactions were a gendered affair) were now able to buy what was formerly common land. Since more land was now available to be bought and sold, wealthy people were more willing to devote resources to improve the land's fecundity, since they could now reap all the financial benefits from their investment. As a result, farms increased in size and productivity.[4] The territorial expansion of private property law's purview also meant that small farmers and herdsmen lost their right of pasturage and were forced to sell their time and labor to landlords.

Yet the most fundamental transformation that occurred at the end of the eighteenth century was the interlacing of capitalism with industrialization in Western Europe. In the past, merchants bought and sold goods for the everyday use of different social classes. Industrial production always had its own historical relationship with commerce and mostly served the needs of merchants. Thus, industry mostly produced what was socially needed. Now commerce began to serve industry. Merchants began trading in the elements of industry. They saw profit in meeting industrialists' growing demand for long-term investments in machinery, raw materials, and infrastructure (and learned to share their distaste for risk).[5]

By the late nineteenth century, British technology and know-how behind agricultural industrialization began to spread to other parts of the world. With the spread of industrialization, capitalism followed. People, goods, and wealth were now travelling around the world at unprecedented speeds and were being bought and sold on a global scale. This was also when the British Empire was at the height of its

[3] *Ibid.*, pp. 73–100. [4] Toynbee, *Industrial Revolution*, pp. 62–3.
[5] Polanyi, *Great Transformation*, pp. 74–5.

power and territorial scope. Imperialism was driven by the dynamic of territorial expansion. As such, it needed new modes of governance to rule on a global scale. By mode of governance, I mean a specific, historically occurring set of social relations through which authority is deployed to direct a certain group's activities by means of violence, organization, and knowledge.

International law was one of the many new modes of governance forged out of empire.[6] The publication of the first international law journal, the *Revue de droit international et de législation comparée*, in 1868, and the creation of the *Institut de droit international* in 1873, marked the moment that international law became the profession that we recognize today. It shifted from being the musings of "professors and philosophers, [as well as] diplomats with an inclination to reflect on the procedure of their craft," to becoming the practice of lawyers.[7]

International institutions were another mode that emerged from the same context of capitalism and imperialism. Today, international law and institutions are deeply intertwined and we now describe international institutions as lawmakers unto themselves.[8] But the history of international institutions does not arise from the optimistic, humanist imagination of the men of 1868 and 1873. Rather, it is a history told in more functionalist and pragmatic terms.[9]

The history of international trade institutions is predominantly drawn from the practice of diplomats, politicians, civil servants, capitalists, and economists. Only recently, with the creation of the WTO in 1994, have lawyers become important protagonists.[10] This is not to say that there was no theory of law informing the work of these non-lawyers over the past century in how they designed and negotiated international trade institutions. But it is because most of the people were not lawyers that today's trade law has not focused on this history.

To determine how international law, international institutions, capitalism, and imperialism are configured and interact is to follow a moving target, since they constantly change over time. I therefore focus on a single, everyday agricultural commodity – sugar – to explain the relationship amongst these histories. I use sugar "as a kind of trace

[6] Anghie, *Imperialism.* [7] Koskenniemi, *Gentle Civilizer*, pp. 17, 41.
[8] Alvarez, *International Organizations as Law-makers.*
[9] Kennedy, "The Move to Institutions."
[10] Hudec, "GATT Legal System"; Weiler, "The Rule of Lawyers."

element, tracking the direction of change,"[11] in order to outline the complex intersections of old and new ideas, interests and institutions.

I investigate three sugar treaties and their concomitant institutions: the 1902 Brussels Convention,[12] the 1937 International Sugar Agreement (ISA),[13] and the 1977 ISA.[14] I examine the text, structure, and preparatory work of the trade treaties within the political context and economic discourse of the time, juxtaposed against the international social history of certain sugar-producing countries. I do so in order to investigate what it means to organize trade through a multilateral institution and discern how institutionalization involves the prioritizing, marginalizing, and exclusion of certain ideas and interests.[15]

We will see that the 1902 Brussels Convention was intended to buttress the British Empire by supporting colonial sugar plantations and to secure the Crown's control over the West Indies. The economic purpose was to stabilize the price of sugar in order to attract private investment to the sugar-harvesting industry in the West Indies. The 1937 ISA was an attempt by the Cuban elite to renegotiate their neocolonial relationship with the US. It was also part of plans by Cuban businessmen and North American financiers to develop the island economically. The 1977 ISA was part of the Third World's demand to redress imperial patterns of global poverty. Former colonies were now newly independent states, but still economically dependent on former imperial masters. International lawyers had little to say about the first two sugar treaties and institutions; it was not until the last sugar treaty that they began to put sugar treaties, and commodity agreements in general, in their sights.

Sugar has always been central to industry and empire, and has transformed global economic history.[16] Slave-driven sugar mills of the seventeenth century were one of the earliest factories.[17] But the history

[11] Grew, "Food and Global History," pp. 1, 6.

[12] International Convention Relative to Bounties on Sugar, Brussels, March 5, 1902, 191 *Parry* 56, 1902 *Foreign Relations* 80, Cd 1535.

[13] International Agreement Regarding the Regulation of the Production and Marketing of Sugar, London, May 6, 1937, League of Nations, *International Sugar Conference*, p. 7; also reprinted in International Labour Office, *Commodity Control*, p. 26.

[14] International Sugar Agreement, 1977, New York, October 28, 1977, 1064 UNTS 219.

[15] For an analysis of how contemporary international regimes affect the international political economy of sugar, see Richardson, *Sugar*.

[16] Higman, "The Sugar Revolution."

[17] Pomeranz and Topic, *World that Trade Created*, p. 225.

of sugar predates these modern developments. It is a history that witnesses the transformation of an unassuming plant into a global commodity. For most of its existence, sugar in the human diet was a luxury that came in the form of sucrose extracted from sugar cane.[18] Only in the nineteenth century did sugar beet become a competitor to sugar cane. And only starting in the 1970s did sucrose start losing out to high-fructose corn syrup and artificial sweeteners that dominate the contemporary industrialized diet.[19]

What began as a grass native to Southeast Asia, was picked up in Persia by Arab traders. They were the first to introduce sugar to the European palate, as the Umayyad Empire expanded into Europe through Spain and Sicily during the seventh and eighth centuries CE.[20] Later, crusaders established sugar cane plantations in the Levant and Mesopotamia, and brought news of what was considered an exotic spice from the Orient. European nobility then started to incorporate sugar as a luxurious additive, elevating the flavor of food and forming part of the stock for apothecaries.[21] By 1440, sugar began replacing honey in the diet of European nobility.[22] Braudel notes that in 1544 there was a German saying, *Zucker verderbt keine Speis* ("sugar spoils no dish").[23]

Sugar first came to the so-called New World on Columbus's second voyage in 1493.[24] This set the foundation for centuries of African slave labor sustaining sugar cane plantations in the Americas.[25] By the seventeenth century, the French and British had acquired a voracious appetite for coffee, tea, and cocoa; because of this hot beverage revolution, sugar was no longer a luxury item and become an everyday good.[26] The British were one of the first nations to move away from a starch-rich diet towards a sugar-rich diet. By the end of the eighteenth century, sugar was a staple in Britain, as many cups of sweet tea were incorporated

[18] I am referencing sucrose throughout this study when I discuss "sugar" unless otherwise noted.

[19] Pollan, *The Omnivore's Dilemma*, pp. 102–3.

[20] For general histories of sugar, see Deerr, *History of Sugar*; Toussaint-Samat, *History of Food*, pp. 552–63.

[21] Geerligs, *Sugar Industry*, p. 5; Fernández-Armesto, *Thousand Tables*, p. 81.

[22] Galloway, *Sugar*, pp. 1–10. [23] Braudel, *Civilization and Capitalism*, p. 191.

[24] Sugar was part of the "Columbian Exchange," which involved the movement of a large variety of plants, animals, foods, human populations, communicable diseases, and ideas between the Eastern and Western hemispheres after 1492, greatly affecting ecological conditions. See Crosby, *Columbian Exchange*.

[25] Mintz, *Sweetness and Power*, p. 32.

[26] Clarence-Smith, "Global Consumption of Hot Beverages."

into the diets of workers, providing a "calorie-laden stimulant that warms the body and blunts the pangs of hunger."[27] Mintz notes that this change in diet coincided with the Industrial Revolution, exemplifying one sort of modernization. According to Mintz, however, it is not entirely clear whether the Industrial Revolution caused the dietary transformation, or if Britons' taste for sweetness facilitated fundamental industrial and social changes in British society.[28]

Sugar is central to the colonial history of the formation of many states and territories, such as Hawaii, Louisiana, Puerto Rico, Brazil, Cuba, Haiti, Indonesia, India, Taiwan, and the Philippines.[29] Some suggest that the desire for sugar was a driving force of imperial expansion.[30] Others propose that imperial expansion reduced the price of sugar, enabling popular consumption.[31] Regardless, sugar (along with coffee, tea, and cocoa) played an important part in the expansion of the British and other European empires.

Sugar may very well have been central to the history of modern trade law because the nature of sugar production lends itself to competing transnational interests. Sugar cane harvested from the fields must be processed into raw sugar. The mill that processes cane into raw sugar must be close to the fields to ensure that the cane does not spoil. One mill would be a center of power fed by multiple peripheral sugar cane fields. As such, mill owners often constituted a sugar elite within their own country, with ties to international capital, or were owned by foreign investors. People could eat moist, raw sugar, but the demand was highest for white, refined sugar. Refining was also where much of sugar's economic value was added. Most refineries were located in industrialized countries. One refinery might source its raw sugar from different points around the world. Thus, there was also a global pattern of an industrialized center drawing sugar from mills in the periphery. All this created a relationship of dependence and disparity of power between sugar growers and sugar refiners.

As I will soon discuss further, international trade institutions emerged when the geography of world sugar production changed with the rise of the sugar beet. Cane sugar's course began in warm climates and traversed through Europe as a luxury export, a slave-produced staple and a colonial good. Early cane-processing technology was

[27] Mintz, *Sweetness and Power*, pp. 45, 80. [28] *Ibid.*, p. 14.
[29] Abbott, *Sugar*, pp. 270–310; Wolf, *Europe*, pp. 333–6.
[30] Fernández-Armesto, *Thousand Tables*, p. 181. [31] Galloway, *Sugar*, pp. 1–10.

principally steam-powered, whereas sugar was first extracted from beetroot during the late eighteenth to early nineteenth century in Prussia, through chemical and mechanical innovations, directly from harvest to refinement. Soon after, beet sugar entered into the quotidian diet in Europe and beetroot spread across the colder soils of Europe and North America.

2 Histories as context

An emphasis on institutions

Before delving into the history of sugar and trade law, I will briefly consider some of the theoretical understandings that informed my research and explain how I structured this book. Each sugar treaty is addressed in a separate part. Each part is comprised of two chapters. The first chapter of each part outlines the broader institutional context in which I situate the treaty. Thus, the 1902 Brussels Convention is about the British Empire. The 1937 ISA is about the League of Nations and US-Cuban imperial relationships. And the 1977 ISA is about how the world of international trade law was constituted by a plethora of institutions, such as the International Trade Organization (ITO), United Nations Conference on Trade and Development (UNCTAD), the General Agreement on Tariffs and Trade (GATT), and international commodity agreements (ICAs) – all against the backdrop of Third World politics. These contextual chapters of each part serve as historiographies. The purpose is to bring different bodies of knowledge into conversation with one another. I have drawn from other disciplines and literatures, and interpreted them in order to understand how and why multilateral trade institutions came about. The second chapter of each part focuses on the specific sugar treaty.

More importantly, however, the contextual chapters are also an argument as to why I think certain institutions provide the best insight into the meaning of free trade. Each sugar institution has been informed by a conception of free trade. But what free trade means is not predetermined and simply formalized in the text of the treaty. Rather, free trade is defined through the struggles, arguments, and compromises that lead to the creation and operation of an institution;

in turn, each institution redefines the meaning of free trade. Indeed, "the task of international lawyers is to think about how concepts move across time and space. The past, in other words, may be a source of present obligations."[32]

The history of trade law is most often an account of the GATT and WTO. The story is often told and there is no reason to repeat it here.[33] For its first decade, the GATT was thought by many to be a small club of rich, industrialized countries.[34] Recently, there has been a re-emphasis on the role of developing countries, from the beginning of GATT negotiations to the end of the Uruguay Round in 1994.[35]

Yet the history of modern trade law remains narrow in space and time. First, on temporality: even those histories that take a perspective of international trade law before the Second World War do so from the perspective of the GATT by noting the history of GATT doctrines in previous centuries. In this way, the GATT acts as the historical centerpoint for modern international trade law in that international trade agreements and doctrines are either pre-GATT or post-GATT. A GATT-centric account has obscured the fact that modern trade law has its origins at the end of the nineteenth century within the context of imperialism – a context most relevant to developing countries. Second, on spatiality: this version of trade law has done away with appreciating the role of multilateral trade institutions such as UNCTAD and ICAs in the regulation of international trade for several decades.

Shifting the historical and institutional context of international trade law opens up free trade to a wider array of understandings. In the most general terms, free trade is the idea that international trade should be free from state intervention. Since this has framed trade law and policy for more than a century, the central issue that people have debated has been what constitutes unwanted state intervention. Questions that soon follow are: What constitutes the state and the market? Where is the line between the state and market? When is state action characterized as

[32] Orford, "Past as Law or History?, pp. 97, 99.

[33] See, e.g., Jackson, *World Trading System*, pp. 31–78; Odell and Eichengreen, "The United States, the ITO, and the WTO"; Weiss, "Havana to Marrakesh," p. 155; Zeiler, *Free Trade*; Gallagher, *WTO: 1995–2005*; Irwin, Mavroidis, and Sykes, *GATT*.

[34] Hudec, *International Trade Law*, pp. 11–12.

[35] See, e.g., Ismail, "Developing Countries in GATT"; Wilkinson and Scott, "Developing Country Participation in the GATT."

necessary to support the market as opposed to an unwarranted intervention? When are exceptions justified?

These questions assume that there is a demarcation between the political and the economic. This assumption is a unique and key characteristic of capitalism. It is also inherently a political act, which means that how the two spheres are separated determines who gets to decide so-called economic matters. The separation reconfigures power and authority in such a way that makes it more difficult to determine how people make choices (as well as coerce and resist) in the market. The result is that capitalists' decisions regarding production levels, which profoundly affect workers' lives, are treated as "economic." As such, they are not as easily subject to political scrutiny or social contestation. From another perspective, the political options available to workers are reduced because the assumption is that they are at the mercy of the impersonal forces of the market, with little hope for the significant redistribution of wealth and power. The problem, therefore, with separating the political from the economic, is that it most often privileges capitalists' interests over labor's interests.[36]

Each sugar treaty has drawn and redrawn the line between the supposedly political, public state and the economic, private market quite differently. Moreover, because these treaties were about the buying and selling of goods across borders, this raised the question of where to construct the line between international and domestic – which was always a matter of negotiation. While sugar allows us to track patterns of capitalism and imperialism, tracing the legal concepts that informed the treaties of the time allows us to understand how these tensions between state and market were understood and contested.

The work of Karl Polanyi provides some guidance in this regard. In *The Great Transformation*, Polanyi set out to understand what caused the political and economic crisis that led to the Great Depression and the Second World War.[37] What makes Polanyi so attractive to read while studying international institutions is that he provides a way of understanding different scales of governance. Inherent in his work is a

[36] Polanyi, *Great Transformation*, pp. 71, 51–55; Wood, "Separation."

[37] Polanyi, *Great Transformation*. On the benefits and limits of using Polanyi, especially in regard to the Third World, see Fakhri, "Law." This chapter is by no means intended to be a definitive reading of Polanyi. While there are disagreements over how to read Polanyi, what I found helpful are the terms of those debates.

transnational sensibility that allows us to navigate the local, national, regional, imperial, international, and global.[38]

Polanyi's first thesis was that historically markets were "submerged" in social relationships and as such can be considered as enmeshed or embedded in society.[39] This meant that social needs dictated markets' function and purpose. People acted not to safeguard their individual interest in material goods, but to safeguard their social standing, social claims, and social assets.[40]

Polanyi was reacting against a theory that assumed that the market was and is separate from society. He was responding to the premise that "instead of economy being embedded in social relations, social relations are embedded in the economic system."[41] Polanyi warned, however, that this theory of a "market society" – which assumed that the political and economic spheres were in fact separate – was a stark utopia that had violent consequences.[42] Evoking William Blake, he pointed to how the destructive nature of markets was most apparent (and acute) during the Industrial Revolution in England, when new technologies radically improved the tools of production, while at the same time drastically disrupting common people's lives through "satanic mills."[43] He was concerned that whenever market forces determined how people interacted with each other, they eroded the structures that enabled people to realize social principles such as reciprocity, redistribution, and householding (producing for one's own use).[44]

In his later work, Polanyi stated that the economy "is embedded and enmeshed in institutions, economic and noneconomic," and described the economy as an "instituted process."[45] By "economy," he meant the interchange of humanity and the "natural and social environment, in so far as this results in supplying him with the means of material want and satisfaction."[46] "Process" was meant to suggest motion – that is, movement in location (through means of production or transportation) or appropriation (through the regulation and administration of goods).[47] Institutionalization of the economy was that which vested the economic process with unity and stability. It also provided structure and definite function in society, thereby adding significance to history, and focused "interest on values, motives and policy."[48]

[38] Block, "New Understanding"; Ebner, "Polanyi Problem."
[39] Polanyi, *Great Transformation*, pp. 45–6. [40] *Ibid.*, pp. 43–55. [41] *Ibid.*, p. 57.
[42] *Ibid.*, p. 3. [43] *Ibid.*, pp. 33–42. [44] *Ibid.*, pp. 51–5. [45] Polanyi, "Economy."
[46] *Ibid.*, pp. 243, 250. [47] *Ibid.*, p. 248. [48] *Ibid.*, pp. 249–50.

Polanyi never explicitly defined what he meant by institution (which he used interchangeably with "system"). Generally, he considered institutions as the social instruments that translate interests into politics. One could extract from his writing that what Polanyi may have meant by an institution was the "established centers, regular meetings, common functionaries, or compulsory code of behavior." Institutions were made up of various laws made effective by customary practice.[49]

This leads to Polanyi's second thesis, regarding the "double movement" created by the market. According to Polanyi, certain social actors benefit the most from the buying and selling of commodities. Driven by a desire to obtain as much profit as possible, their interest is to try to create a market society by transforming as many items and endeavors as possible into a commodity. Time and time again, these actors – merchants, financiers, landowners, and the like – successfully push the market to become the principal institution structuring economic life (as opposed to redistributive or reciprocative institutions). This first move causes the market to have a destructive social effect, by unleashing poverty, dislocation, and hardship. Other social actors, in turn, organize their political power and respond with a countermovement, demanding and creating laws and institutions in order to ameliorate the ensuing social disruption. To Polanyi, a market society remains in tension between the (market) move and (social) countermove.

Such a conception of change requires social actors to act based on their interests. Polanyi provides a dynamic sense of how to determine interests and class, which formed when "not the economic but the social interests of different cross sections of the population were threatened by the market, persons belonging to various economic strata unconsciously joined forces to meet the danger."[50] Class is a historically contingent concept, and determining interests is neither obvious nor economically determined. Groups and individuals coalesce depending on the political and economic conditions of their time in an effort to protect themselves from social hardship and calamity. It was from these interests being put into operation that institutions were formed. Notably, laws and institutions not only reflected certain interests, but they also had the effect of changing people's perception of their social

[49] Polanyi, *Great Transformation*, pp. 8, 262.
[50] *Ibid.*, pp. 155–6. *Cf.* Rasulov, "'Nameless Rapture'."

reality.[51] Thus, institutions also had the effect of influencing what interests in the future came together as a common social class.

Polanyi did not only look at interests, but also accounted for how ideas themselves shaped what social actors considered possible choices. Polanyi took stock of how European policy-makers believed in liberal market policies and theories of laissez-faire as creed.[52] So, for example, during the major currency fluctuations in the 1920s, "belief in the gold standard was the faith of the age."[53] Herein lay the paradox that could only be explained by how influential the theory of the time was. Most policy-makers believed that currencies should be stabilized by any means necessary, especially since a stable currency was sought to ensure the flow of foreign trade. All foreign policies were directed towards stabilizing currencies in service of the gold standard. Nonetheless, to ensure a stable currency, they had to enact laws and policies that in effect restricted trade and foreign payments. Governments sacrificed their economies by reducing trade and closing markets in order to ensure a stable currency. To Polanyi, these sorts of economic dogmas were what created a sense of an automatic march to the Great War. He had been deeply horrified by how surreptitiously the world found itself in conflict, and sought to understand how decisions that were intended to avoid global political and economic crisis actually contributed to triggering war and depression.

Context as argument

Polanyi suggested that the market was embedded in social structures, yet he never provided a definition of society. Not surprising, then, that the word "embedded" has now become a term of art with different meanings and uses.[54] But Polanyi's lack of definition of society is not necessarily an analytical shortcoming.[55] I suggest that defining what is "society" is part of the effort involved in the double movement. It is the ideational and political struggle over defining society that shapes the market and respective institutions.

From a researcher's perspective, this means that determining the appropriate institutional context is not self-evident. An argument

[51] Polanyi, *Great Transformation*, pp. 77–85. [52] *Ibid.*, pp. 135–62. [53] *Ibid.*, p. 25.
[54] Beckert, "Embeddedness"; Dale, *Polanyi*, pp. 188–206; Buğra and Agartan, *Reading Karl Polanyi*, pp. 4–5.
[55] Burawoy, "Sociological Marxism."

regarding which institutions matter reveals one's own intuitions about what constitutes society. By arguing that the 1902 Brussels Convention, 1937 ISA, and 1977 ISA were some of international trade law's most defining multilateral institutions, I am suggesting that trade law is about constantly redefining capitalism and imperialism, and negotiating between agriculture and industry. A propensity for the GATT most likely arises from a partiality for manufactured products alongside an assumption that capitalism is inevitable and imperialism was historically extraneous to trade law.

Reading Polanyi makes me think that while social actors struggle to determine how institutions will configure the market's role in society, they look to law as a central object of contestation. Indeed, Polanyi's imagery of a market as always enmeshed within institutions aligns with the work of legal realists such as Robert Hale and Morris Cohen.[56] Polanyi, like Hale and Cohen, argued against the notion that the idea of the market and interventionism are mutually exclusive terms:

> For as long as [the system of a self-regulating market] is not established, economic liberals must and will unhesitatingly call for the intervention of the state in order to establish it, and once established, in order to maintain it. The economic liberal can, therefore, without inconsistency call upon the state to use the force of law.[57]

In reading Polanyi, Hale, and Cohen, we can think of markets as institutions in and of themselves, constantly interacting with other social institutions. There is no separation between law and the market, or state and the market. Rather, the law and the state are constitutive of the market. Like Polanyi, legal realists argued that "a free market system could not be distinguished in a significant sense from a regulatory system."[58]

In *The Great Transformation*, laws (which constitute institutions) were created to establish and re-establish the market's role as the primary institution structuring society. Laws were also created as a pushback dynamic of the double movement to compensate for the market's destructive effect. Moreover, laws and institutions reflected a compromise or uneasy tension between market actors and other social actors. Law is not simply characterized as representing the interests of the

[56] Hale, "Coercion"; Cohen, "Property"; Cohen "Basis of Contract." See Rittich, *Recharacterizing Restructuring*, pp. 127–52.

[57] Polanyi, *Great Transformation*, p. 149.

[58] Singer, "Legal Realism Now," 482.

ruling class; rather, it exemplifies the mix of societal interests and structures. Society's laws and institutions therefore contain within them the conflict and tension of competing social interests.

This complexity means that law can represent the interests of social actors who benefit from the primacy of the market, or social actors reacting against the transformative nature of the market, or a compromise amongst a number of social actors. With this sort of analysis, law is the terrain of conflict and negotiation for both aspects of the double movement – law structures the market and is also part of the countermovement against attempts to create a market society.[59]

Recall that according to Polanyi, prevailing ideas and institutions determine what choices are possible. For example, once the international gold standard was institutionalized, the idea was further legitimized and prevailed over all domestic and international economic policy. What actual decisions are then taken leads to the creation of new institutions. In turn, those new institutions condition how future social actors understand their interests and how policy-makers understand what changes may be possible. Institutions provide the authority to certain ideas, thereby providing social actors with the repertoire of tools to make choices.[60] As such, to argue over the appropriate institutional context is a debate over what choices are possible.

[59] Dale, *Polanyi*, pp. 201–2. [60] David, "Institutions."

PART II

The 1902 Brussels Convention and the beginnings of modern trade law

The earth seemed unearthly. We were accustomed to look upon the shackled form of a conquered monster, but there – there you could look at a thing monstrous and free. It was unearthly, and the men were – No, they were not inhuman. Well, you know that was the worst of it – this suspicion of their not being inhuman. It would come slowly to one.

Conrad, *The Heart of Darkness*, p. 62

THE CONTROL OF THE FACTORY. A modern factory must be conducted from the mill to the distillery as a huge chemical experiment, and efforts be made to account for every pound of sugar entering the factory; the losses should be located, and where possible corrected; where canes are purchased, not only should their weight be systemically checked, but what is as important as their actual weight, the time between cutting and milling should be strictly controlled, and perhaps, most important of all, the economic limit of mill extraction with maceration processes should be carefully determined for the conditions of the particular factory in question.

Deerr, *Sugar and the Sugar Cane*, p. 281

3 Free trade as an imperial project

The 1902 Brussels Convention was arguably the earliest modern international trade treaty that established a multilateral institution. The treaty was the result of negotiations mainly among the UK, Germany, Austria-Hungary, and France. The primary conflict was between British sugar cane producers in the West Indies and sugar beet producers in continental Europe. West Indian planters were frustrated by the European system of sugar subsidies; they believed that European subsidies were undue government interference in the sugar market, thereby destabilizing (and lowering) world sugar prices. Thus, "the sugar question became international."[61]

The treaty's principal purpose was to discourage governments from subsidizing sugar production. It did so by allowing countries to impose countervailing duties against subsidized (or "bounty fed" in the language of the time) sugar from any country, regardless of whether the sugar originated from a non-signatory country. As such, the treaty created an incentive for signatory and non-signatory countries to do away with their bounty system as soon as possible if they wanted access to the UK, which was the largest sugar-consuming market in the world. In effect, the treaty ended in 1912–13, when the UK refused to renew its membership.[62]

[61] Lapeyrade, *La Question des Sucres*, p. 152.

[62] Great Britain refused to sign the agreement protocol on March 17, 1912 and declared that it would withdraw from the Convention as of September 1, 1913. See Despatches to His Majesty's Minister at Brussels Respecting the Signature and Ratification of the International Sugar Union, Cd 6146 (1912); Correspondence Relating to the Withdrawal of His Majesty's Government from the Brussels Sugar Convention, Cd 6325 (1912); Correspondence Relating to the Withdrawal of His Majesty's Government from the Brussels Sugar Convention, Cd 6877 (1913).

The Brussels Convention has mostly been a minor historical note in the study of international trade law and international institutions. As such, one has to determine how to situate it in time and space. Despite the sugar treaty's origins in the late nineteenth century, I suggest that the Brussels Convention provides one of the earliest examples of how modern free trade was institutionalized. Further, we can only determine the relevant global power dynamics for the purposes of understanding this treaty if we take into account the fact that sugar was extracted from the tall canes towering in warm European colonies and former colonies, as well as from the stubby beetroots growing in the ground of colder continental Europe. While I focus on the British West Indies and nineteenth-century British Empire (and, to a lesser degree, continental Europe) in the next chapter, I first present some global context and touch upon various prominent sugar markets. I briefly address exporters such as Cuba, Brazil, and Java, and importers such as the US.[63] In the next chapters, we will see how these other areas indirectly affected decisions that led to the creation of the Brussels Convention.

The world's first modern multilateral trade institution

A modern institution

The Brussels Convention created an international trade institution (sometimes called the Sugar Union) that in many respects we would recognize as contemporary in form and function. What I mean by "modern" is that the 1902 institution included many mechanisms that can be found in contemporary trade agreements. The treaty included a "most favored nation" clause (Art. V), regulated against subsidies (or "bounties") (Art. I), allowed for countervailing duties and retaliation (Art. IV), and addressed matters of "like" or "analogous" products (Art. I).

The 1860 Cobden-Chevalier Treaty is often credited as one of the earliest free trade treaties. But this treaty was simply a bilateral agreement between the UK and France. Sometimes the 1815 Central Commission for Navigation on the Rhine or the 1885 General Act of the Berlin Conference on West Africa are noted as being the earliest multilateral free trade treaties. However, these treaties governed trade through the negotiation of territorial access and rights. Whereas the Brussels Convention, like

[63] During this time, British India produced a significant amount of sugar. But it was also a major consumer and therefore a net importer of sugar.

treaties of today, governed trade by regulating the movement (and production) of an actual good through a permanent multilateral institution.

The 1902 Brussels Convention was most "curious and anomalous" for its time, since its Permanent Commission exercised an unprecedented amount of power over the signatory states.[64] Like the WTO, the treaty established a permanent organizational structure, the Permanent Commission, that not only held administrative duties of collecting and publicizing information, but also functioned to resolve disputes and to ensure adherence to the agreement (Art. VII). The Permanent Commission was composed of delegates of the Contracting States. The Permanent Commission was aided by a Permanent Bureau that addressed matters of collecting and disseminating technical information. One early scholar of international organizations goes so far as to consider the Brussels Convention "the first [agreement] to give an international committee power to dictate policy."[65] This power to determine policy led the few, early scholars of international organizations to portray the Brussels Convention as an exemplar for other international institutions.[66]

I also characterize the Brussels Convention as modern because it coincided with innovations in sugar harvesting and refining technology, food production, and data gathering and processing. These advances allowed for new modes of governance through the use of statistics and monitoring. This parallels Foucault's account of how the technical science of statistics paved the way for modern modes of governmentality.[67] The Permanent Commission collected information from every country regarding the details of industrial output and unique systems of domestic regulation, accounting for different grades and colors of sugar.[68] This information was thought to be necessary to calculate the amount that sugar was subsidized and the appropriate countervailing duty. It would not have been possible to establish this international system of economic management without the sugar-related innovations in statistics in the late nineteenth century. During this time, a great number of statistical firms arose in Europe which collected data for the purpose of predicting future trends in the sugar market. Franz

[64] Woolf, *International Government*, p. 246. [65] Mander, *Foundations*, p. 237.

[66] See, e.g., Reinsch, *Public International Unions*, pp. 50–1; Sayre, *Experiments*, pp. 15–16.

[67] Statistics allowed technocrats to define a "population," thus shifting the model of government away from the family and towards the state. Foucault, *Security, Territory, Population*, pp. 104–5.

[68] Geerligs, *Sugar Industry*, pp. 378–80.

Otto Licht established one of the first German sugar statistical firms, which remains today as the one of the most influential publishers of sugar reports and journals;[69] his son, Friedrich Otto Licht, took over in 1885 and was one of the expert authors of a report to the World Monetary and Economic Conference, providing recommendations to the League of Nations as to how to regulate the international sugar market. F. O. Licht's influential work may have been the driving force behind Germany's suggestion that the Permanent Bureau establish a uniform system of collecting statistics.[70]

Sugar production has always been linked to the development of new technologies. W. Arthur Lewis, renowned development economist and St. Lucian, noted that sugar was the only tropical crop to experience a (harvesting and refining) scientific revolution before 1914.[71] This phenomenon likely correlates to the fact that sugar was also the only tropical commodity produced on a large scale in Europe.[72] There is evidence that West Indian and European sugar producers were informed of each other's respective innovations, especially as experts traveled between Europe and the sugar colonies.

Innovations in distribution were also relevant. Sugar was now a staple food in the Western diet. The increase of sugar consumption in Europe was part of the broader trend from *c.* 1850 to 1913, when demand for staple food dramatically increased, and transportation and production costs radically decreased.[73]

While the sugar treaty was driven to some degree by European demands for sweetened foods at home and hot beverages like tea, coffee, and cocoa, it was also at a historical cusp of new consumption habits: people were starting to eat an increasing amount of sugar through confectionaries and newly developed processed foods. During the late nineteenth century into the early twentieth century, sugar claimed a central role in US cookbooks.[74] But the most important technological innovation affecting consumption habits around the time of the 1902 Brussels Convention was the development of factory-processed food,

69 Moreno Fraginals, "Caribbean Plantations," pp. 19, 23; Bruhns, "Zur Geschichte der Firma F. O. Licht."

70 Further Findings of the Permanent Commission Established Under Article VII of the Sugar Convention of March 5, 1902 and Further Reports of the British Delegate, Cd 2094 (1904), pp. 39–40.

71 Lewis, "Export Stimulus," pp. 13, 19.

72 Albert and Graves, "Introduction," pp. 1, 3.

73 Nützenadel and Trentmann, "Mapping Food," pp. 1, 5.

74 Galloway, *Sugar*, pp. 1–10.

high in sugar, quickly prepared, and quickly eaten.[75] Sugar, industry, and commerce intertwined in a way that became a mainstay in the Western diet, exemplified by the 1904 World's Fair in St. Louis, Missouri. Indeed, the fair itself may have changed the way the Western world ate and snacked. The World's Fair made eating on-the-go popular and acceptable, which until then had been considered vulgar. Dr. Pepper, Coca-Cola, Hires Root Beer, ginger ale, and iced tea were showcased. Ice cream was placed in a cone for one of the first times. Jell-O was given away for free, along with recipes in order to allow people to prepare this fast food at home. Forerunners to popsicles and cotton candy were also introduced at the fair.[76]

The curious and anomalous Permanent Commission

How, then, did this new, modern institution function? Even though the new international institution was revered for its ability to generate its own policies, law was understood to remain solely in the purview of states. Policy-makers and lawyers understood the function and purpose of the Sugar Union to be about coordinating domestic laws towards a common economic policy.

In order to avoid theoretical and political dilemmas associated with questions of sovereignty, efforts were made to ensure that the Sugar Union would not be characterized as creating a law unto itself. For example, one of the few extensive legal studies argued that when the Commission was resolving a dispute, it was not ruling as a body of the Sugar Union, but as an ad hoc arbitration court established by the agreement of the litigants.[77] The disputes themselves were framed within the Commission as disputes of fact and interpretation. There was also some trepidation in granting the Commission full recognition as a diplomatic force unto itself, much less any sort of legal personality; the Commission was to communicate to the states via the Belgian government and vice versa (Art. VII). The debate over the legal nature of the Permanent Commission and questions of sovereignty were not only theoretical dilemmas. Politicians, such as British opposition parliamentarians, were the most vocal critics of the Sugar Union, on the grounds that the international institution exercised too much

[75] Mintz, *Sweetness and Power*, p. 80.

[76] Vaccaro, *Ice Cream Cone*; Abbott, *Sugar*, pp. 349–52.

[77] Politis, "L'organisation," 7.

autonomous and juridical decision-making power over national sugar production, thereby infringing upon the state's sovereignty.[78]

But the question of how the treaty delegated power between signatory states and the Commission was not a clear ceding of power. The treaty enacted a more relational notion of sovereignty, where the state and Sugar Union derived their power and authority over sugar from each other. The Permanent Commission's role was not to enforce the treaty directly; rather, it was to supervise the execution. This suggests that the Commission had some power over the state, but the state had to actually enact the terms of the treaty. In fact, the treaty required states to ensure "continuous supervision, both by day and night," of sugar refineries and factories by state Revenue Officers, for the purpose of guaranteeing "against the surreptitious removal of sugar" (Art. II). The treaty actually empowered these state agents, allowing them "the right of entry into all parts of the factories" (Art. II).

The *chapeau* provided that the treaty's purpose was to "equalize the competition between beet and cane sugar from various countries and increase sugar consumption by abolishing bounties and limiting surtax." A state's ability to impose countervailing duties (Art. IV, referred to as the "penalty clause") was thought to be the most effective enforcement measure. In fact, it was the key component of the whole system. Before the treaty, a state always had the ability to unilaterally impose countervailing duties. Because of the treaty, states had to work with the Commission to determine the amount of countervailing duties. While, on one hand, one could interpret the Commission as limiting state power, on the other hand, the treaty now legitimized countervailing duties as a legitimate international policy tool in order to serve a common international economic policy.

States were also empowered through flexible language, thereby preserving their political will. Contracting Parties would generally "engage to do X."[79] This was distinct from how the Permanent Commission,

[78] See, e.g., Hansard, HC, vol. 118, cols. 59–105, February 17, 1903; HC, vol. 126, cols. 587–627, July 28, 1903; HC, vol. 126, cols. 759–807, July 29, 1903; HC, vol. 126, cols. 1653–709, August 5, 1903; HC, vol. 130, cols. 730–1, February 23, 1904; HC, vol. 130, cols. 1545–84, March 2, 1904; HC, vol. 141, cols. 108–41, February 14, 1905; HC, vol. 141, cols. 1494–551, February 28, 1905; HC, vol. 142, col. 410, March 6, 1905.

[79] E.g. Art. IV: "The High Contracting Parties *engage to impose* a special duty on the importation into their territories of sugar from those countries which may grant bounties either on production or on exportation" [emphasis added].

Permanent Bureau, and factories were always ordered that they "shall do X."[80] The Commission was not treated as a forum for debating what economic policy was best or managing diverse economic systems; rather, it was the mechanism through which the agreed upon economic policy was implemented and managed.

The assumption, therefore, was that all the economic policies were to be determined during the negotiations. Each sugar-producing country in continental Europe had its own complex system of tariffs and duties which subsidized domestic beet sugar, generated revenue for the government, and acted as a means of income redistribution.[81] Germany and Austria-Hungary had a "direct bounty" system in which consumers paid a high amount of excise duty and sugar refiners received subsidies for export. France had a system of direct bounties, but also had a system of "indirect" bounties (such as subsidized transportation costs) that favored sugar production by sugar planters and old sugar cane refineries.[82]

The central problem during negotiations was to determine how to regulate every different European country's unique system of sugar subsidization under the auspices of one international institution. This was a huge logistical and analytical endeavor. But, of course, it was also political – the issue of defining bounties was so contentious during the Brussels negotiations that Russia, which had the most centralized system of subsidization, insisted that its system was not a bounty and refused to sign the Brussels Convention (later joining in 1907).[83]

[80] E.g. Art. VII: "The duty of the Commission shall be limited to findings and investigations."

[81] Hagelberg, "International Sugar Agreements." For excellent summaries of the various bounty systems, see Chalmin, "Important Trends," pp. 9, 12–14; Deerr, *History of Sugar*, pp. 21–35.

[82] At first, France had first started negotiation of the Brussels Convention adamant that its system of indirect bounties was not negotiable, but later changed its position in 1901, after side negotiations with Germany and Austria-Hungary. Correspondence Relating to the Sugar Bounty Conference, Cd 1013 (1902), p. 19.

[83] Each year, the Russian government determined the amount of sugar necessary for home consumption, allowing for sugar surpluses to be exported and taxed at a lower rate than domestic sugar. US Senate Committee on Finance, *Proceedings of the Conference on the Question of Bounties, held at Brussels, Jun 7–25, 1898* (Blue Book Commercial No. 6, 1898); *Protocol Respecting the Accession of Russia to the Sugar Convention on March 5, 1902 and the Additional Act of August 28, 1907* (December 19, 1907) 206 *Parry* 56, *British Treaty Series* 12 (1908), Cd 3968 (entered into force March 31, 1908). See also Correspondence Respecting the Adhesion of Russia to the Brussels Sugar Convention of March 5, 1902, Cd 3877 (1908).

Bounties were finally defined in Article I in the following way:

The High Contracting Parties engage to suppress ... the direct and indirect bounties by which the production or exportation of sugar may profit and not to establish bounties of such kind ...

The preceding paragraph applies to all advantages derived directly or indirectly; by the several categories of producers, from State fiscal legislation, and in particular to–

Direct bonuses granted on exportation;
Direct bonuses granted to production;
Total or partial exemptions from taxation which profit a part of the products of manufacture;
Profits derived from the excess of yield;
Profits derived from too high a drawback;
Advantages derived from any surtax in excess of the rate fixed by Article III.

As any student of WTO jurisprudence would know, this hardly solved the dilemma of regulating subsidization. Matters of treaty interpretation quickly arose, emphasizing Holmes's point that "General propositions do not decide concrete cases."[84] Most disputes and appeals made to the Permanent Commission were presented as disputes of fact as to what was a country's legislation, determining whether the legislation created a bounty, and measuring amounts of sugar production. Despite delegates' best efforts to characterize the Commission's role as one of determining facts and implementing economic doctrine, the Commission in effect exercised powers of interpretation. For example, just as in debates regarding "like" products in the WTO,[85] disagreements arose over what constituted a "notable proportion" of sugar in analogous products such as biscuits.[86] Another debate of interpretation was over determining when a surtax constituted enough of an "advantage" as to warrant being treated as a bounty.[87]

During this same debate over the surtax, the British delegate was concerned that the Commission's actions misconstrued its dispute settlement capacity. The Commission was empowered to "pronounce" as to whether states met the treaty criteria and to "deliver an opinion on contested questions" (Art. VII(d)). The British delegate successfully

[84] *Lochner* v. *New York*, 198 US 45 (1905), 74. [85] GATT Art. III:4.

[86] Further Findings of the Permanent Commission Established Under Article VII of the Sugar Convention of March 5, 1902 and Further Reports of the British Delegate, Cd 2094 (1904), p. 26.

[87] Further Findings of the Permanent Commission Established Under the Sugar Convention of March 5, 1902, Report of the British Delegate and Appeal of His Majesty's Government Against Certain of those Findings, Cd 2349 (1905), p. 3.

argued that certain practices of the Permanent Commission were becoming rules that were being applied more generally and that instead the text needed to be interpreted in light of the carefully examined facts of each particular case.[88]

While there may have been debate over the nature of the Commission's interpretive powers, the negotiators of the treaty quite consciously granted the Commission executive powers.[89] The treaty made exceptions for countries that produced sugar but did not export. If those exceptional countries changed their domestic legislation in an effort to stop subsidizing and start exporting, the Commission would decide if their new laws conformed to the treaty (Art. VI). Once these countries were no longer deemed to be exceptional, they would be more regularly judged and scrutinized by the Commission. The Commission could determine if there were bounties in non-signatory countries and decide the appropriate amount of countervailing duties that signatory countries could impose (Art. VII). The broad language of Article I granted the Commission a significant amount of leeway to determine what constituted a bounty. The Commission also decided who could be a member and participate in the Sugar Union. This was remarkable for the time, since states could join other international unions simply by request and ratifying the appropriate treaty. So, for example, when Peru decided to join the Brussels Convention, the Commission first examined Peru's legislation and then decided when Peru's legislative changes conformed to the treaty. The Commission exercised executive judgment and limited its own power, when it ruled that communications and inquiries by private firms and individuals were not to be accepted by the Commission, but would be referred to the respective governments.[90]

Histories of international trade, international institutions, and public international law

Since trade law has mostly ignored the Brussels Convention, the next most obvious context would be to situate the sugar treaty within the history of international organizations. The Brussels Convention was part

[88] *Ibid.* [89] Politis, "L'organisation."
[90] Further Findings of the Permanent Commission Established Under Article VII of the Sugar Convention of March 5, 1902 and Further Reports of the British Delegate, Cd 2094 (1904), pp. 26–7.

of the trend *c.* 1815–1913 when over thirty "International Administrative Unions" or "Public International Unions" were created. These unions were often international organizations that administrated the global machinations of things like communication, transportation, measurements, meteorology, and public health.[91] The first problem in situating the sugar treaty in this context is that these historical international administrative unions do not garner much attention from lawyers; they are usually treated as administrative bodies focused on technical questions.[92] Therefore, the Brussels Convention, as part of this trend, might have been thought of as legally and politically uninteresting. Moreover, the study of international organizations by lawyers usually begins with the League of Nations.

Of course, that does not explain why an international institution that was granted unprecedented power when compared to all the international unions of the time has not garnered more attention. During and after the creation of the League, the Sugar Union was often mentioned as an example of an effective international institution that developed its own policy. Yet we must be careful not to be teleological in how and whether we situate it as a prototype for the League of Nations or other international institutions.[93] It was never characterized as *the* exemplar.[94] Nor was it clear that it affected how and why the League was created. After the time of the League, it was more or less ignored except as a minor historical reference.[95] The Brussels Convention therefore had very little direct impact on the creation of the League of Nations, other than as a rhetorical device that allowed supporters of the League to point to the

[91] Murphy, *International Organization*, pp. 46–152; Kingsbury, Krisch, and Stewart, "Administrative Law," 19–20; Wolfrum, "International Administrative Unions."

[92] This is likely to change with the advent of the Global Administrative Law project. See www.iilj.org/gal (accessed May 27, 2014).

[93] The other international institution of the time with significant legal and political power was the Permanent Court of Arbitration (PCA), created by the 1899 and 1907 Hague Peace Conferences. Even though today the PCA occasionally administers investment treaty arbitrations, it usually does so under the rules set out by a particular investment treaty. Moreover, its historical antecedents in the nineteenth century emerged out of the desire to prevent war and enable peace rather than encourage commerce. Ando, "Permanent Court of Arbitration."

[94] See, e.g., Hill, *League of Nations*, p. 12; McClure, *World Prosperity*, p. 50; Sayre, *Experiments*, pp. 117–24; Hicks, *New World Order*, pp. 267–8; Mander, *Foundations*, p. 237; Zimmern, *League of Nations*, pp. 58–60.

[95] See, e.g., Lyons, *Internationalism*, pp. 103–10; Murphy, *International Organization*, p. 95; Reinalda, *History*, pp. 126–8; Richardson, *Sugar*, pp. 54–7.

fact that creating an international institution with significant policy-making power had been done before.

It is even more difficult to place the sugar treaty within the history of international legal thought. In searching the journals that would define the public international legal profession in the nineteenth century, I found that very little was written about the sugar treaty.[96] Koskenniemi is right to warn us not to treat legal thought of the nineteenth century as a "uniform datum ... [or] homogenous experience."[97] Nevertheless, using a rough periodization that places the end of the long nineteenth century at 1914, we can see that public international lawyers during this time were preoccupied with configuring territory, society, and the so-called native in different ways through doctrines of sovereignty.[98]

Not surprisingly, those few international jurists who did write about the sugar treaty mostly addressed issues of sovereignty.[99] For example, a young Nicolas Politis (before he went on to play a prominent role at the League of Nations and be a regular agent for Greece before the Permanent Court of International Justice) wrote one of the most perceptive studies on the Sugar Union. To him, it provided a new theoretical and practical way of understanding sovereignty that was not absolute. Rather, it was an innovation that was the product of a long process of states trusting each other and giving up bits of sovereignty.[100] To Westlake, the fact that states signed such a treaty that granted an international institution a great deal of decision-making power was a foremost exercise, not a renunciation, of state sovereignty.[101] As one

[96] This includes the *American Journal of International Law*, *Revue de droit international et de législation comparée*, *Revue générale de droit international public*, and *Annuaire de l'institut de droit international*.

[97] Koskenniemi, "Legacy," pp. 141, 145.

[98] Kennedy, "International Law"; Koskenniemi, *Gentle Civilizer*, pp. 11–288; Anghie, *Imperialism*, pp. 32–114; Sylvest, "International Law"; Ala'i, "Leopold and Morel"; Pitts, "Boundaries"; Lobban, "International Law."

[99] Though some small number of jurists were more concerned that countervailing duties, which differentiated between and punished states, was not legally compatible with the most favored nation principle, which was based on treating all states equally. Visser, "La clause," 165–76; Kaufmann, *Welt-Zuckerindustrie*; Hornbeck, "Most Favored-Nation Clause," 640–5.

[100] Politis, "L'organisation." See also André, "La convention"; Kaufmann, *Welt-Zuckerindustrie*.

[101] Westlake, *International Law Part I*, pp. 309–11; Westlake, *International Law Part II*, pp. 322–4. Oppenheim had nothing substantive to say about the sugar treaty; see Oppenheim, *International Law*, 1st edn., pp. 496, 498, 582; Oppenheim, *International Law*, 2nd edn., pp. 515, 517, 616.

member of the German Reichstag stated during debates regarding the Brussels Convention:

> In answer to the question raised – as to why we should allow the foreigner to interfere in German tariff legislation – he is not interfering with ours any more than we are with his; every Tariff and Commercial Treaty binds both parties, and cannot be looked upon as undue interference of a third Party.[102]

Others overcame this question regarding the new international institution's relationship to sovereignty by emphasizing how the so-called Sugar Union was a practical and specific response to a serious problem.[103]

Nonetheless, much like in discussions about international institutions or international trade law today, many of the discussions of the time used functional language that focused less on theoretical dilemmas of sovereignty, and instead characterized the Sugar Union as a trade institution designed to solve a global issue pragmatically.[104] It is therefore difficult to reconcile the Brussels Convention with its contemporaneous public international legal thought. This complicates our understanding of the nineteenth century. Whereas nineteenth-century jurists developed international law as part of their project to reflect civilized society, policy-makers created the Brussels Convention to ensure that the world sugar market functioned correctly. International law's defining doctrine was sovereignty over territory, while the sugar treaty's central tenet was the free trade of goods. The so-called native referenced in treaties like the Berlin Act was nowhere to be found in the sugar treaty text.

Thus, the sugar treaty was not characterized at the time as a principal subject of public international law. Nor was it squarely in the realm of private international commercial law. This area was thought to include issues such as: "the commercial acts of traders; terrestrial, marine and life insurance; crashes, collisions and wrecks; carriage contracts; general or sea-risk loans; seafarers; benefits; letters of exchange; bankruptcy."[105]

Geography of interests

All this configuring of market and sovereignty needs to be situated somewhere if we are to understand how and why the 1902 treaty

[102] Correspondence Relating to the Sugar Bounty Conference, Cd 1013 (1902), p. 58.
[103] Reinsch, "International Administrative Law," 14. See also André, "La convention," 688.
[104] Kennedy, "Law and Policy," 59; Jackson, *Sovereignty*; Klabbers, *Introduction*.
[105] Pradier-Fodéré, "Le Congrès," 231.

arose, what was at stake, and what conditioned the institutional design. Where a market is geographically located is just as important as how it is institutionally constructed in order to understand how it operates.

The 1902 Brussels Convention may not have garnered much attention from international lawyers, but it was central to political, economic, and social debates of the time. The UK was the financial center of the world's sugar trade and had the largest number of sugar consumers in the world. There was not, however, a world sugar market as such. Rather, there were a number of more-or-less distinct regional markets. The European market was by far the largest and most internationally influential.[106] The US and its market in the late nineteenth century only indirectly influenced Europe's treaties and would not enter into multilateral sugar agreements until after the collapse of the Brussels Convention. Asian countries and territories, with the exception of British India and Dutch Java, would not directly enter into multilateral agreements with European countries until the 1930s.[107]

The history of the conditions of sugar production within the British West Indies, the imperial politics between the West Indies and London, and continental European sugar beet politics provide the best insight into the advent of the Brussels Convention. Before honing in on the British Empire and continental Europe, however, it is worth taking some note of the other significant sugar markets of the world in order to appreciate how the different major sugar-producing countries and regions may have at least indirectly influenced one other, but did not directly contribute to the creation of the treaty.[108]

USA, Cuba, and Brazil

In the mid-nineteenth century, Cuba and Brazil were the largest producers of cane sugar in the world.[109] Despite this fact, Cuban and Brazilian cane sugar made little headway into the UK and continental Europe, for several interrelated reasons. European countries, such as France and Germany, essentially kept out foreign sugar through their respective systems of high tariffs and subsidies. These policies also

[106] Chalmin, *Sugar Giant*, pp. 16–17. [107] Galloway, *Sugar*, pp. 197–217.

[108] I am aware of the different regional delineations, such as the West Indies or the Caribbean. Also, I acknowledge that each particular island had its own political and economic system. I tend to refer to the "British West Indies," since that is often how they were referenced in British political thought of the time.

[109] Mintz, *Sweetness and Power*, p. 36.

allowed for continued investment and innovation into beet sugar extracting and harvesting technology, so that by the 1870s, sugar beet provided a more efficient way of producing sucrose. This also meant that British consumers' cheapest source of refined sugar was from Europe.[110]

Another reason that Cuban and Brazilian sugar gained little presence in the UK was an influential campaign calling for consumers to boycott slave-produced sugar.[111] Cuba and Brazil were among the last sugar-producing countries to abolish slavery (1886 in Cuba and 1888 in Brazil). Also, many British consumers considered the quality and taste of Brazilian refined brown sugar, which after 1854 was priced similarly to European sugar, to be one of the most inferior in the world.[112] In addition, Brazil had preferential trade agreements with Portugal and Germany; the result was that Brazil supplied approximately one-third of Germany's sugar in 1844 and 83 percent of Portugal's sugar in 1870. Besides, in the mid-nineteenth century, the Brazilian sugar industry was starting to give way to burgeoning coffee production.[113]

Cuba's principal sugar consumer was the US, and by 1880, 82 percent of Cuban sugar went to the US. In 1903, the US granted a newly independent Cuba preferential access to its market.[114] Prior to this point, the US's main sources of sugar were cane sugar from Louisiana (territory bought from France in 1803),[115] Hawaii (which it had annexed in 1893),[116] and the Philippines (US government provided preferential access to Filipino sugar after annexing the islands in 1898; US capital had developed the sugar industry).[117] With these preferential agreements and annexations, combined with a system of countervailing duties on subsidized sugar,[118] the US had developed its own broad-based regional sugar market.[119] As one US economist proudly noted in

[110] Moreno Fraginals, "Caribbean Plantations," p. 23.

[111] Mintz, *Sweetness and Power*, p. 62; Galloway, *Sugar*, pp. 120–42; Chalmin, "Important Trends," p. 11; Delson, "Sugar Production."

[112] Delson, "Sugar Production," pp. 66–7.

[113] *Ibid.*, p. 66; Clarence-Smith, "Sugar and Rum." [114] Abbott, *Sugar*, pp. 270–80.

[115] *Ibid.*, pp. 280–302.

[116] The US annexation of Hawaii ended the Hawaiian monarchy. Some argue that the US annexed the islands for the purpose of maintaining its US-owned sugar plantations. Pomeranz and Topik, *World that Trade Created*, pp. 123–5.

[117] Galloway, *Sugar*, pp. 216–17.

[118] The respective pieces of legislation were the 1890 McKinley Bill, the 1894 Wilson Bill, and the 1897 Dingley Bill. See Deerr, *History of Sugar*, vol. II, pp. 507–8.

[119] Even though the US never participated in the multilateral sugar trade conferences, the US valuation of countervailing duties later acted as a temporary system to be used

1904 in regard to the insulation of the US sugar market from international market influences, "Hamburg no longer fixes the price of sugar in American markets."[120] The US was increasing its appetite for sugar and would not develop its sugar beet industry until the twentieth century.[121]

Java

Sugar cane has been grown on Java for as long as anyone can remember.[122] One of the earliest historical mentions of sugar on the island was in 424 CE, by Fahian, a Chinese traveler. Sugar was first exported from Java by the Dutch East India Company in 1637. From then on, sugar exports ebbed and flowed with the tides of Dutch national and imperial history.

Starting in 1816, the newly formed Kingdom of the Netherlands formally governed colonies in Java. The Netherlands subsidized and supported the sugar industry in Java until around 1896. The Dutch government's plan from the beginning was to gradually reduce government support in an effort to ensure that the sugar-producing industry in Java would only rely on the market. It succeeded in its plan despite two calamities: first, the price of sugar in 1882–4 dropped to historical lows, below the cost of production; and second, a mysterious disease decimated all the cane on the island.

Dutch capitalists rallied and invested heavily in order to save the sugar industry in Java. Private investment not only salvaged the island's sugar industry, but also improved the industry in such a way that made Java a major world exporter of cane sugar. After 1880, the Netherlands no longer imported sugar from Java since its beetroot sugar industry took off. From that point, a great amount of Java sugar went to the UK and the US. However, when the US began to obtain more of its sugar supply from its own colonies, Java exported more to China (via Hong Kong), Japan, and British India. When the Netherlands signed the Brussels Convention in 1902, the Javanese sugar industry no longer received any subsidies. Yet, due to the historic subsidies and influx of

by the Brussels Agreement Permanent Commission, until the Commission was able to make its own assessment. See Findings of the Permanent Commission established under Article VII of the Sugar Convention of March 5, 1902, and Report of the British Delegate, Cd 1632 (1903), pp. 5–6.

120 Stubbs, "Sugar," 97. 121 Abbott, *Sugar*, p. 303.

122 This section draws heavily from Geerligs, *Sugar Industry*, pp. 115–20, 139–41.

capital, the sugar cane industry in Java was one of the most technologically advanced in the world.[123]

Rise of the continental European sugar beet

It is significantly more expensive and technically complicated to extract sugar from beet than it is from cane. How is it, then, that beet became a principal source of sugar, thereby challenging the prominence of cane? Traces of the changes that would lead to the Brussels Convention start in the early sixteenth century, when European agriculturalists first discovered that beet contained sugar. And then, like Mary Shelley's *Frankenstein*, the story of sugar and modern international trade institutions takes off, with a turn away from alchemy and towards the new practice of chemistry. In 1747, Andreas Sigismund Marggraf, a Berlin professor and one of the earliest modern chemists, succeeded in extracting sugar from a beet. Franz Karl Achard, Marggraf's student, industrialized this method with the financial backing of King Friedrich Wilhelm III of Prussia, and set up a sugar beet factory in Cunern, Silesia, in 1801. Interest in Achard's work quickly spread across Europe, especially to France and the Netherlands.[124]

During the time of the Napoleonic Wars (*c.* 1800–15), the UK's naval blockade and France's embargo of goods cut off continental Europe's supply of cane sugar (which mostly came from Cuba, Brazil, and the West Indies). By this time, sugar had become a mainstay in the common French diet – in 1792, crowds in Paris rioted to protest the increased cost of sugar.[125] Napoleon, to ensure a domestic source of sugar, invested heavily in expanding the continental European sugar beet industry. Moreover, Haiti's slave revolt and independence in 1791 cut off France's largest source of sugar cane (and launched Cuba's sugar industry as French technicians fled to Cuba).[126]

The French state invested the necessary financial and technical resources to develop the infrastructure of the beet sugar industry. It did so by training "technical cadres." In 1812, Napoleon launched schools that, by 1817, had produced effectively trained middle-level personnel. Very soon, this new cadre of sugar technicians was far more skilled and knowledgeable than their counterparts in the West Indies. To Moreno

[123] *Ibid.*, pp. 37, 120.

[124] Deerr, *History of Sugar*, vol. II, pp. 474–8; Moreno Fraginals, "Caribbean Plantations," pp. 20–1.

[125] Stein, *French Sugar*, p. ix.

[126] Abbott, *Sugar*, pp. 270–340.

Fraginals, one of the most important results of these schools is that they brought together all the different sugar interests within France.[127]

A the end of the Napoleonic War in 1815, cheaper sugar from sugar cane flowed back into continental Europe, causing the sugar beet industry to collapse. However, France retained a unique position in the sugar trade, since it sourced its sugar from both domestic sugar beet and from French cane sugar from colonies in the Caribbean and the Indian Ocean. Within France, there was competition between colonial and shipping interests, which defended colonial sugar, and agricultural and industrial interests, which defended domestic sugar. During the Napoleonic Wars, France's colonial holdings were diminished, which also reduced the influence of colonialists in France. By 1830, France's remaining sugar-producing colonies, Guadeloupe, Martinique, and Réunion, could not keep up with French sugar consumption. Therefore, as France's colonial holdings in the Caribbean dwindled and the subsidized domestic sugar industry grew, it was easier for the domestic sugar beet growers to ensure that France's foreign policies reflected their interests. This meant that by the middle of the nineteenth century, France was heavily subsidizing domestic sugar beet agriculture by way of high tariff barriers against cheaper sugar from Cuba and Brazil.[128]

Certain agricultural elements also influenced the development of sugar beet production in continental Europe. Improvements in Russian agriculture had increased the yield in wheat, and the surplus was sent to Europe. This reduced the price of wheat, which was detrimental to continental wheat farmers. The inclusion of beet into crop rotation not only provided farmers with relief from relying on devalued wheat and cereals, but also enriched the soil, thereby increasing the yield of other crops. Also, the by-product of beet harvested for the purpose of sugar extraction provided valuable feed for cattle during a time when animal husbandry was more lucrative than growing cereals.[129]

French consumption never came close to that of the British. Mintz notes that in 1775, British consumption was ten times higher per capita than French consumption.[130] This pattern of consumption continued into the nineteenth century, making the UK the largest market for sugar in the world, and home to major refining centers. This also meant that

[127] Moreno Fraginals, "Caribbean Plantations," pp. 21–2.

[128] Stein, *French Sugar*, pp. 50, 88–9; Moreno Fraginals, "Caribbean Plantations," p. 22.

[129] Chalmin, "Important Trends," pp. 9–10; Timoshenko and Swerling, *World's Sugar*, pp. 235–7.

[130] Mintz, *Sweetness and Power*, p. 189.

decisions and conditions in the UK significantly influenced the global sugar trade.[131]

British imperialism and free trade colonialism

The free trade debates within the UK provide the discursive context for the debate surrounding the 1902 Brussels Convention. From these debates, different ideas about free trade shaped how competing groups argued amongst each other, and informed what they understood to be their own interests. By the latter half of the nineteenth century, free trade discourse had seeped through the general British consciousness, and by around 1879, many politicians and civil servants in the British government had adopted free trade with almost religious fervor.[132] The unifying idea was that free trade was a policy of maintaining as little government involvement as possible in the import and export of goods. The dividing question was what counted as illegitimate government intervention in the market.

These debates were not only about different understandings of free trade, but also about the British Empire. The treaty would not have emerged without West Indian colonial governors demanding that London improve the economic conditions of sugar production in the colonies. What gave urgency to their petitions, as I touch upon below, was the fact that black workers were expressing their social, economic, political, and cultural discontent by burning sugar cane fields and politically organizing through labor unions and legislatures. The result was that the Brussels Convention assembled prevailing theories of free trade in such a way that it created a sort of "free trade colonialism" – that is, it employed a particular conception of free trade doctrine which had the intended effect of maintaining British power over the colonies in the West Indies, and ensuring that raw material from the colonies reached European industries and consumers in the metropole.

It is common to characterize *c.* 1815–70 as the period when the British state secured and expanded its power overseas. British power during this time, however, was not usually exercised through the establishment of formal colonies. Rather, British global power and influence was mostly constituted through corporate charters, trade treaties, and gunboat diplomacy.[133] In fact, the policy of free trade was understood at

[131] Chalmin, *Sugar Giant*, pp. 18–22, 47–67; Galloway, *Sugar*, pp. 120–42.
[132] Beachey, *British West Indies*, p. 54. [133] Hyam, *Britain's Imperial Century*, pp. 1–73.

the time to be the opposite of colonial policy; free trade was considered to be a more efficient means of obtaining necessary goods and maintaining political influence.[134] It also opposed the tariffs and monopolies that went with colonial rule.

Robinson and Gallagher coined the phrase "free trade imperialism" to describe British overseas policy during this period.[135] They suggested that in order to determine the contours of British Empire, one had to account for informal influences, namely through trade and commerce, and not only formally annexed colonies. By "formal," they meant legalized state control over territory. Informal did not mean that law was not involved. In fact, they argued that the free trade treaty was the most common way that the UK exercised its informal power over weaker states. By doing so, they also challenged another commonly held notion, that to support free trade necessarily made one an anti-imperialist. Thus, we are well advised to treat arguments regarding free trade as separate but related to arguments regarding imperialism.[136]

The 1902 free trade treaty, however, was concluded during a period (*c.* 1870–1914) when British imperial policies were less about informal rule and focused more on expanding its power by ruling overseas territory through formal colonies. Thus, the Brussels Convention was an example of how free trade discourse could also make room for an imperial policy exercised through formal colonies.[137] Joseph Chamberlain, while he was Secretary of State for the Colonies, championed the 1902 treaty for its imperial ambitions – but to be sure, the treaty's most favored nation clause, countervailing duties, and refusal to allow for imperial preferences placed the treaty squarely within free trade discourse of the time, and not within the purview of Chamberlain's explicit anti-free-trade policy of high tariffs and imperial preferences.[138]

The Brussels Sugar Convention, with its use of free trade doctrine, institutionalized a specific version of empire.[139] This was a vision of imperialism that focused on the movement of raw material from the peripheries to the industrialized center. This was a different project

[134] Koskenniemi, *Gentle Civilizer*, pp. 110–12.

[135] Gallagher and Robinson, "Imperialism." See also Howe, "Global Order"; Bell, *Greater Britain.*

[136] Semmel, *Free Trade Imperialism.*

[137] Drage, *Trade*, pp. 141–2, 184–5, 318.

[138] See *Hansard*, HC, vol. 126, cols. 759-807, July 29, 1903; Chamberlain, *Imperial Union.*

[139] This is discussed more fully in the next chapter.

than the civilizing mission of public international law, with its paternalism and tutelage towards the native, and its preoccupation with territory and sovereignty. Nor was this how Lord Lugard famously described British imperialism – a dual mandate of industrial benefit for Europe and progress for the native races of the colonies.[140]

[140] Lugard, *Dual Mandate*.

4 The institutionalization of international trade

The 1884–5 sugar crisis

During the 1880s and 1890s, free trade was one of the most important ideas through which issues about domestic, imperial, and global relations were debated. And sugar was central to these debates over the domestic and world economy.[141] The 1902 Brussels Convention was ratified and took effect only because shifts in free trade discourse coincided with changes in the transnational production of sugar and the UK's imperial politics. Indeed, the sugar debates of the 1880s and 1890s galvanized interests and political alliances within the British Empire in such a way that would continue into the next two decades.[142]

The pivotal event that changed the conditions of sugar production, and trade theory and policy, was the 1884–5 sugar crisis. For most of the nineteenth century, nearly all of the world's sugar came from cane. Achard's first sugar beet factory in 1801, however, paved the way for an innovative and productive beet sugar industry in continental Europe. Sugar beet productivity began to rise dramatically in the 1850s, challenging sugar cane's dominance. Since European capital was invested in both colonial cane and continental beet, European states attempted to devise an international sugar trade treaty that would liberalize the sugar trade. Nevertheless, from 1863 to 1902, European sugar diplomacy went from "failure to failure," through eleven conferences and two multilateral treaties.[143]

[141] For two articles which exemplify arguments for and against the Brussels Convention, see Taylor, "Sugar"; Lough, "Brussels."

[142] Howe, *Free Trade*, pp. 204–13; Trentmann, *Free Trade Nation*, pp. 136–7, 154–61.

[143] Chalmin, "Important Trends," pp. 9, 14. See also Myers, *Collections*, p. 475; Pigman, "Hegemony"; Moura Filho, "Pioneering Multilateralism."

Sugar was the most important commodity in the British West Indies, since the colonies' entire socio-economic structure depended on the production – that is, the harvesting and processing of cane sugar – for the purpose of export to refiners. British sugar cane producers in the West Indies struggled to keep up with the rising production levels of their continental European sugar beet counterparts. That competition eventually culminated in a crisis. And that crisis raised the stakes of concluding a multilateral sugar treaty. Sometime between 1881 and 1883, the amount of beet sugar produced in the world surpassed cane sugar for the first time.[144] This coincided with a significant drop in sugar prices in London in 1884–5, caused by an influx of beet sugar that was "dumped" onto the British market, mostly from Germany and Austria-Hungary (meaning that it was surplus sold at less than the cost of production). The price of sugar in the UK, the world's largest sugar consumer, dropped by approximately 50 percent from 1872 to 1884–5.[145]

The sugar crisis's clearest origins were in the 1870s, when countries in continental Europe, such as Germany, Austria-Hungary, and France, started to adopt a novel system of bounties and duties that shielded local industry from foreign competition and stimulated local industry. Consequently, sugar producers invested in new technologies that increased the extractable sugar content of beetroot. The bounty system also created an incentive to increase sugar production for the purpose of export.

The British West Indies historically sold most of its sugar to refiners in the UK, who further processed the sugar for the purpose of consumption. By the latter half of the nineteenth century, however, West Indian planters were economically depressed and were no longer selling their sugar to the British market. Planters blamed the European bounty

[144] Shephard, "Sugar Industry," 151. Data regarding the production of cane sugar in the nineteenth century are not entirely accurate; therefore, there are different sets of statistics, placing the actual date and production output at slightly different amounts. Some commentators consider that beet sugar production rose from 14 percent of world sugar production in 1853 to 65 percent in 1900, and surpassed cane sugar production in 1883. See Griffin, "Legislation," 5; Poggi, "German Sugar Beet," 81–2; Chalmin, "Important Trends," 12. Others found that beet sugar production rose from 10 percent of world sugar production in 1850 to approximately 60 percent in 1900, and surpassed cane sugar production in 1881. See Deerr, *History of Sugar*, vol. II, pp. 490–1; Galloway, *Sugar*, p. 132.

[145] Deerr, *History of Sugar*, vol. II, pp. 503–5; Galloway, *Sugar*, pp. 238–9; Chalmin, *Sugar Giant*, pp. 23–4.

system for the price of sugar dropping so rapidly, thereby causing the sugar crisis.

There was, though, more at stake with the sugar crisis than the price of sugar. The words of Gerald Balfour, President of the Board of Trade (a committee of the Privy Council), in the House of Commons captures one prevailing British sentiment as to why the Brussels Convention was necessary:

> In the case of the [British] sugar-refining industry, even supposing that that industry is altogether squeezed out of existence by the unfair competition to which I have referred, it would be still possible for those who were engaged in it to be gradually absorbed in other occupations. The case of the West Indies is different. We have there to deal, not merely with a section of the population engaged in one among a large number of different industries, but with the condition of whole societies. *What is at stake in the West Indies is the fate of entire communities under the British Crown.* Take away the export trade from the West Indies, and you take away from them the means of maintaining a civilised Government. Of all the exports of the West Indies, in the majority, at all events, of the islands, sugar is by far the most important; so much so that if you were to destroy the sugar industry you would practically destroy the Power of those Governments to raise a revenue or to carry on the work of administration in a proper and efficient manner. [emphasis added][146]

Thus, this sugar crisis was not only an economic question of sugar industries, but also a political issue – the British Empire was at risk. If the West Indies sugar industry failed, the British Crown would have to bear the cost of the increasing economic and political instability in that region.

Conditions that led to the treaty

Sugar production in the British West Indies

The late nineteenth century was not only a key moment in the intellectual and political history of free trade, it was also a turning point in the relationship between the UK and the British West Indies. There had always been tension between West Indian planters, who organized themselves via the colonial legislatures, and the Crown represented by the colonial governor.[147] The competing interests of the British Crown, the West Indian planters, black and so-called colored workers,

[146] *Hansard*, HC, vol. 115, cols. 256–7, November 24, 1902.
[147] Richardson, *Caribbean's Past*, p. 40.

and indentured workers, primarily from India and China, informed the UK's negotiation and eventual accession to the Brussels Convention.

In 1846, the Sugar Duties Act was passed in the UK, which led to the gradual removal of all duties on sugar and ended the protection and preference that West Indians previously enjoyed in the UK.[148] Free trade advocates treated this legislation as a considerable ideological victory. The planters, however, were infuriated. They argued that allowing for duty-free slave-produced sugar from Cuba and Brazil (which was assumed to cost less than free wage-labor-produced sugar) would ruin West Indian economies and uphold slavery.[149] These arguments implied that the resulting economic distress would potentially lead to violence from recently emancipated slaves, who would find themselves destitute.[150] With the emancipation of slaves in the West Indies in 1834, and, later, the passing of the 1846 Sugar Duties Act, a number of West Indian planters moved to India and reinvested their capital in sugar estates and factories.[151] West Indian planters were further frustrated by the 1847–8 commercial crisis in the UK, which led to the bankruptcy of several prominent West Indian merchants and banks.[152] Some plantations in Jamaica were abandoned and left to crumble, or sold into smaller lots to local, black peasants.[153]

Another socio-economic change arose from the fact that former slaves began to reorganize their relationship with white planters a decade after their emancipation. Each particular island in the West Indies had its own consequent system, which depended on how willing ex-slaves were to move away from the plantation, and on the ensuing relationship with white planters if ex-slaves did decide to move away.[154] A commission of inquiry appointed in 1842 under the chairmanship of Lord Stanley concluded that there was a labor shortage in the British West Indies because former slaves were leaving plantations to buy or rent their own plots of land.[155] Lord Bentick chaired another commission of inquiry, appointed in 1848, to investigate the effects of the Sugar Duties Act in the West Indies. He reiterated the problem of labor shortages and called for financial assistance to help planters with

[148] The sugar duties were completely removed in 1874. See Beachey, *British West Indies*, p. 44.

[149] Delson, "Sugar Production," pp. 59, 62–3. [150] See, e.g., Questel, *Appeal*.

[151] Deerr, *History of Sugar*, vol. II, p. 56. [152] Look Lai, *Indentured Labor*, pp. 10–11.

[153] Black, *Jamaica*, pp. 174–5. [154] Look Lai, *Indentured Labor*, pp. 3–4.

[155] Different islands were affected differently, with Jamaica, Trinidad, and British Guiana experiencing the largest exodus of black workers. *Ibid.*, p. 5.

an immigration project to bring in workers. Starting in the 1840s and lasting into the early 1900s, this demand for labor pulled large numbers of indentured servants from China and India. This was a period of immigration and experimentation in the West Indies that changed the ethnic make-up of the region forever.[156]

By the 1860s, most of the West Indies had recovered from the financial crisis, with the exception of Jamaica.[157] However, because Jamaica was the largest and most populated island in the British West Indies, its unique circumstances eventually affected the relationship between the West Indian sugar colonies and the British Crown. Jamaica had trouble recovering from the financial crisis for several reasons. First, there were ecological reasons. There had been a cholera epidemic in 1850, followed by a smallpox epidemic in 1852 combined with a severe drought, all of which had ruined many plantations.[158] Second, there was a critical labor shortage in Jamaica, resulting from a large number of emancipated slaves relishing their new freedom and refusing to work on plantations.[159]

In response to these concerns, the UK offered West Indian sugar colonies financial support to aid in developing immigration programs (as per Lord Bentick's 1848 report). However, economic conditions in Jamaica were so dire, and workers' wages so low relative to nearby islands, that by 1858, agricultural workers, the small number of black and colored members of legislature, Baptist missionaries, and citizen groups banded together. They successfully organized to keep immigrant workers to a minimum for decades by campaigning against immigration legislation. Their fear was that the influx of indentured servants would weaken the position of black and colored workers by reducing already low wages.[160]

Black workers also feared the return of legal slavery. In 1848, these workers heard a rumor that the US was asked to annex Jamaica, which would then reinstate slavery. The Governor of Jamaica had to issue a proclamation denying the rumor and emphasizing that there was no possibility of slavery returning to the island.[161] The workers' concerns were not unfounded. Some Jamaican political parties (most political

[156] *Ibid.* Look Lai also examines the conditions in China and India at the time, in order to understand how these workers were "pushed" from their respective domiciles.

[157] *Ibid.*, p. 11; Beachey, *British West Indies*, pp. 40–4.

[158] Burns, *History*, pp. 669–70.

[159] Deerr, *History of Sugar*, vol. II, pp. 362–78; Beachey, *British West Indies*, pp. 43–4, 105–11; Look Lai, *Indentured Labor*, p. 4.

[160] Look Lai, *Indentured Labor*, pp. 18, 184–7.

[161] Burns, *History*, p. 653.

parties represented the interest of planters) were so infuriated by the introduction of the 1846 Sugar Duties Act that they suggested that payment of taxes to the UK cease and that the island be annexed to the US.[162]

In October 1865, political disenfranchisement and economic adversity led to a revolt by the black community in Morant Bay, Jamaica. Governor Eyre declared martial law and British troops were sent in to reclaim order. The uprising was quelled through the burning of houses, and the flogging and execution of hundreds of men and women without trial. The majority of the Members of the Jamaican House Assembly feared a general "Negro uprising," especially against the backdrop of Haiti's slave revolt and independence in 1791. As a result, the Jamaican legislature passed legislation granting more power to the executive. Other islands soon followed suit, especially after the Confederation Riots in Barbados in 1876, marking a shift of power in the British West Indies from the colonial legislature to the Crown represented by its governor.[163]

The sugar crisis meant that landowners and sugar farmers often tried to save costs by paying sugar harvesters and workers less, working them harder and for longer hours, for the same pay, or by reducing the number of workers. As such, working conditions deteriorated as the price of sugar declined. In response, workers retaliated across the West Indies from 1884 to 1902, by secretly burning sugar fields. Starting in 1897, workers became more organized, and the regions' earliest unions were formed in Jamaica, Trinidad, and Guyana. Now that the different islands in the British West Indies were Crown Colonies (with the exception of Barbados, which was a self-governing colony), the UK had a direct political hand in trying to maintain order.[164]

By the 1890s, relationships between former slaves and white planters, and between white planters and the British Crown, were overwrought.[165] Joseph Chamberlain, who became Secretary of State for the Colonies in 1895, was becoming impatient with the colonial governments and wanted them to end these conflagrations and keep their respective houses in order.[166] Moreover, Chamberlain, like many in London, considered most non-whites in the West Indies as "near savages." The Morant Bay Rebellion was evidence to many in the mother country that black people were not fit for political leadership. Those in London

162 *Ibid.*, p. 659.
163 Richardson, *Caribbean's Past*, p. 40; Hyam, *Britain's Imperial Century*, p. 156.
164 Hart, "Working Class." 165 Richardson, *Caribbean's Past*, pp. 40, 162.
166 *Ibid.*, pp. 123, 181–2, 191–2.

generally underestimated the increasingly sophisticated, broad-based local groups agitating against local governments to improve their conditions. These opinions also failed to appreciate the trend of increasing literacy, growing numbers of black and brown professionals, and the centrality of English culture within this group of emerging elites.[167] In other words, London only considered how the West Indian colonies benefited the British metropole, and not the reverse.

Imperialism and free trade

Sugar was central to the British West Indies, and the British West Indies were an important part of the British Empire. It is not self-evident, however, what role the sugar colonies played in the Empire. One reason is because there has never been conceptual consensus as to what is meant by the "British Empire." Another reason is that the historical character of the British Empire was always changing, especially since different parts of the Empire were acquired for different reasons.

The British Empire was one of the largest empires that the world has ever known. Throughout history, the British exercised control through a variety of methods, including formal territorial annexation, corporate expansion, and free trade treaties. They devised a variety of forms of territorial control, including self-governing dominions, Crown colonies, protectorates, and mandates. Moreover, imperial power in any one area depended on the nature and degree to which different aspects of indigenous communities engaged with British imperialists. Sometimes indigenous actors were duped, sometimes they were deferential, and at other times they were collaborators. Thus, the British Empire was a diffuse mix of interests, held together through different ideas in a way that did not add up to a coherent whole.[168]

British attitudes towards the Empire also varied. In the late nineteenth century, imperialists could be found in both the Liberal and Conservative parties. More interesting, however, are the varieties of anti-imperialists of the time. We must be careful and note that "anti-imperialist" is a historical term of art. This is because those who described themselves or were described as anti-imperialists were rarely against empires as such, especially settler colonies. Rather, they were against the expansion of existing empires and advocated for imperial reform.[169] By the end of

167 *Ibid.*, p. 191; Hyam, *Britain's Imperial Century*, p. 155.
168 Hyam, *British Empire*, pp. 18–21.
169 Porter, *Critics of Empire*; Taylor, "Imperium et libertas?"; Matikkala, *Imperial Ambition.*

the nineteenth century, most people in Europe did not have the cultural and political means to imagine a world without the existence of some form of empire.[170]

For example, J. A. Hobson is often hailed as one of the earliest theorists and critics of imperialism because of his 1902 monograph, *Imperialism: A Study*. Yet to be sure, Hobson was not against the British Empire per se. Rather, like many other anti-imperialists, he was criticizing "imperialism," which was defined as the rapid expansion of the British Empire, which began in the 1870s, through newly acquired territories that were ruled as formal colonies. Hobson's main argument was that jingoistic support for the British imperial expansion, for purposes of political prestige, Christian proselytizing, personal adventure, or psychological desire, rarely served the UK's economic interest. He called, instead, for some sort of imperial federation of self-governing colonies.[171] Thus, anti-imperialists distinguished between the British Empire, which they wanted to reform but not dismantle, and imperialism as it was being practiced, which they opposed.

Hobson, like many of his fellow anti-imperialists, also repudiated imperial expansion because it contravened principles of free trade.[172] Since the unquestioned world political geography of the time was an imperial picture of some sort, everyone's theory of trade had to work within and reconcile itself with an imperial landscape – free trade was not employed to dismantle empires all together.

There was a wide array of economic theories as to how to organize the British Empire, from both imperialists and anti-imperialists. Sometimes people agreed on the trade policy, but disagreed about imperial policies. Other times, people agreed on an imperialist agenda, but disagreed on the appropriate trade policy. Or, more commonly, people disagreed on both imperial and trade policies, but for a variety of reasons.

[170] Said, *Culture*, p. 24. There are some notable exceptions. In politics, some Cobdenites called for an abandonment of empire altogether. Howe, *Free Trade*, p. 215. In literature, Jules Verne's Captain Nemo in *Vingt mille lieues sous les mers* (1870) and *L'Île mystérieuse* (1874) was one of the few characters in Western literature who exemplified the native hero who rebelled against empire and oppression. Early English translators edited out these sentiments from Verne's novels. Dasgupta, "Jules Verne."

[171] Hobson, *Imperialism*, pp. 74, 179, 245, 251, 347–76.

[172] *Ibid.*, pp. 22, 112; Hobson, "Abandonment." Hobson's thinking about the relationship between free trade and imperialism changed over time; see Cain, "Hobson."

Howe outlines four policy models which different people employed at different times when debating how to structure the British Empire. Each model was a prescription for some conception of empire tied to a particular trade policy. First, there was the idea of a free trade empire that would be comprised of self-governing colonies, which would set their own tariffs only for the purpose of raising revenue; this would create a system of uniform tariffs for goods and do away with differential tariffs based on place of origin. This was a central idea of the Liberal Party during Gladstone's time. Second, there was the idea of an imperial customs union, which would mean that colonies would agree to a common revenue-only imperial tariff; this would increase a sense of imperial political integration. This idea was popular with some members of the Conservative party, but did not gain much traction. Third, the idea of an imperial *Zollverein* imagined free trade within the British Empire, but allowed for high, protective duties against foreign goods. Chamberlain championed this idea, along with various imperialist and fair trade organizations. Fourth was a proposal that involved the UK granting the colonies a mix of preferences for imperial goods and protectionist duties against foreign goods. After 1902, this idea informed Chamberlain's "tariff reform" campaign; this idea arose only after other models of empire more consistent with free trade principles had been ruled out.[173]

We must also be careful how we parse out the different positions of the time regarding free trade. During the latter half of the nineteenth century, free trade discourse had seeped through the general British consciousness: by 1879, free trade principles were zealously adopted in certain parts of government, and by the 1890s, free trade dominated economic thinking by both the public and politicians.[174] The most ardent challenge to free trade theories and policies was organized by the "Fair Trade" movement, which peaked in the 1880s and had fizzled out by the early 1890s.[175]

The unifying idea of the time was that "free trade" was a policy of maintaining as little government involvement as possible in the import and export of goods. The dividing question was what counted as illegitimate government intervention in the market. In the 1890s, free trade principles were debated and reworked not in the annals of

[173] Howe, *Free Trade*, pp. 213–16. [174] Beachey, *British West Indies*, p. 54.

[175] Zebel, "Fair Trade." Not surprisingly, the Fair Trade movement also had a complicated, varied relationship with imperialism.

international jurists or tomes of economic and social theory, but in the everyday policy debates of the financially wealthy and formally educated.[176] Arguments about free trade - and imperialism - were published in pamphlets and high quality, elite newspapers of the time.[177]

Shifts in interests and ideas

Coalescing of interests

There were two types of sugar-refining industries in Great Britain in the nineteenth century. Moist sugar refiners were mostly found in Liverpool and on the river Clyde, and used both foreign and colonial cane sugar. Loaf sugar refiners, which constituted a smaller industry, were mostly found in London and Bristol. They preferred cane sugar from places like Java, Havana, or Mauritius, rather than muscovado cane sugar from the West Indies, because they believed that were able to get more yield out of the former. Loaf sugar refiners competed directly with the subsidized, refined beet sugar that came in from Europe and represented the most vocal opposition to the European bounty systems when they first appeared. Most British West Indian sugar went to moist refiners, so West Indians voiced little concern regarding continental European sugar bounties prior to 1875.

One reason that sugar conferences did not lead to operational treaties for four decades was because during this time, the British government was in part responding to demands by the loaf sugar refiners in Britain and this industry did not wield significant political influence.[178] West Indian planters had been pressing their interests in London, but with very little traction until the 1880s.[179] Whereas the sugar-using industries (such as jam, confectionary, and biscuit manufacturers) were a powerful force within British politics at the time, especially since the rapid drop in prices that led to the sugar crisis had lowered their production costs. The 1890s were when iconic British confectioners Cadbury and Rowntree incorporated and started mass-producing milk chocolate bars.[180] Thus, when an international sugar treaty was signed at a conference in 1888, it failed to be ratified by the British Parliament

[176] Howe, *Free Trade*, p. 194. [177] Matikkala, *Imperial Ambition*, p. 18.

[178] Beachey, *British West Indies*, pp. 48–50. [179] See, e.g., Cropper, *Relief*.

[180] Nestlé Rowntree, "History of Rowntree," available at www.nestle.co.uk/aboutus/nestle-history (accessed May 28, 2014); Cadbury, "The Story," available at www.cadbury.co.uk/the-story (accessed May 28, 2014).

because the leader of the opposition raised the interests and concerns of those manufacturers.[181]

The turning point came around 1876, when the following groups found that their concerns coalesced around declining sugar prices: those who were harmed by the declining price of cane sugar, those who competed with the rising level of imported beet sugar, and those who supported the British West Indian planters politically. By now, British West Indian planters had aligned their interests with the now collapsing British refining industry.[182] By 1882, the National Anti-Bounty League formed as an umbrella group, representing all those who opposed European sugar bounties and supported what later became the Brussels Convention. The League's main voice was a combination of the West Indian Committee (a lobby group representing West Indian planters' interests in London), members from the sugar-refining industry, and "sugar capitalists" (those whose invested capital was at stake), who provided the League with financial assistance. The League explicitly set out in its Constitution that its purpose was to advocate for free trade, not protectionism.

Accordingly, those who opposed the Brussels Convention and did not want to challenge the European bounty system organized themselves through the Cobden Club. This group derived its name from the then-deceased Richard Cobden, who had led the campaign of "free trade" to repeal the Corn Laws in the early nineteenth century ("corn" being the word for any grain, in this case, wheat).[183] This not only included those politicians and industrialists who supported sugar-using industries, but also academics professing a certain theory of free trade that opposed countervailing duties, as well as those who represented the interests of British consumers.

Changes in continental Europe were also key. Because the European bounty system was significantly buttressed by excise taxes, citizens had to bear the brunt of this system directly. In 1884, when France adopted the German-style bounty system, this triggered a "bounty war," primarily between France and Germany, as each nation competed for access to consumer markets in the US and the UK. This not only led to the sugar crisis and a rapid drop in prices, but also significantly increased the

[181] Deerr, *History of Sugar*, vol. II, p. 506. The confectioners were also among the principal supporters of the Liberal government, which later withdrew from the Brussels Convention. Chalmin, *Sugar Giant*, p. 41.

[182] Beachey, *British West Indies*, pp. 50–3; Chalmin, *Sugar Giant*, pp. 45–67.

[183] Howe, *Free Trade*, pp. 191–229; Grampp, *School of Economics*.

practice of citizens' taxes being directed towards the bounty system. Sugar consumers throughout Europe demanded lower sugar prices and were frustrated to see British consumers having access to sugar two to three times cheaper. National treasuries could no longer bear the burden of bounties. European consumers were also becoming weary of, in effect, subsidizing the British confectionary industry.[184]

Moreover, there were political changes in France, where Napoleonic ideas of agricultural self-sufficiency were still influential. French refiners were now gaining political power and challenging the historic position of the ardent agriculturalists. All this occurred while French colonialist power was waning within the French political system.

Countervailing duties, free trade discourse, and the invention of the international trade institution

In the midst of these social, political, and economic changes, the way people thought and argued about free trade also changed. Debates raged in London as to what caused the 1883–4 economic crises and what was to be done. Most scholars and parliamentarians during the debates of the late nineteenth century identified themselves as "free traders." They differed in opinion as to whether foreign subsidization of exports constituted a violation of the principles of free trade, and whether countervailing duties were warranted against this bounty. Similarly, West Indian planters, British refiners, British confectioners, and British consumers all argued within the terms of free trade principles in order to press forward their particular desires regarding sugar, while also claiming that they employed the true concept of free trade.[185]

Historically, free traders opposed countervailing duties since they were thought to be direct government interference in the market. In theory, the UK could have imposed countervailing duties unilaterally. The newly elected Conservative Unionist government was responding to West Indian governors' demands, and the UK was considering the

[184] Martineau, *Question of Sugar*, pp. 7–13; Beeton, *Truth*, pp. 137–40; Malinvaud, *Les Primes Sucres*.

[185] The common way of understanding the historical British debate is to divide the positions between "protectionists," who were against foreign bounties and supported countervailing duties, and "free traders," who were not against foreign bounties if it benefited the British consumer, and were against countervailing duties. They were all, however, arguing within the tenets of free trade. At this point, "protectionist" was used more as an insult.

use of countervailing duties with regards to bounty-fed sugar.[186] This not only curtailed subsidization, but it also allowed the British government to control European production levels by unilaterally adjusting their countervailing duties at any time. European sugar beet producers were now worried because countervailing duties would shut them out of the UK market (they were already blocked from the US market because of high tariffs and countervailing duties.)[187]

While unilateral countervailing duties may have granted the British great international political power, according to free trade principles this would destabilize the sugar market, because it allowed for the whims of government rather than the nature of supply and demand to dictate production levels. Moreover, countries in the past had imposed countervailing duties in order to protect local industries. As such, the British government had a historic aversion to countervailing duties. For example, at the 1888 sugar conference, the British scuttled negotiations by citing free trade principles and refused to include an allowance for a countervailing duty system.[188]

As Taussig, one of modern free trade theory's foundational thinkers, noted during the time of the Brussels Convention, countervailing duties were now necessary because:

> the situation [of sugar bounties] was so exceptional that even a convinced free-trader might accede to this drastic mode of ending it. The bounty system was certainly a greater violation of the principle of free-trade than the prohibition or taxation of bounty-fed imports. It was well-nigh certain to topple over sooner or later from its own weight; and, the sooner it was ended, the better.[189]

Taussig welcomed the Brussels Convention, for it did away with the bounty war and eased relations between nations. Recall that free trade was a policy that was allergic to state power in the market. A new mechanism was therefore needed to keep state power at bay, whether in the form of unilateral countervailing duties or subsidies, and to correct the market. Moreover, along this same line of thought, this new mechanism needed to be guided by free trade principles (and not politics), in

186 "Colonial Office to Treasury (Appointment of Royal Commission)" (November 9, 1896), Correspondence Relating to the Sugar Industry in the West Indies, C. 8359 (1897), p. 100.

187 See, e.g., Correspondence Relating to the Sugar Bounties, C. 8780 (1898), p. 24.

188 Deerr, *History of Sugar*, vol. II, 506. As mentioned above, this was both an ideological aversion to countervailing duties and part of advancing British confectioner's interests.

189 Taussig, "Sugar Bounties," 133–4.

order to determine when bounties were excessive enough to warrant exceptional action. And this was why diplomats and statesman created a novel type of international institution.[190]

To many in the West Indies, these "exceptional" bounties detrimentally affected their economic conditions. Planters and governors from British Guiana, Trinidad, Antigua, Barbados, Jamaica, and St. Lucia increased their complaints of economic depression, and petitioned the British government to take action against what they thought was the cause of the depression - the European bounty system.[191] West Indian planters assumed that the bounty system blocked their access to the British consumer market because it significantly reduced the price of sugar.

Some in Europe had little sympathy for the West Indian governors' and planters' argument because, by the late nineteenth century, most West Indian sugar was exported to the US. After 1846, West Indian sugar no longer had privileged access to its traditional market in the UK. Planters increasingly began to export their sugar to the US, such that by the 1890s, the US was the primary destination for West Indian sugar. However, what added to the colonialists' pessimism was that negotiations to establish a preferential trade agreement between the US and the West Indies failed in 1884–5. Therefore, West Indian planters no longer had access to the US market because of high tariffs, nor to the UK market because of the dumping of European continental sugar.[192]

Petitioners also thought that the bounty system diminished confidence in the West Indian sugar industry's production capacity because it slowed down the flow of capital investment from London; this was thought to be necessary to modernize the colonial sugar industry. In contemporary terms, colonialists made free trade claims for a system of countervailing duties to oppose foreign subsidization, alongside arguments for access to more developed markets and capital investment in local industry. Today, those appeals are made from poorer countries

[190] The earliest countervailing duties were also in the context of sugar, but were structured through domestic law and not within a free trade scheme. The US's 1890 McKinley Tariff included a system of countervailing duties and high tariffs that created a highly protected regional sugar market. See Findings of the Permanent Commission established Under Article VII of the Sugar Convention of March 5, 1902, and Report of the British Delegate, Cd 1632 (1903), pp. 5–6.

[191] Correspondence Relating to the Sugar Industry in the West Indies, C. 8359 (1897); Correspondence Relating to the Sugar Conference At Brussels 1901–1902, Cd 940 (1902).

[192] Beachey, *British West Indies*, pp. 139–40.

(which we now call developing) to richer countries (which we would call developed). The twist is that the richer nation that the West Indies was appealing to was the "mother country"; that is, planters and governors couched their interests as part of the UK's interest.

This aligned well with how Chamberlain understood imperialism. Chamberlain was the official instigator behind passing the Brussels Convention through the British Parliament, and was one of the most persistent, high-level politicians who supported imperialism. As Secretary of State for the Colonies, his methods were unique, for he regularly drew on his personal experiences in the world of commerce. He preferred to rely on his business contacts and private capital rather than legislative or bureaucratic devices in order to improve economic conditions in the West Indies.[193]

By examining debates within the UK between the Anti-Bounty League and the Cobden Club, we can see how countervailing duties found their way into British free trade discourse. The Anti-Bounty League's arguments can be summarized as follows.[194] The problem with the bounty system is not that it reduces the price of sugar. Rather, the problem is that it does not allow for the "natural" price of sugar because of bounties. "Natural price" means the price dictated by the market without any government interference. This is problematic because the purpose of free trade is not simply for consumers to receive goods at the cheapest price, but for consumers to receive goods at the cheapest natural price. Bounties create "unnatural" prices because they are dictated by government policy and are a form of protection; they disallow sugar from outside to enter, exploit the use of national taxes to sell sugar in free trade countries, and create instability in cane sugar industries due to the fear that beet bounties will increase at any moment. Countervailing duties, therefore, compensate for this economic transgression and restore sugar to its natural price. Countervailing duties do not contravene most favored nation (MFN) clauses in bilateral commercial treaties. This is because the spirit of MFN clauses concerns equality, and therefore they do not apply in this instance because the bounties constitute such a disparity of competitive conditions. Thus, countervailing duties are necessary in exceptional circumstances.

[193] Hyam, *Britain's Imperial Century*, pp. 248–9.

[194] I am drawing from Smart, *Sugar Bounties*; Anti-Bounty League, *Report of Proceedings*; Beeton, *Truth*; Carrington, *Colonies*; Beeton, *Twenty Years*; Beeton, *"Open-Door"*; Shepheard, "Most-favoured-nation."

These arguments for countervailing duties, made popular and refined because of the Brussels Convention, still resonate in free trade debates today. The argument and concerns regarding domestic industries is similar to the theory informing GATT Article VI and the WTO Agreement on Subsidies and Countervailing Measures, which allow for countervailing duties. The GATT provision is intended to ensure that products maintain a "normal value," by preventing subsidization for products intended for export (Para. 1). Subsidies are prevented by allowing for countervailing duties, which are defined as "a special duty levied for the purpose of offsetting any bounty or subsidy bestowed directly or indirectly upon the manufacture, production or export of any merchandise" (Para. 3). The GATT provides for a factual test in which a countervailing duty is authorized only when the "subsidization ... is such as to cause or threaten material injury to an established domestic industry, or is such as to retard materially the establishment of a domestic industry" (Para. 6(a)).[195]

The Anti-Bounty League considered those who supported the bounties and were against countervailing duties to be protectionists who had misread Adam Smith's and Cobden's work. The League derided members of the Cobden Club for assuming that the role of government was to ensure that citizens are left to be free in the market and allow competition to rule everyday life. This laissez-faire view, League members argued, ignores the role government already plays through laws regarding commerce, factories, education, and land. However, they argued, laissez-faire is a policy of government inaction and does not necessarily equate with free trade.

This argument mirrors the critique of the idea of a self-regulating market by Polanyi and some American legal realists. The early US legal progressives (such as Oliver Wendell Holmes, Jr.) and early legal realists, contemporaries of the Anti-Bounty League, provided an account of the market which outlined how the state always played a regulatory role in its relationship to the market. They showed that the state enacted the laws which determined, whether through action or inaction, how wealth and power would be distributed through the market.[196] This also parallels arguments that the regulation of domestic markets is

[195] I only highlight GATT Article VI because the WTO Agreement on Subsidies and Countervailing Measures (SCM) is more complex. The SCM follows a similar general logic regarding countervailing duties.

[196] See, e.g., Holmes, "Privilege"; Pound, "Liberty"; Cook, "Labor Unions"; Hale, "Coercion"; Cohen, "Property."

inextricable from, but does not necessarily determine how, international trade should be internationally organized.[197]

The Cobden Club argument was as follows.[198] Countervailing duties are against principles of free trade mainly because they demand government intervention in the market. This was problematic because the government is ill-equipped to regulate the market. Moreover, MFN clauses were a paramount concept in free trade; thus, because countervailing duties treated goods from different countries differently, the duties offended principles of free trade and MFN clauses in commercial treaties.

The Cobden Club members also unwittingly foreshadowed contemporary arguments that establishing legally specific definitions for economic concepts, and ensuring that all the different definitions were theoretically coherent, would be difficult, if not impossible, in an international trade treaty.[199] For example, the Cobdenites argued, it is extremely difficult to define exactly what counts as a bounty – are investments in infrastructure, such as roads and railroads, bounties?[200] They also argued that it would be difficult to determine what should be the appropriate countervailing duty.

Even though the ideational debates regarding free trade of the late nineteenth century have contemporary equivalents, the stakes behind the ideas were particular to the time and do not carry over to current arguments. Ideological differences regarding the role of the state, the role of the market, and definitions of free trade were not the only differences between the two positions. Each position also connected to particular positions about the British Empire.

The arguments of the Anti-Bounty League (and its supporters) included imperialist plans to support, if not expand, the British Empire. They considered the role of the West Indies to be crucial to the British Empire. Some were concerned that if the British Empire were weakened, then the German Empire would fill in the gaps.

Members of the Cobden Club were predominantly anti-imperialists. They discounted the economic role of the West Indies in the British

[197] A most prescient argument at the time, though not published with reference to the Anti-Bounty League, was Amery, *Fundamental Fallacies*. For a contemporary argument, see, e.g., Ruggie, "At Home Abroad"; Howse, "Politics to Technocracy"; Unger, *Free Trade*.

[198] I am drawing from Farrer, *Free Trade*; Johnson, *Sugar Tax*; Cooke, "Sugar Convention"; Cooke, "Sugar and the Tariff"; Cooke, "Amended Sugar Convention."

[199] Tarullo, "Logic"; Driesen, "What Is Free Trade?". [200] Sykes, "Subsidies Regulation."

Empire and assumed that the British confectioners were a more viable industry. Any depression in the West Indies, they assumed, was exaggerated, and not necessarily caused by the bounty system in Europe. Each country had such a complex and different system of tariffs and duties, they argued, that it was not clear how to establish its relationship to the price of sugar. Moreover, they believed that if the low price of sugar were a result of foreign bounties, it was not a concern of the British government because it was a benefit to the British consumer at the expense of foreigners, and was not sustainable by foreign governments and thus would probably collapse on its own.

By 1886–7, the Anti-Bounty League vision of free trade significantly influenced British government policy. This is evidenced by the appointment of two Royal Commissions whose mandate was to address the 1884 crises in Great Britain and the West Indies. The first of these, the Royal Commission on the Depression in Trade and Industry,[201] was headed by Neville Lubbock, chairman of the West India Committee (and who later served as an expert for the British delegation to the conference that led to the Brussels Convention).[202] The Cobdenites in Parliament decried this nomination because they thought that Lubbock's appointment was indicative of the Commission's general "protectionist" bias.[203] In 1886, the Commission produced a majority and minority report. The majority report affirmed the older view of free trade and did not propose any changes to the British policy of reducing tariffs via MFN policies. The minority report (which Lubbock signed), however, reflected a rising opinion that the British government should grant colonial goods duty-free access and should levy duties against countries that did not provide adequate market access to British goods. This would not be the trade policy exemplified in the Brussels Convention, but it did reflect how orthodox thinking about trade was being challenged. More importantly, to many scholars and policy-makers of the time, the minority report was more accurate in its assessment of the problem.[204]

The West India Royal Commission was appointed to examine the state of the sugar industry in the West Indies. It was one of the most significant and innovative official investigations of the West Indies in

[201] Final Report of the Royal Commission Appointed to Inquire into the Depression of Trade and Industry, C. 4893 (1886).

[202] Correspondence Relating to the Conference at Brussels on the Question of Sugar Bounties, C. 8938 (1898), p. 1.

[203] Beachey, *British West Indies*, p. 137.

[204] Zebel, "Fair Trade," 174–5.

the nineteenth century.[205] Chamberlain's primary concern was that the West Indies depended solely on sugar, and that if the industry were to collapse, there would be no other industry to compensate for the unemployed, thereby causing great political instability and financial strain for the UK.[206] The West India Royal Commission concluded, in 1897, that the West Indian sugar industry was on the verge of extinction and that this had likely been caused by the European bounty system.[207] This provided factual detail supporting the ideological shift within free trade discourse and Chamberlain's political support for strengthening Britain's empire.

Institutionalization of free trade colonialism

The delegates at the opening of the conference proceedings that led to the signing of the Brussels Convention, despite their perfunctory nature, capture the political and economic conceptions that permeated the final agreement.[208] The German delegate's statement was the exception that made the British the rule. According to the delegate, Germany was in transition to a bounty-less condition. The delegate stated that the German bounty system was only intended as a temporary measure to benefit manufactures until they could produce without government aid. The German delegate's remarks captured continental European countries' "infant industries" economic policy (an idea expounded by Alexander Hamilton[209] and commonly attributed to Friedrich List[210]). The continental European sugar industry, however, was now mature, and governments, after nearly a century of subsidizing their domestic sugar industry, needed a mechanism to give them leverage against politically powerful domestic sugar producers; the Brussels Convention ensured access to the lucrative UK sugar-consuming market only if subsidization ceased. Thus, sugar producers could be weaned off government subsidization, and be sure of access to the UK market without having to compete with sugar producers from other countries who were subsidized by their respective governments.

[205] Lobdell, "British Officials," pp. 195, 199.
[206] Correspondence Relating to the Sugar Industry in the West Indies, C. 8359 (1897), p.103.
[207] Report of the West India Royal Commission, C. 8655, 8656, 8657, 8669 (1898).
[208] US Senate Committee on Finance, *Proceedings of the Conference on the Question of Bounties, held at Brussels, Jun 7–25, 1898* (Blue Book Commercial No. 6, 1898), pp. 20–2.
[209] Hamilton, *Manufactures*. [210] List, *Political Economy*.

The British delegate's opening remarks were straight out of the pages of Anti-Bounty League pamphlets. He stated that principles of free trade demanded that products everywhere be sought at their natural market price, without the artificial hindrance of bounties. When expressing his concern that unnatural effects on price create uncertainty for the consumer and destroy industries not favored by the state, the delegate noted the depression of sugar industries in British colonies and refineries.

Even though the West Indian colonies were a principal reason why the Brussels Convention was created, they were treated as an explicit exception in the treaty. The general rule was that the treaty should apply to all parties' colonies (Art. XI). The Permanent Commission decided that this meant that all colonies were allowed preferential access to their respective "mother country." For example, in assessing sugar produced in Cuba and the Philippines and then refined and exported from the US, the Permanent Commission decided that the fact that the US granted preferential treatment to sugar from Cuba and the Philippines (all non-signatories) was akin to a formal colonial relationship, and therefore was not considered a bounty.[211] This was similar to how John Stuart described England's historical relationship to the West Indies:

> Our West Indian colonies, for example, cannot be regarded as countries with a productive capital of their own ... [but are, rather] the place where England finds it convenient to carry on the production of sugar, coffee, and a few other tropical commodities. All the capital employed is English capital; almost all the industry is carried on for English uses; there is little production of anything except for staple commodities and these are sent to England, not to be exchanged for things exported to the colony and consumed by its inhabitants, but to be sold in England for the benefit of the proprietors there. The trade with the West Indies is hardly to be considered an external trade, but more resembles traffic between town and country.[212]

This, in effect, was the premise of the Brussels Convention, since it considered the West Indies and the UK as an integrated political unit, but separate economic units. But the nature of this relationship was modified during treaty negotiations. An explicit exception was made in Art. XI for British (and Dutch) colonies. In light of the British sugar colonies' persistent demand for financial support and Chamberlain's

[211] International Sugar Commission Spring Session 1905, Report of British Delegate and Correspondence, Cd 2531 (1905), pp. 17, 23.

[212] Mill, *Political Economy*, Book III, Ch. XXV, para. 17.

imperial policies, the British delegates tried to negotiate as much flexibility as possible, to allow the UK to support the West Indies financially.[213] Late in the negotiations, British delegates argued that they wanted to retain the right to provide bounties to the West Indies and that the penal clause only applied to Europe. This, of course, generated surprise amongst the other delegates and talks almost broke down on this issue.[214] The end result was an annex to Article XI, which is worth reproducing in detail:

> (A) 1. The Government of Great Britain declares that no bounty, direct or indirect, shall be granted to the sugar of the Crown Colonies during the continuance of the Convention.
>
> 2. It also declares, *as an exceptional measure*, and reserving in principle entire liberty of action as regards the fiscal relations between the United Kingdom and its Colonies and Possessions, that, during continuance of the Convention, *no preference will be granted in the United Kingdom to colonial sugar* as against sugar from the Contracting States. [emphasis added]

This was to commit the UK to two things. First, the UK explicitly renounced its ability to subsidize sugar from the West Indies. Second, the UK agreed not to provide the West Indies with preferential access to its home market (most of the British colonies in the West Indies were by this time "Crown Colonies"); even though the provision is written in the language of exceptionality, it was understood that the British would have to pay a high political cost to other Convention members if they granted their colonies an imperial preference.

The treaty thereby aligned more with different anti-imperialist conceptions of the British Empire which emphasized economically independent colonies that were politically held together through some sort of federation or commonwealth. The treaty also made it significantly more difficult for Chamberlain to install his ideal system of imperial preferences. Thus, the treaty economically disconnected the sugar colonies from the center of the British Empire. And yet it employed a theory of trade that allowed for countervailing duties which aligned with the assumption of imperialists that trade policy should serve to strengthen British imperial power. It was a theory of trade, with its desire to stabilize sugar to its natural price, tied to Chamberlain's

[213] See, e.g., Correspondence Relating to the Sugar Bounty Conference, Cd 1013 (1902), pp. 19, 24.

[214] *Ibid.*, pp. 36–40.

affinity for private capital. It is not surprising, then, that when the Liberal party took power in 1905, they maintained British membership in the treaty, but suspended the penal clause.[215]

The treaty also marginalized the West Indies in the formalized international sugar market by making them the exception to the exception. In effect, the treaty built in a disadvantage against other sugar producers. The treaty allowed for an infant industry exception for countries that produced but did not export sugar, since they did not have to remove any of their bounties (Art. VI). Only when these countries become exporters did the bounty-removal requirements apply. This exceptional status was a privilege limited to the enumerated countries (Spain, Italy, and Sweden). These exceptional sugar-producing, non-exporting countries were still allowed to evoke the penal clause, thereby allowing them to subsidize domestic sugar industries and block foreign subsidized sugar through countervailing duties or import prohibition. Thus, exceptional countries could develop their domestic sugar industry until they were able to compete internationally without public financial support. In one final move to cement this arrangement, the Commission decided that it did not have the power to admit new members under the exceptional category.[216]

Conclusion: the treaty's effects

The sugar trade

Regardless of how the Brussels Convention actually impacted the West Indian sugar industry, many in the UK and the West Indies adamantly believed that the treaty, and the ideas it embodied, was in the best interest of preserving economic and political stability in the West Indies. The British were trying to negotiate an early enforcement date, based on the assumption that the sooner the treaty was signed, the

[215] Correspondence Respecting the Additional Act to the Brussels Sugar Convention of March 5, 1902, signed at Brussels, August 28, 1902, Cd 3780 (1907). This had the effect of making the sugar treaty a more traditional MFN trade treaty.

[216] *Protocol Relative to the Accession of Switzerland to the International Convention Concerning the Regime of Sugars of March 5, 1902*, June 26, 1906, 202 *Parry* 79, Cd 3301 [admitting Switzerland as an sugar-producing, non-exporting exception, but not allowing it to vote; entered into force September 1, 1906]. See also Further Findings of the Permanent Commission Established Under the Sugar Convention of March 5, 1902, Report of the British Delegate and Appeal of His Majesty's Government Against Certain of those Findings, Cd 2349 (1905), p. 3.

sooner the British West Indies could benefit.[217] Colonial governors held the same beliefs, and in 1906–7 petitioned the newly elected British government to remain a party to the Convention;[218] despite their de facto marginalization by the treaty, the governors maintained their faith in the treaty's potential to improve conditions in their sugar colonies throughout the span of the UK's membership.[219]

Richardson notes that in Barbados, the site of the worst political protest arsons, the number of sugar cane fires had dropped by April 1902, and in the rest of the region by 1905. Richardson doubts that the Brussels Convention had enough time to have affected the islands and leaves it open as to why sugar cane fires began to decrease in 1902.[220] One reason could be that sugar workers were starting to form new unions and were therefore increasingly expressing their grievances through organized labor rather than unruly fire.[221]

All this suggests that the Brussels Convention was part of a trend of shifting conditions in the West Indies rather than an instigator of change. But the treaty may have contributed indirectly to local conditions. There is evidence that the treaty generated the confidence necessary to increase investment in the sugar colonies[222] – and this change in perception may have been its most notable contribution to the West Indies. The main issue was that sugar needed to be processed near where it was harvested before it was sent to the refinery. Even though old mills that crushed sugar cane were gradually being replaced by steam-driven mills, it was not until 1874 that the first central factory was constructed in the British West Indies (in St. Lucia).[223] With the 1884 crisis, there was little financial confidence or political will to invest in central factories and very few were built.[224] After the crisis, many sugar producers in Jamaica sold their machinery to Cuban producers.[225] Colonial governors desired the capital and legal authority from London to be able to widely establish central factories. London, however, did not support the idea of central factories until around 1897.[226]

[217] Correspondence Relating to the Sugar Bounty Conference, Cd 1013 (1902), p. 37.

[218] Papers Relating to the Brussels Sugar Convention, Cd 3565 (1907). [219] *Ibid.*

[220] Richardson, *Caribbean's Past*, p. 124. [221] Hart, "Working Class," pp. 43–7.

[222] Burns, *History*, p. 706; Taylor, "Brussels," 354–6. [223] Shephard, "Sugar Industry."

[224] See, e.g., Correspondence Relating to the Sugar Industry in the West Indies, C. 8359 (1897), p. 56.

[225] Moya Pons, *History*, p. 265.

[226] Correspondence Relating to the Sugar Industry in the West Indies, C. 8359 (1897), p. 100. See also Beachey, *British West Indies*, p. 86 (Beachey mistypes "1827" for "1897").

To the West Indian planters and supporters of the agreement, signing of the Brussels Convention provided the stability needed to instill confidence in the market.[227] British Parliament granted £250,000 to cover the immediate needs of sugar planters for the year between the signing of the treaty and its coming into force, in anticipation that the West Indies would need help catching up with all the previously subsidized, industrially advanced sugar industries.[228] In places like the Leeward Islands and Jamaica, laws and policies were put forward that encouraged the building of central factories.[229] The central factories that were built during this time shifted control of sugar production from planters to factory owners. Many of the resulting changes endure today, both in terms of technology and dynamics of power between estate owners, cane farmers, and central factories.[230]

Yet local conditions were not all that West Indian planters had to worry about. Global interests also shifted after the Brussels Convention. Both supporters and opponents of the treaty assumed that it would benefit colonial sugar cane growers to the detriment of sugar consumers and sugar-related industries; they vehemently disagreed over the normative implications of this perceived benefit. What does not seem to have been anticipated was that even though the treaty did allow for unsubsidized sugar cane to have increased access to the growing British and European appetites, the source would not be the West Indies. Latecomers to the treaty such as Peru, and non-signatories such as Argentina, which had subsidized their local sugar industry in the past, changed their domestic system of tariffs and duties in order to gain access to the world's largest market of consumers in the UK and continental Europe.[231] Similarly, Cuba and Hawaii, which had benefited from US preferential treatment, also made headway into the expanding European market.[232]

[227] Castelot, "Sugar Conference"; Taussig, "Sugar Bounties"; Castelot, "High Prices"; Martineau, "Sugar Convention"; Geerligs, *Sugar Industry*, p. 209; Beachey, *British West Indies*, p. 171.

[228] Geerligs, *Sugar Industry*, p. 209. See also Correspondence Relating to the Sugar Bounty Conference, Cd 1013 (1902), p. 37. To give a rough sense of what this meant, in 2005, that would have been approximately equivalent to £14,200,000. See www.nationalarchives.gov.uk/currency (accessed May 28, 2014).

[229] Correspondence Relating to the Sugar Conference at Brussels 1901–1902, Cd 940 (1902), p. 37; Galloway, *Sugar*, p. 148.

[230] Galloway, *Sugar*, pp. 148–82. [231] *Ibid.*, pp. 180, 188.

[232] Timoshenko and Swerling, *World's Sugar*, p. 240.

The Brussels Convention, therefore, may actually have hampered the development of the sugar industry in the West Indies. The West Indies were so technologically less advanced than bounty-fed sugar producers, that even with the UK's injection of capital right before the treaty was signed, West Indian sugar producers could never match the industrial efficiency of others. In effect, the treaty, by disallowing subsidies, blocked West Indian sugar from the British and European markets, since it could not compete with the more technologically advanced sugar producers. This meant that the Brussels Convention had the effect of "kicking away the ladder" from under the feet of West Indian sugar producers.[233]

The British had a distaste for cheaper, unrefined, viscous, brown Caribbean muscovado sugar, and a preference for more expensive, refined, granulated, white European sugar.[234] Thus, Caribbean sugar had to be refined to reach British consumers (and there were hardly any refineries to speak of in the West Indies). By 1902, however, the cane sugar-refining industry in the UK was practically extinct.[235] After the Brussels Convention, most of the sugar consumed in the UK was refined beet sugar from Europe.[236] This could be an indication that Europe's bounty system had generated an efficient and productive sugar industry that could compete in the British market without subsidies. But it also indicates that consumers' gastronomical preferences, regardless of price differential, had economic consequences.[237] The British West Indies' sugar industry was saved because of Canada's growing consumer market, with its gastronomical partiality for muscovado and its preferential trade agreement.[238]

Free trade ideas

When colonial governors and imperialists started to express their demands through free trade ideas, the conclusion of a trade treaty became possible after four decades of failed attempts. Subsidizing the

[233] Chang, *Kicking Away the Ladder*.

[234] Beachey, *British West Indies*, pp. 143–4; Deerr, *History of Sugar*, vol. II, pp. 109–10, 528–30.

[235] Beachey, *British West Indies*, p. 172. [236] Chalmin, "Important Trends," p. 15.

[237] I do not assume that taste is a biological given or simply a matter of personal preference. Historians remind us that taste is the result of a complex mix of psychological and cultural forces, along with social, economic, and political conditions. Trentmann (ed.), *History of Consumption*.

[238] Beachey, *British West Indies*, pp. 139–40, 173–4.

West Indies sugar industry was not an option, because of anti-imperialist political pressure and because of how free trade discourse dominated all aspects of British policy-making. Thus, the only means of holding the British Empire together through acceptable principles of free trade was through countervailing duties.

Theoretically, countervailing duties could be unilaterally implemented; they were the exercise of state power against another state subsidizing its sugar production. In practice, however, unilateral countervailing duties were most often employed to protect domestic industries from foreign imports (as was done in the US with the 1890 McKinley Tariff). But in this instance, countervailing duties were being innovatively deployed as a means to increase the flow of trade.

Thus, policy-makers turned to the new mode of governance of the time. An international institution would have to monitor the complexities of sugar technologies and domestic fiscal laws in order to determine when a subsidy was a derivation from the natural market and ensure that appropriate remedies were implemented. Member state governments agreed that their common purpose was to do away with subsidies. The institution's function, therefore, was to arbitrate between states over the different ways one could define the complexities of the sugar market.

Recall that from the perspective of international lawyers, this involved ceding sovereignty to an international institution. From the perspective of commercial and imperial actors, however, the integrity of the market was their priority. They experienced the sugar market as inherently interconnected, and sovereignty was already a porous idea: the fiscal policies of continental European countries supported a domestic industry, but affected the global price of sugar and rattled the British Empire; sugar worker rebellion in the West Indies changed British imperial structures and challenged European fiscal policies; and the British propensity for sweet tea and confectionaries put the British Empire at the center of the transnational sugar market. Therefore, the task was to more formally institutionalize the market in a way that adhered to free trade principles and attended to political agendas. For the UK and West Indies colonial governors, this was in order to ensure stable market conditions that would encourage private investment in the sugar colonies. For the continental European governments, this was to grant them leverage against their subsidized domestic sugar industries and to push them to compete in the British consumer market.

What remains is to question why the British government agreed to the marginalization of the West Indies in the Brussels Convention, and why West Indian governors were pleased by the final results. One reason is that only in hindsight are we able to discern the treaty's economic and political effects. But also, the government officials' powerful faith in the ideas of free trade – with its competing conceptions and respective divergent distributive consequences – made it more difficult for them to clearly assess the effects of the Brussels Convention.

The Brussels Convention's greatest outcome was how it influenced ideas about free trade. It gave intellectual credence to the notion that subsidies are an unnatural intervention into the market and that countervailing duties are a necessary remedy. After 1902, within the Cobden Club and at the earliest international free trade conferences, some referenced the Brussels Convention as an exemplar of a liberal free trade agreement. It was praised for restricting the "artificial pampering" of the European sugar industry and increasing consumer demand through stable prices.[239] Similar characterizations of the Brussels Convention as an example of a liberal trade treaty were made throughout the 1920s and 1930s.[240] Countervailing duties are still a controversial issue in economic theory, but remain a component of free trade discourse partly because the WTO includes an Agreement on Subsidies and Countervailing Measures.[241]

[239] Welby *et al.* (eds.), *Proceedings*, pp. 120, 269, 560. (The International Free Trade Congress, the first of its kind, was an international gathering of "free traders" organized by Cobden Club. The opening address was by Winston Churchill, who was at the time the President of the Board of Trade and representative of His Majesty's Government.) Even some Cobdenites had been won over in the debates leading up to the treaty. Howe, *Free Trade*, p. 208.

[240] See, e.g., Notz, "Private Agreements," 676; Viner, *Dumping*, pp. 185–6; Wilk, "International Affairs," 863.

[241] See, e.g., Krugman, Obstfeld, and Melitz, *International Economics*, pp. 179–80; Sykes, "Subsidies Regulation."

PART III

The 1937 ISA, Cuba, and the League of Nations

Like motor-cars, wireless telephony, aviation, prohibition, fluctuating exchanges, Russian bolshevism, Italian fascism, American opulence and European impecuniosity, the League was a "fact" which the "student of contemporary affairs" could either praise or damn but simply could not ignore.

William Rappard (then Rector of the University of Geneva and member of the Mandates Commission), 1926, quoted in Pemberton, "New Worlds," 315

Alas, Miranda has blazing cane
Palmarito has blazing cane
Santa Lucía has blazing cane
What is happening in my Cuba
That cane is now hardly being sold
I'm dying for the price to go up
What is happening to the Good Neighbor
He is buying very little cane from me
I'm shouting at the Good Neighbor
"You need to raise the quota"

Lorenzo Hierrezuelo and Duo Los Compadres, *c.* 1930, quoted in McGillivray, *Blazing Cane*, p. 1

5 Economic aspects of the League of Nations

From Brussels to Havana and Geneva

When the Brussels Sugar Convention was signed in 1902, one of Cuba's great "sugar barons," Manuel Rionda y Polledo, hoped that the UK would turn to Cuba for its demands for sugar. Cuba had just gained its independence from Spain and Cuban delegates were negotiating the terms of their neocolonial relationship with the US. Rionda, who, like other members of the Cuban commercial elite, had his money tied up in US banks, US refineries, Cuban sugar fields and Cuban mills, benefited from preferential access to the US. However, Rionda worried, and was proven correct, that the US would only provide duty-free access to sugar from its colonies and annexations in the Philippines, Puerto Rico, and Hawaii.

The Brussels Convention provided the Cubans with hope of duty-free access to the world's largest sugar consumer – the UK. Buttressed by the confidence that the Brussels Convention provided, Rionda warned US Senator Platt (author of the Platt Amendment which would define the US–Cuba relationship) that if the US did not act quickly, Cuba would "slip through their hands." Regulating how sugar from Cuba would enter the US for decades to come, the Platt Agreement provided Cuban sugar with preferential access to the US market, though not duty-free access.[242] As the price of sugar radically fluctuated and declined after the First World War, Rionda envisaged a "League of Nations of Sugar" to stabilize the world sugar trade.[243] This story of Rionda would not only mark the future of how US and Cuban interests would intertwine,

[242] McAvoy, *Sugar Baron*, pp. 43–4. [243] *Ibid.*, p. 2.

but would also foreshadow the role of sugar and international trade agreements in shaping the League of Nations.

Even though the 1902 Brussels Convention lay at the origins of the modern multilateral *trade* institutions, during the time of the League, many looked to the Brussels Convention as a formal exemplar for the institutional design of the League as a whole. Sometimes the sugar treaty was highlighted as an example of multilateralism because it was thought to have successfully managed the world economy and diverse national policies.[244] Some looked to the Brussels Convention as an important antecedent to the League as a whole, because its Permanent Commission was thought to be the first example of a permanent international body that effectively influenced domestic policy.[245] What is telling is how the 1902 Brussels Convention was characterized during the time of the League, because it was in line with the trend of the time to deemphasize the League's economic aspects.[246]

Rarely was the 1902 Brussels Convention examined as an international economic agreement regulating international agriculture, despite the fact that its subject was the sugar trade. One League report commissioned to research the prospect of an international sugar agreement and summarizing the findings of retained experts, made the point that the experts could only agree on one issue – that the principles of the 1902 Brussels Sugar Convention did not apply to the context of the sugar crisis they were studying (in 1929).[247]

Nevertheless, the negotiators of the subsequent international sugar agreements looked to the 1902 Brussels Convention as evidence that that a multilateral agreement regulating international sugar trade was feasible.[248] This led to two international sugar agreements during the interwar period: the 1931 Chadbourne Agreement[249] and the 1937 ISA.

[244] Economic and Financial Section, *Report and Proceedings*, vol. I, p. 89; Schüller, [no title], p. 113; Grossman, *Rapprochement*, p. 26; Viner, *Memorandum*, p. 18; Hirsch, *Monopolies*, p. 23.

[245] See, e.g., Sayre, *Experiments*, pp. 117–24; Hicks, *New World Order*, pp. 267–8; McClure, *World Prosperity*, p. 50; Zimmern, *League of Nations*, pp. 58–60; Mander, *Foundations*, p. 237; Hill, *League of Nations*, p. 12.

[246] One exception is McClure, *World Prosperity*, pp. 49–50, 368 (suggesting that the 1902 Brussels Agreement was the blueprint for devising the tariff scheme for League agreements relating to hides, skins, and bones. To him, this latter agreement was one of the earliest multilateral trade treaties.)

[247] Economic Committee, *World Sugar*, p. 15. [248] McAvoy, *Sugar Baron*, pp. 223–34.

[249] Reprinted in "The Brussels Sugar Convention of 1931" (1931), 33 *International Sugar Journal* 391.

On its face, the Chadbourne Agreement was a private agreement between world sugar producers. It was named after Thomas Chadbourne, a Wall Street lawyer selected by Cuban sugar mill owners and American and Canadian financiers to stabilize the world sugar market. Since the signatories of the Chadbourne Agreement acted in their commercial capacity, one could contrast it against the 1937 ISA, which was an intergovernmental agreement, signed under the auspices of the League of Nations. It is, however, more accurate to understand both of these agreements as early experiments in transnational governance.[250]

What this means is that these trade agreements were informed by no clear delineation between things like the state and market, public and private, or domestic and international.[251] As such, these agreements structured how these categories were understood and negotiated. For example, to one jurist, the 1937 ISA "represented a considerable modification of the principle of absolute state sovereignty," since the more a state imported or exported sugar, the more voting power it wielded within the concomitant sugar institution.[252] Moreover, there was no preconceived sense of what it meant in practice for an agreement to be signed under the auspices of the League rather than outside of it. And, as always in diplomacy, the line between the personal and professional was often blurred.

Regardless of their formal status as League or non-League conventions, both the 1931 Chadbourne Agreement and 1937 ISA were significantly informed by the League's economic doctrines. Which League doctrines were taken up and how those doctrines were refined and implemented in order to structure the world sugar market was determined by the fact that the sugar conventions were deeply embedded within the Cuban political economy. In this chapter, I outline the underappreciated history of the League's economic doctrines. The reason that I survey the most popular doctrines (rather than argue that one doctrine was better than another) is in order to set out the array of choices that was readily available to the rising Cuban sugar elite. The League was not only a reflection of North American and Western European interests. These emerging leaders of commerce and governance turned to League

[250] Trentmann, "Shortage," pp. 13, 15. See also Clavin and Wessels, "Transnationalism."

[251] von Graevenitz, "Changing Visions." On transnational law, see Zumbansen, "Transnational Law."

[252] Freeman, "Administrative Law," 979.

ideas, prowess, and prestige in order to increase the economic power of the Cuban state. Thus, in Chapter 6, I focus on transnational sugar political economy and the history of the Cuban state in order to outline one of the few cases in which League economic doctrines were put into operation. By taking Havana as the hub of the transnational sugar trade and looking out to Geneva, Washington DC, New York, and Toronto, we gain a clearer theoretical sense of how transnational governance was put into practice.

Of course, the Cuban story is not the only one that can be told in order to understand the sugar treaties or the League. One could look at life in Java and its relationship to the "home country" of the Netherlands. Java dominated sugar production in the Eastern hemisphere. Dutch delegates were the primary protagonists in trying to advocate for lower tariffs in the world; their particular trade ideology and engagement in League debates was likely affected by conditions in the sugar cane fields of Java and sugar beet fields of the Netherlands.[253] Moreover, others have noted the competition between cane growers in Java and Cuba.[254] Nevertheless, Cuban delegates were the principal advocates for an international sugar treaty, which was one of the League's few successful economic treaties. Thus, Cuban experiences and contexts can provide some insight into the economic functions of the League.

The League of Nations as an international economic institution

League historiography

Surveys[255] and histories[256] of the League of Nations often characterize it as a political institution, occasionally as a social institution, and rarely as an economic one. If economic matters are discussed, it is usually in the context of outlining the League's general institutional structure or listing its conferences. This oversight likely arises because the League is usually examined through the lens of the Covenant where

[253] Boomgaard, "Treacherous Cane," p. 157; Rowe, "Sugar," pp. 23, 25–6.

[254] See, e.g., Stocking and Watkins, *Cartels*, pp. 20–2; von Graevenitz, "Changing Visions," 733–5.

[255] See, e.g., Oppenheim, *League of Nations*; Levermore, *First Yearbook*; Howard-Ellis, *Origin*; Eppstein, *Ten Years*; Hudson, *Progress*; Beer, *League of Nations on Trial*; Webster and Herbert, *Theory and Practice*; Fanshawe and Macartney, *What the League Has Done*; Zimmern, *League of Nations*.

[256] See, e.g., Walters, *History*; Mangone, *International Organization*; Claude, Jr., *Swords into Ploughshares*; Dexter, *Years of Opportunity*; Scott, *Rise and Fall*.

there is only one very limited reference to any "economic" matters in Article 23(e).[257]

Research into the economic functions of the League has been reinvigorated.[258] Many of these studies focus primarily on the intellectual significance of the practice of economists employed in or by the League.[259] Two things are missing from these works. First, there is little examination of the League's doctrines – that is, the system of principles, rules, and procedures intended to implement the ideas derived from expert economic advice and delegates' demands. We will see how three doctrines dominated the League's economic discourse of the time: rapprochement, rationalization, and freer trade. Rapprochement was the general principle that political *and* economic cooperation were necessary to ensure peace. Rationalization was the theory that it was necessary to stabilize and control economic conditions of production, distribution, and consumption in a way that ensured economic efficiency and improved a community's welfare. And freer trade was the idea that domestic tariffs levels would eventually be reduced over time, but how fast and to what degree was a matter for negotiation.

If any doctrine is mentioned in the few works that examine the economic aspects of the League, it is freer trade, and, to a lesser degree, rapprochement, whereas rationalization has been ignored or lost. Yet the one League treaty that attempted to implement the League doctrine of freer trade was not popular amongst many League delegates and it never came into operation.[260] Conversely, the 1937 ISA epitomized rationalization and was one of the League's few successful economic treaties.

Indeed, delegates from relatively newly independent Cuba employed the doctrines of rapprochement and rationalization and became some

[257] Art. 23(e): "[the Members of the League] will make provision to secure and maintain freedom of communications and of transit and equitable treatment for the commerce of all Members of the League. In this connection, the special necessities of the regions devastated during the war of 1914–1918 shall be borne in mind." This provision is referred to as the "Economic Equality" provision.

[258] The most groundbreaking work is Clavin, *World Economy*.

[259] Endres and Fleming, *International Organizations*, pp. 105–32; Clavin and Wessels, "Transnationalism."

[260] International Convention for the Abolition of Import and Export Prohibitions and Restrictions, Geneva, November 8, 1927, 97 LNTS 391; Hill, *League of Nations*, pp. 45–7; McClure, *World Prosperity*, p. 366; League of Nations, *Commercial Policy*, pp. 33–45, 93. The treaty was riddled with conditional ratifications, and was brought into force by special arrangement on a short-term basis on January 1, 1930. By the middle of 1934, the treaty was renounced by all the parties.

of the primary instigators of the 1937 ISA. This leads to the second point: recent accounts primarily focus on the role of industrialized countries in League debates and operations, and do not take into account the role that so-called underdeveloped countries played in the institutional formation and innovations of the League.[261] Cuban delegates agitated for an international sugar agreement from 1927 until the final League sugar treaty was concluded in 1937. Sugar was one of only two agricultural products that were regulated by an international trade agreement under the auspices of the League (the other was wheat).[262] To many Cuban officials and businessmen, the story of the League was one of success, since the sugar treaty was an important aspect of the relatively new Cuban state.

Economic conceptions of the League

The few authors who focused on the League's economic aspects still characterized the League's primary purpose to be about achieving political stability. They also considered the scope and efficacy of the League's economic work to be limited by the political will of states, which was thought in turn to be shaped by domestic policy.[263]

When the League's institutional structure was being negotiated, not everyone conceded to this political conception of the League. In December 1918, Jan Smuts, the prominent white South African and British Commonwealth statesman and military leader, published his famous pamphlet, entitled *The League of Nations: A Practical Suggestion*.[264] Smuts started by noting that one popular conception of the League imagined it to have economic functions; its usefulness lay not in preventing wars but in "the domain of ordinary peaceful [economic] intercourse between members of the League."[265] To Smuts, this economic function was not controversial, for he used that as a springboard to outline a version of the League that extended into "much more as a great organ of the ordinary peaceful life of civilization."[266] Even though

[261] A notable exception is Symposium, "League of Nations."

[262] Baer, *International Organizations*, p. 159.

[263] See, e.g., League of Nations, *Ten Years*, pp. 178–206; Heilperin, "Financial Issues," p. 50. Notable examples of writings in the English language which primarily examine the economic aspects of the League are McClure, *World Prosperity*; Hill, *League of Nations*; League of Nations, *Better Economic World*.

[264] Smuts, *League of Nations*. Smuts would also influence the advent of the United Nations. See Mazower, *No Enchanted Palace*.

[265] Smuts, *League of Nations*, pp. 7–8. [266] *Ibid.*, p. 8.

Smuts's pamphlet influenced how the League was constructed, his prescriptions were not incorporated into the Covenant.

During the Paris Peace Conference in 1919, a voice of dissent was concerned that the Wilson-inspired Covenant did not include significant economic provisions. John Maynard Keynes wrote a scathing and influential indictment against the Peace Conference, and resigned from the conference as principal representative of the British Treasury in the midst of negotiations.[267] His primary frustration was that the emerging consensus for the League by and large ignored the necessity of economically reconstructing Europe and had the effect of economically punishing Germany and Austria. Keynes proposed a plan, outlining what international action was necessary to ensure international economic stability and the economic development of Europe.[268] Keynes's opinions aligned with broader criticisms that proposals for the League were too focused on ethnic, strategic, and political considerations, leaving out the economic and financial causes and consequences of war.[269]

Economic functions of the League

Despite the criticisms of the Paris Peace Conference and the ensuing Covenant, the narrow scope of Article 23 did not predetermine the actual scale of economic and financial organization of the League. In 1923, not long after the League was created, scores of industry groups, commercial groups, and co-operative organizations petitioned the Secretary-General of the League to put the issue of free trade and the reduction of tariffs on the international agenda. The letters sometimes made their way through to the League's Economic and Financial Section. But the standard answer from the Office of the Secretary-General was that this issue was beyond the scope of the current League activities and that larger commercial policies should be brought by state governments.[270]

In practice, within the League, a great amount of time, effort, and resources went into examining international economic issues and attempting to form international consensus on how to organize

[267] Keynes, *Economic Consequences*. See also Markwell, *Keynes*, pp. 54–89.

[268] Keynes, *Economic Consequences*.

[269] See, e.g., Garvin, *Economic Foundations*; Frank, "Economic Nationalism," p. 184.

[270] Correspondence with the various free trade associations, LON, R402, 10/28784/28790; 10/28790/28790. Groups included the International Committee to Promote Universal Trade, the Free Trade Union, the British Section of the Women's International League for Peace and Freedom, the Netherlands Society for Free Trade, the Scottish Co-operative Wholesale Society Ltd, and the International Arbitration Society.

international economic life. The organizational structure was such that the League Assembly and Council directed international economic questions to its permanent staff and through a series of world economic conferences. The League's Assembly oversaw six committees.[271] The Second Committee, which was entrusted to attend to "technical organizations," was composed of several sections addressing economics, finance, health, communications and transit, and technical questions. The Economic and Financial Organization (EFO) was the largest of the "technical organizations" within the League and the most active.[272] But one should not overlook the fact that economic and commercial issues also arose in other parts of the League, such as the Permanent Mandates Commission and the Health Organization.[273]

The Economic and Financial Section of the EFO was staffed by civil servants and economic experts. Their formal role was to provide a comprehensive collection of statistical information relating to economic matters, and to use economic theory to interpret this information for the purpose of devising practical solutions to international economic problems.[274] The official position put out by the Economic and Financial Section was that League's authority to address economic questions was the following:

> There is only one direct reference in the Covenant (Article 23) to economic cooperation – the undertaking to "make provision to secure and maintain freedom of communications and transit and equitable treatment for the commerce of all Members of the League." But a large part of the work done under the auspices of the League finds its raison d'etre in its general purpose, as defined

[271] The League Assembly, which comprised representatives from all the member countries, each country having one vote, is often understood as performing more legislative functions. The League Council, which was composed of four permanent members and up to ten rotating non-permanent members, is often understood as having an executive role. The six committees under the auspices of the Assembly were: (1) Constitutional and Legal Questions; (2) Technical Organizations; (3) Reduction of Arms; (4) Budget; (5) Social and Humanitarianism; (6) Political and Minorities Questions. Howard-Ellis, *Origin*, p. 135.

[272] Aufricht, *Guide*, pp. 212–14; McClure, *World Prosperity*, pp. 21–3; Hill, *League of Nations*, p. 109. The organization of sections within the 2nd Committee changed over the years. From 1922 to 1931, the Economic and Financial Sections functioned as separate but related entities under the same secretariat.

[273] Anghie, "Colonialism"; Clavin, *World Economy*, pp. 165–72.

[274] Hill, *League of Nations*, pp. 1–11. In October 1931, when Arthur Salter stepped down as director, the Economic and Financial Section was split into two separate sections. After 1931, EFO comprised the Economic Section, the Financial Section and the Economic Intelligence Service.

in the widely drawn Preamble to the Covenant – "to promote international co-operation and to achieve international peace and security."[275]

Article 23 treated commerce in the context of communications and transit. By situating economic and commercial issues within broader questions of peace and security, the Economic and Financial Section cast a wide methodological and ideological net. The result was that League meetings, conferences, and publications constituted a debate amongst some of the world's leading economists over a wide range of issues, such as tariffs, cartels, subsidies, finance, money, industrial policy, agriculture, and labor. Famous economists (or those who would later become famous), such as Gustav Cassel, Bertil Ohlin, Gunnar Myrdal, Jacob Viner, and Gottfried Haberler, were either employed by the Economic and Financial Section or were commissioned by the section to write reports; it was here that they developed some of their more popular ideas.[276]

Even though the work of these international bureaucrats and experts was often characterized as technical and non-political, the members of the section were astute political actors who, in practice, worked with a significant degree of autonomy.[277] One could interpret the decision to characterize economic issues as technical as a way to ensure that the economic functions of the League would not formally derogate from the Covenant and infringe upon the definition of political as enumerated in the rest of the Covenant. This meant that the Economic and Financial Section's permanent staff significantly influenced the League's economic functions by defining the remaining economic sphere through institutional practice.

To a small number of observers, the Economic and Financial Section was an essential component to the formation of world order.[278] This was in part because the section provided all the information that formed what was assumed to be relevant background for the series of world economic conferences held under the auspices of the League. This is where League permanent staff exercised their political power – by influencing the global policy ideational agenda.

The three conferences that addressed general world economic problems were the 1920 International Financial Conference (the League's first conference of any kind), the 1927 International Economic Conference (commonly known as the World Economic Conference), and the 1933

[275] Economic and Financial Section, *Economic Work*, p. 3.
[276] Clavin, *World Economy*, p. 37. [277] *Ibid.* [278] See, e.g., Greaves, *League Committees.*

International Monetary and Economic Conference (sometimes called the 1933 World Economic Conference). The League's experts determined the problems that needed to be addressed and devised the agenda that structured the international conferences. The section would retain external experts to provide memoranda outlining the intellectual and statistical background on certain topics. The information provided by the League's permanent staff and expert memoranda was often referenced during conference discussions and debates as authoritative sources.

The first two world economic conferences were not constituted by government officials representing their respective countries' official position.[279] Instead, governments sent their own experts of high-level civil servants, academics, industry leaders, union leaders, and the like. After the delegates spent some time deliberating and when they could find a theoretical and practical consensus, the results were submitted to conferences of the plenipotentiary representatives of the national governments to be put into form as conventions.[280]

Experience of war and rule by experts

After the Great War, a great amount of intellectual and artistic energy went towards attempting to create a "new world order,"[281] "new era,"[282] or "new man."[283] Many conceived the League as part of this effort to create a new world of international solidarity.[284] Despite this desire to break away from the past, the experience of war had a great influence on how the League's economic activities were devised.

Even with their different opinions regarding the importance of the League's economic activities, both Wilson's[285] and Smuts's[286] thinking of how the League would address economic problems was influenced by the inter-allied efforts to ensure a supply of primary commodities (for food and industry) and equipment. During the war, the Allies responded to naval blockades and shortages of supply by co-coordinating their

[279] The International Monetary and Economic Conference, 1933, had both experts and representatives of national governments attending as delegates.

[280] McClure, *World Prosperity*, p. 101.

[281] See, e.g., "Woodrow Wilson," online: The White House www.whitehouse.gov/about/presidents/woodrowwilson (accessed May 28, 2014).

[282] See, e.g., Boyden (ed.), *Economic Consequences*, pp. 53, 92, 101.

[283] See, e.g., Clair (ed.), *1930s*.

[284] Pemberton, "New Worlds," pp. 314–18.

[285] Woodrow Wilson, "Letter to Secretary Redfield" (October 29, 1918), in Baker (ed.), *Woodrow Wilson*, vol. VIII, p. 587.

[286] Smuts, *League of Nations*, p. 7.

efforts and organizing the supply of goods. They created a series of inter-allied organizations, which at first coordinated shipping purchases for the armed forces, and later controlled commodities for civilian needs.[287] These organizations linked together government departments by creating ongoing relationships: "[t]he French wool official dealt with the British and Italian wool officials and was not concerned with what his colleagues for cotton or timber or coal were discussing with the corresponding experts."[288]

This experience of the war, in effect, transformed the conceptualization of the economic function of the state.[289] The experience of wartime organization provided evidence that governments could effectively and efficiently plan and manage the production and distribution of goods. The system of coordination was thought to be so successful that plans were made to use the organizations for the purpose of European economic relief and reconstruction – an idea that was supported by the fact that the inter-allied organization coordinated a large number of neutral countries' foodstuffs during the war.[290]

Sir J. Arthur Salter headed the inter-allied coordination efforts and carried this new conceptualization of the state through to the economic functioning of the League. Salter was the director of the Economic and Financial Section of the League from 1922 to 1931, and was considered by many to be one of the section's most influential and active directors.[291] He attributed the efficacy of the inter-allied system to the fact that there was no external authority, but that "it was national organizations linked together for international work and themselves forming the instrument of that work."[292] Salter, like many other internationalists at the time, believed that the war was caused by excess centralization of state power. These internationalists also mistrusted leaving the market to its own devices. Therefore, they looked to the League as the institution that would decentralize political power and coordinate economic activity.[293] It is worth reproducing Salter's words in detail, since in them are the traces of the concepts of rapprochement and

[287] Hill, *League of Nations*, pp. 14–18. [288] Salter, *Shipping*, p. 252.
[289] Hill, *League of Nations*, p. 13.
[290] McClure, *World Prosperity*, pp. 66–74; Hill, *League of Nations*, pp. 15–16.
[291] McClure, *World Prosperity*, pp. 66–74; Hill, *League of Nations*, p. 109; Zimmern, *League of Nations*, p. 404; Russell, "Political Scepticism," p. 108. Salter later described this time as the "happiest period of my work life." Salter, *Memoirs*, p. 17.
[292] Salter, *Shipping*, p. 252. [293] Trentmann, *Free Trade Nation*, p. 262.

rationalization (discussed below) that would permeate the League's economic policies and conferences:

> [International administration] will work through the executive organization of national Governments. It will influence, co-ordinate, perhaps control their work. But it will not replace them. It will obtain its power, not from an authority conferred by delegation, but by continuous pressure and influence on the centres of national power. … Sometimes its objects may be achieved merely by securing that national decisions, even if still made nationally and on national grounds, are made after full recognition of their effect upon other countries and of other countries' views and opinions. … the method of direct contact over a wide surface, of linking these departments together by the association of their crucial officers, will prove more effective and successful than any form of external influence and control. The method is capable of infinite variations for particular needs, but in one form or another it will be applied to most of the really important work touched by international administration. This principle, valuable as an instrument of administration, is the more interesting and important because it is in accord with the fundamental purposes and policy of the League of Nations.[294]

Salter's ideas were part of a larger trend of the time. Arthur Lewis, one of the early doyens of economic development, described the interwar period as a time when "[d]emocracies and dictatorships alike resolved that society should no longer be at the mercy of economic events, and sought gropingly, and in conflicting and contradictory ways, to control events by government agency."[295]

Keynes was also significantly influenced by wartime efforts when thinking about the League. Right before the outbreak of the Second World War, he examined and promoted the idea of governments controlling the supply of commodities (which he discussed with his friend, Salter).[296] Keynes would further promulgate the desire for state action to play a decisive role in managing international economy in a way that influenced the creation and structure of the Bretton Woods institutions and the International Trade Organization.[297]

Around the turn of the twenty-first century, some argued that we live in an unprecedented, though underappreciated, "new world order,"

[294] Salter, *Shipping*, pp. 253–4. Salter noted that his experience during the war informed his work as head of the Economic and Financial Section. Salter, *Memoirs*, p. 177.

[295] Lewis, *Survey*, p. 12.

[296] John Maynard Keynes, "Letter to Sir Thomas Inskip (with copies sent to Oliver Stanley and Arthur Salter)" (August 23, 1938), and Arthur Salter, "Letter to John Maynard Keynes" (August 31, 1938), in Moggridge (ed.), *Collected Writings*, vol. XXI, pp. 471, 474.

[297] Markwell, *Keynes*, pp. 140–1, 165.

ruled by networks of government officials and experts.[298] According to this account, the network of government officials must be further supported and improved in order to respond to economic globalization, as well as to the global networks of "terrorists, arms dealers, money launderers, drug dealers, traffickers in women and children, and the modern pirates of intellectual property" which threaten the world.[299] Nevertheless, the experience of the First World War had already buttressed the idea, promoted by Salter and the League, that governments should coordinate their experts and officials (not heads of state). The purpose was for the experts and officials to establish ideal policies for the control of global social development. This was part of a transnational "new world order," which was expected to rationally ensure peace and prosperity after the Great War.[300]

Economic doctrines

The League's economic purpose was understood by many to be twofold. It was thought that the League had the ideational purpose of guiding public opinion, which meant citizens and governments, towards the adoption of sound economic and financial policies. Its practical purpose was considered to be the economic reconstruction of Europe.[301] The method of implementing these purposes was through several economic doctrines. The most debated doctrines – rapprochement, rationalization, and freer trade – provided the context for how the League regulated the world sugar trade.

Rapprochement

The President of the 1927 World Economic Conference began his closing speech by outlining the overriding spirit of the conference:

> It was necessary to clear away through the thicket and chaos of the problems which hindered the nations of the world in their progress. It was necessary to bring into harmony the conflicting policies and desires of many interests and many great movements. . . . The danger of confusion and of controversies, which

[298] Slaughter, *New World Order*. For a more normatively tentative approach, see Kingsbury, Krisch, and Stewart, "Administrative Law." For a more critical assessment of (but not against) rule by experts, see Kennedy, "Invisible College."

[299] Slaughter, *New World Order*, p. 1. [300] Clavin and Wessels, "Transnationalism."

[301] See, e.g., League of Nations, *Ten Years*, pp. 178–206; Salter, "Recovery of Europe."

many pessimists considered practically certain, has, thanks to the generous effort at *rapprochement*, not only been avoided but actually eliminated.[302]

This principle of rapprochement was similar to the *doux commerce* thesis first articulated by Montesquieu.[303] To Montesquieu, commerce had the natural effect of leading to peace among nations and also civilized peoples, by "polishing and softening" barbarous manners.[304] According to League doctrine, commerce would lead to the desired peace and prosperity.

The first "General Resolution" from the Conference recognized "that the maintenance of world peace depends largely upon the principles on which the economic policies of nations are framed and executed," and recommended that "recognized principles [be] designed to eliminate those economic defficulties [*sic*] which cause friction and misunderstanding in a work which has everything to gain from peaceful and harmonious progress."[305]

The League experts could not reach a definitive consensus regarding what specific mechanisms of economic cooperation would lead to peace and progress. One expert report, written by Eugene Grossman as preparatory material for the conference, distinguished between political and economic approaches to "economic rapprochement."[306] The three political methods were multilateral commercial treaties, bilateral preferential systems, and customs unions. Grossman noted that multilateral commercial treaties, regulating states' systems of tariffs and duties, were ideal, but very difficult because of the complex character of classifying goods. He was reluctant to endorse bilateral preferential treaties because he thought they led to high tariffs and hindered free trade. He thought a customs union was ideal for Europe, which could model itself upon how the different states in the US functioned as one market. The 1902 Brussels Sugar Convention was examined as an ideal model for the multilateral regulation of commerce and as a basis for a customs union.[307] Grossman defined the economic approach as international cooperation among producers.

[302] League of Nations, *Final Report*, p. 118. [303] Montesquieu, *Spirit of the Law*, p. 338.

[304] *Ibid.* But see Montesquieu, *De L'Esprit des Lois*, vol. II, p. 501 (suggesting that Montesquieu did not use the term "commerce" to include all economic activity and international commerce at large; he may have excluded agriculture in his use of the word).

[305] League of Nations, *Final Report*, p. 51. [306] Grossman, *Rapprochement*. [307] *Ibid.*, p. 26.

But he concluded that economic approaches are problematic because they grant producers too much power.

Amongst these different options, delegates at the economic conferences focused most on and fiercely debated between two specific doctrines of economic rapprochement: the economic method in the form of industrial agreements under the doctrine of "rationalization," and the political method in the form of multilateral commercial treaties under the doctrine of "freer trade" or "liberty of trade."

Rationalization

The final report for the 1927 World Economic Conference defined rationalization to be:

> the methods of technique and of organization designed to secure the minimum waste of either effort or material. It includes the scientific organization of labour, standardization both of material and of products, simplification of processes and improvements in the system of transport and marketing.[308]

As one World Economic Conference delegate commented, "the heading 'rationalization', a word like 'solidarité' and 'homme de bonne volonté', seems to thrive in the air of international conferences."[309] It remained quite popular even after the 1927 conference. Some businesses, such as Rowntree, the iconic British confectioner, wanted to know more about the League's work regarding ideas of rationalization.[310] The International Management Institute, which was co-funded by the League, the International Labour Organization (ILO), and private philanthropic foundations, took up rationalization as part of its research mandate.[311]

Even though a large number of experts advocated for increased rationalization, there was disagreement as to what was the best method. The debate ranged between two approaches. Those who advocated "scientific management" wanted to leave rationalization to standardizing products, materials, machines, tools, and methods.[312] From industry's perspective, rationalization's purpose was to stabilize and control economic conditions of production, distribution, and consumption in a way that

[308] League of Nations, *Final Report*, p. 41.

[309] Runciman, "World Economic Conference," 468. See also Jacobsson, "Theoretical Solution," pp. 43, 49; Pemberton, "New Worlds."

[310] Wallace to Loveday, June 15, 1928, LON, R2823, 10D/5204/3705.

[311] International Management Institute Constitution, LON, R2824, 10D/17804/3705.

[312] See, e.g., Pearson, "Scientific Management"; Houston, *Rationalization*.

increased a community's welfare by cheapening, multiplying, and improving the quality of commodities produced.[313]

The others that called for "cartels" or "industrial agreements" wanted to control and coordinate production and distribution (with an eye to influencing consumption) through mechanisms such as quotas, granting of monopolies, or the formation of trusts.[314] These agreements would not determine the price "by marginal or average cost, but [act] as an instrument for the administration of industry, so as to prevent the fluctuations which take place around the market."[315] The main criticism against the industrial agreement argument was that the price system of the market, rather than government-imposed monopolies, was the most efficient mechanism to regulate the flow of labor, goods, and capital.[316]

In the debate over rationalization, everyone agreed that it involved a blurred line between the state and the market. People differed over where to draw that blurry line; there was no shared assumption whether any form of rationalization, be it scientific management or industrial agreements, demanded more market or state mechanisms. Economic policies and commercial institutions involved the participation and coordination of state and market actors.

This made it very difficult for people to determine clearly when certain ideas or institutions should be characterized as public or private. There was clear consensus that government policy was public. But it was not clear when commercial laws and policies were public or private. This opaqueness between the public and the private was rationalization's defining feature. In fact, the International Management Institute was well situated to study rationalization because it was deliberately structured to be a mix of the public and private, and "to promote collaboration as between official and individual interests." The International Management Institute worked closely with governments and businesses, but it only undertook inquiries regarding rationalization from the League's EFO or the ILO. The theory was to "keep its work scientific and technical and free from political entanglements with either governments or employers or workers."[317] In other words, the

313 Spitzer, "Rationalization and Cartels."

314 MacGregor, *International Cartels*; de Rousiers, *Cartels and Trusts*; Wiedenfeld, *Cartels and Combines*.

315 MacGregor, *International Cartels*, p. 6.

316 Cassel, *Monopolistic Tendencies*.

317 International Management Institute to Salter, January 18, 1930, LON, R2824, 10D/17804/3705.

international institutions would mediate between the state and the market, the public and the private. The League (whether the delegates or permanent staff) took on economic issues only if it was thought to be within the League's public intergovernmental purview.

The general understanding of the 1927 World Economic Conference was that rationalization was an attempt to establish the economic conditions necessary for rapprochement.[318] As already mentioned, one view, reflected by Grossman's report, was that rationalization was an economic instance of rapprochement, but was also inherently problematic.[319] Another view, as expressed in different expert reports and by some delegates at conference, was that the cordial relationships established through rapprochement provided the conditions necessary to ameliorate or prevent the detrimental effects of rationalization. Economic rationalization was desirable, but the worst of its "contingent abuses" had to be tempered by technical and commercial coordination amongst experts and officials.[320]

There were some delegates who questioned the merits of rationalization as a viable way to improve the conditions of industry.[321] This debate was framed as whether rationalization, an idea thought to have proved successful in practice in the US, was applicable in Europe at this time. Many questioned whether Europe's devastated infrastructure and economy was actually capable of implementing rationalization policies.[322] Others were concerned that rationalization would decrease wages and employment, thereby further exacerbating dire work conditions.[323] The *Secrétaire de l'Union syndicale Suisse á Berne* had existential concerns akin to the anxieties from across the political spectrum, as expressed in the films *Metropolis* (1925) and *Modern Times* (1936); he feared that rationalization would have psychological effects on people because their whole life would be enslaved to efficiency demands made by the machines in factories.[324]

Freer trade

The theory of free trade was so contentious that many felt it wise that conference delegates deliberately avoided the issue between

318 League of Nations, *Final Report*, pp. 7–10. 319 Grossman, *Rapprochement*.
320 de Peyerimhoff, "Rationalisation," pp. 129, 132. See also Hirsch, *Monopolies*; Oualid, *Social Effects*.
321 League of Nations, *Final Report*, p. 11. 322 See, e.g., Lammers, "Cartel Question."
323 Economic and Financial Section, *Report and Proceedings*, vol. II, pp. 129–47.
324 *Ibid.*, p. 145.

"free-traders" and "protectionists."[325] Conference delegates at the world economic conferences, authors of conference final reports, and commentators in articles emphasized that they were advocating for "liberty of trade" or "freer trade," which was not to be confused with "free trade."[326] "*Freer* trade" was defined as policies geared towards reducing, and maybe eventually removing, tariffs.[327]

War and naval blockades forced countries to adopt economic policies of self-sufficiency. According to Salter, high tariffs were instilled soon after the war to ensure that countries could remain economically self-sufficient and maintain home industries, in order to avoid sudden radical economic changes that would lead to severe unemployment and dislocation.[328] During this time, despite the experts' best efforts to convince governments and the public of what they felt was a pragmatic policy, rising tariff levels and economic policies of "self-sufficiency" continued after the First World War and into the Second.[329]

The freer trade debate was about how quickly tariffs should be lowered. There was consensus that eventually tariffs should be removed and that trade should be made "free," but the divisive question was about how soon and to what degree tariffs should be reduced (much like debates within the WTO).[330] Salter's words are worth quoting at length:

> from our present point of view of the peace of the world and international good will, it is not so much tariffs as the arbitrary methods by which they are framed, imposed and changed that are a serious element in international relations. From this point of view, therefore, it may be well to concentrate attention rather on tariff-making methods than on the general issue of Free Trade or Protection. Free Trade may be preferable in the interests of general world prosperity, and if it could be secured might also involve the removal of many serious dangers to international relations. *But in existing circumstances* we may secure a larger return by concentrating upon a more immediately practicable goal than that of abolishing tariffs. What we most need is to reform their abuses.[331]

[325] Salter, "Contribution," pp. 1, 5.

[326] See, e.g., League of Nations, *Final Report*, p. 10; Economic and Financial Section, *Report and Proceedings*, vol. I, pp. 21–7.

[327] League of Nations, *Final Report*, p. 31. [328] Salter, "Economic Conference," 353.

[329] Hermes, [no title], pp. 65, 73; Webster and Herbert, *Theory and Practice*, pp. 231–2.

[330] See, e.g., Economic and Financial Section, *Report and Proceedings*, vol. II, p. 118.

[331] Salter, "Economic Causes of War," pp. 1, 14–15 (emphasis added). See also Preparatory Commission of Experts, *Monetary and Economic Conference*, p. 3. Despite the 1927 Convention for the Abolition of Imports and Export Duties failing to come into

Those labeled as "free traders" thought that the ideal policy was the complete removal of tariffs as soon as possible.[332] Others, critically labeled "protectionists," or sympathetically called "tariff reformers,"[333] were concerned that "the protagonists of this school of thought [free trade] fail to take into consideration the varying level of economic development among the different nations of the world. The economic relations of one country towards other foreign countries must depend on its own material prosperity, which in turn depends on the development of its own powers of production, either of manufactured goods or agricultural products."[334] To some, a policy of "tariff reform" allowed for a way of thinking akin to the idea of "infant industries." The delegates from British Raj India articulated this theory when they argued that states with infant or immature industries must be protected from imports and allowed to develop until they reach a stage that they are able to compete with other nations' industries, not for the purpose of self-sufficiency, but in order to attain an ability to trade with other nations. In other words, protection of an infant industry was an exceptional and temporary measure until conditions allowed for free trade.[335]

What is telling about arguments to maintain tariffs for the support of infant industries is that they remained under the rubric of what was common for the time – that "free trade" was *indicative* of normal international economic relations, and that the unchecked rise in tariffs would lead to the breakdown of rapprochement. The orthodox thinking amongst League experts was that rising levels of tariffs was symptomatic of an international economic system that was not functioning normally. The tariffs were thought to be remnants of exceptional wartime economic policies emphasizing self-sufficiency and prohibiting imports and exports. Therefore, League experts made a determined effort to remove the barriers to trade in order to revert to pre-war "normal" trade relations.[336] It was thought that certain political and financial preconditions had to be met before trade could be free; there needed to be political stability, financial and monetary stability, and

operation, not everyone felt that lowering tariffs was entirely untenable under the League. See, e.g., Viner, "National Monopolies."

332 See, e.g., Colijn, "World Economic Conference."

333 See, e.g., Power, "Comments."

334 Balfour, "International Chamber of Commerce," 127. See also Keynes, "Pros and Cons."

335 League of Nations, *International Financial Conference*, vol. II, p. 95; Rhodes, [no title].

336 See, e.g., Information Section, *Monetary and Economic Conference*, p. 66–7.

the improvement of transportation, before trade could return to what was thought to be "normal."[337]

For example, when addressing the two major economic crises after the Great War – the 1920s reconstruction of Europe and the 1930s Great Depression – the consensus was that financial currencies needed to be stabilized[338] and the matter of war reparations needed to be resolved,[339] in order to provide the "normal" economic preconditions that allow for free trade. During the interwar period there was always a crisis at hand (postwar European reconstruction, the global agricultural crisis, and the Great Depression), so many thought the preconditions for freer trade were not met. As such, rationalization was a very influential economic doctrine within the League.

This line of thinking, where "free trade" is the norm unless exceptional circumstances warrant policies to improve national economic development, also manifested itself in how the League addressed other economic exceptions. So, for example, Article 23(e) of the League Covenant, the "economic equality" provision, stated that the Members of the League "will make provision to secure and maintain freedom of communications and of transit and equitable treatment for the commerce of all Members of the League." But then, countries such as France and Belgium wanted "special protection" during the period of European reconstruction.[340] Therefore, Article 23(e) also provided the exception that "special necessities of the regions devastated during the war of 1914–18 shall be borne in mind."[341]

To some, economic equality could only be provided among equally civilized nations. In other words, only when countries have similar economic, political, and social status can they then be treated equally,

337 See, e.g., League of Nations, *International Financial Conference*, vol. I, pp. 22–3.

338 For comments espousing that the International Financial Conference Brussels 1920 was the necessary precursor to addressing tariffs and trade, see, e.g., Economic and Financial Section, *Agenda*, p. 21. For comments espousing that currencies needed to be stabilized before tariff negotiations within the context of the Great Depression and the 1933 World Monetary and Economic Conference, see, e.g., Salter, *World Trade*, p. 65; Keynes, "World Economic Conference." But see Ohlin, *World Economic Depression* (who also characterized the cause of the depression as a financial problem, but thought the restoration of the flow of investment capital was a priority).

339 See, e.g., Keynes, *Economic Consequences*, pp. 113–225. Later, the 1932 Lausanne Conference concluded the issue of reparations with a call for a world economic conference which enabled preparations for the 1933 World Monetary and Economic Conference. See Information Section, *Monetary and Economic Conference*, p. 15.

340 Wilson, *Origins*, p. 97.

341 See, e.g., Miller, *Drafting*, vol. I, pp. 23–4.

leaving exceptional states that are less developed to be treated by exceptional means.[342]

Indeed, the hierarchy established within the Mandate System confirms this view that the less civilized a nation was, the less the normal rules of "free trade" were applicable. The Mandate System of the League was devised to provide supervision for the peoples of the Middle East, Africa, and the Pacific, who were previously ruled by Germany or the Ottoman Empire.[343] The stated purpose in the League Covenant was to shepherd these colonial nations into becoming civilized, sovereign nations. Mandates were classified according their degree of advancement: "A" mandates were considered the closest to being civilized and accorded the most independence, followed by "B" mandates; "C" mandates were considered to be the most backward and therefore required the Mandatory power to administer them as an integral part of its own territory.[344] "A" and "B" mandate treaties contained detailed policies of when and how economic equality applied, whereas treaties for the less civilized "C" mandates provided no guarantees for economic equality, implying that these mandates were not developed enough to warrant international competition.[345] Mandatory countries imposed extremely high tariffs in their "C" mandates, without any controversy from the Permanent Mandates Commission, which provided the Mandatory power privileged access to the mandate's goods. This was in line with conceiving of colonies as sources of agricultural products, and was consistent with the provision that "C" mandates be considered as internal to the Mandatory power.[346]

[342] *Ibid.* [343] Anghie, "Colonialism." [344] Art. 22.

[345] Gerig, *Open Door*, pp. 15–16, 109–12. Within the context of colonies and mandates, the "economic equality" policy was also known an as the "open door" policy.

[346] McClure, *World Prosperity*, pp. 390–2. Several countries raised complaints to the Permanent Mandates Commission, contesting how other countries were (mis) applying the economic equality provision in "A" and "B" mandates.

6 Developing a Cuban state and renegotiating American imperialism

The intertwining of Cuban and League history

At the 1927 World Economic Conference, Luis Marino Pérez, the Cuban commercial attaché in Washington DC and League of Nations delegate, was careful to articulate Cuba's interests as part of efforts of post-world war rapprochement. In his opening speech, he emphasized how the economies of Europe and America (meaning the countries of Central and South America) were interdependent in a way that did not challenge the notion that the European economy was paramount in the world economy. Rather, he linked European interests to American interests. Marino criticized the conference for focusing predominantly on the highly industrialized nations of Europe, and not on the countries of America which mostly depended on agriculture and raw materials as a source of wealth. But he immediately followed his sharp remarks by shifting the emphasis to Europe, maintaining that the conclusions of the conference were as crucial to the Americas as they were to Europe, "because whatever tends to increase the prosperity of the Old World will also substantially and directly benefit America."[347]

Marino's words epitomize the Cuban's government's strategy in the 1920s and 1930s of clearly articulating its interest, but in a way that was not antagonistic to North American and European interests. It is also telling that the Cuban government turned to the League of Nations in order to implement its economic policies. Cuban delegates employed the economic doctrines of the League and successfully advocated for an international sugar agreement, the 1937 ISA. The Cuban political

[347] Economic and Financial Section, *Report and Proceedings*, vol. I, p. 149. The delegate was looking to devise an agreement regulating the production of sugar and to gain increased access to the European market.

and economic elite used the League and the sugar treaty to buttress a broader state-building project that began with Cuba's independence from Spain in 1902. What is remarkable is that, despite the lack of accord at general League economic conferences, the 1937 ISA put into effect a particular conception of rationalization popular with many at the League: that international agreements and coordinated government policies were necessary to rationally stabilize markets before tariffs could be reduced.

Marino's clear economic agenda for Cuba and political deference to the more politically powerful states also reflected the position of the Cuban state. Cuba successfully fought for its independence from Spain, but found itself in 1902 in an imperial relationship with US. Nevertheless, Cuba was a rising economic power. Cuba was a case of a former colony that benefited from the "European" war. Because European sugar beet fields were ravaged by war, the Allies needed to ensure a steady supply of sugar. They turned to Cuban sugar producers, who in turn benefited from a huge increase in demand.

Europeans, of course, experienced the Great War differently and looked to the League with different interests. The following statement from the *Final Report* of the 1927 World Economic Conference captures the apprehension of many European delegates that their countries had lost their economic position to newly industrialized countries:

> After a whole century, during which other countries were willing to supply Europe with raw products in return for the manufacturers which Europe alone was in the position to make, a careful observer in 1905 or 1906 – or possibly twenty years earlier in the case of the United States – could have perceived a new chapter was opening in the history of these distant countries, the chief characteristic of which was the endeavor to establish manufacturing industries of their own. The war greatly stimulated this development by restricting and diverting foreign trade between Europe and the rest of the world. But at the moment of facing this new situation, Europe finds herself severely handicapped.[348]

This frustration that former colonies that used to supply Europe with raw material had economically surpassed Europe during the war made agriculture an "international" problem. The predominant sentiment expressed by European and North American League delegates was that access to raw materials for industry and foodstuffs was necessary to

[348] League of Nations, *Final Report*, p. 19.

ensure that Europe recovered after the war.[349] This meant that within the context of the League, European interests were a priority. If there was concern for the economic prosperity of the "indigenous inhabitants," it was secondary to ensuring that Europe received its necessary agricultural products.[350]

European interests influenced the League economic agenda in a way that framed many issues in terms of ensuring that the agricultural periphery served the industrial core. The common assumption was that Europe's economic recovery was the best way to ensure world peace and prosperity, and was a necessary precondition to resuming normal trade relations. This assumption, in turn, informed the notion that Europe's economic recovery was understood to be of international interest.[351] Europe's access to agricultural products was thought to be necessary for its recovery, and the world's interest was Europe's interest. In the words of one author examining the League's economic functions, agricultural products and other raw materials were the "world's heritage."[352] Therefore, raw materials had to be internationally regulated for the greater good of the world, understood as Europe's interest.

Cuban delegates championed the notion that a stable world sugar market was necessary as part of rapprochement. They emphasized that respective governments, in order to ensure rapprochement, should rationally regulate the world sugar market. Cuban delegates also adopted the League assumption that the agricultural periphery had to ensure that the industrialized core obtained the primary commodities necessary for manufacturing.

But through the 1937 ISA, Cuban delegates subtly challenged the underpinning power dynamic between core and periphery, and actually increased Cuba's international economic power. Cuban geopolitical sugar concerns were intertwined with domestic socio-economic needs. The League delegates from Europe gave speeches and wrote articles arguing against policies of "economic nationalism" and "self-sufficiency," because they feared that countries would raise tariffs with little regard for the political and economic consequences in the world.[353] This

[349] See, e.g., Wallace and Edminster, *International Control*, pp. 6–23; International Institute of Agriculture, *Agricultural Problems*; Preparatory Committee for the International Conference, *First Session*, pp. 7–9; Gautie, Hermes, and Lindsay, *Agriculture*; League of Nations, *Final Report*, pp. 33, 46–8.

[350] League of Nations, *Final Report*, p. 50.

[351] See, e.g., Lammers, "Cartel Question," 150.

[352] McClure, *World Prosperity*, p. 410.

[353] *Ibid.*, pp. 410–13; Hill, *League of Nations*, pp. 1–13.

resonated with Cuban delegates, since the Cuban economy was extremely dependent on the export of sugar to the US – and the US's high tariffs and self-sufficiency policies ruined many lives in Cuba. Some Cubans argued against this dependency on one commodity, or called for socio-economic changes that would make the domestic sugar economy more equitable.

It was during this time that renowned Cuban intellectual, Ramiro Guerra, wrote the first edition of his influential book, *Azúcar y Población en las Antillas*, which turned attention towards Cuba's imperial relationship with the US. His words stand in contrast to the contemporaneous League *Final Report*:

> By supplying cheap sugar at a very low price to the consumer, the producer country becomes an economic fief of a distant metropolis, and its working class lives in poverty so that the country that dominates or exploits it can live better and more cheaply.[354]

Agriculture was an international problem for a different reason than the one promulgated by the League report. Foreshadowing dependency theorists' arguments in the 1960s and 1970s, Guerra's concern was that the US was the metropolis that benefited from the high price of sugar, leaving Cuba little opportunity for economic development.[355]

Transnational sugar interests and imperial negotiations

Cuba's dependency on sugar

The Cuban delegates could have pursued a sugar treaty independent of the League. Why, then, did they turn to the League? One reason is that the League staff provided the significant intellectual and logistical resources necessary to draft and ratify a complicated agreement. Another reason has to do with transnational sugar interests of the time; the League was thought to be the only institution that could bring together all the world's sugar-producing and -consuming nations. The final reason is related to the Cuban state's relationship to the US: Cubans used the League as the space to negotiate their imperial relationship with the US.

354 Guerra, *Sugar and Society*, p. 76.
355 *Ibid*. Guerra did not take an anti-US stance, but was arguing to improve conditions in Cuba.

Republican Cuba was highly dependent on sugar.[356] In 1913, sugar made up 72 percent of Cuba's exports, and by 1920 it was 92 percent.[357] Sugar not only provided people in Cuba with a principal source of income from exports, but it also structured social and economic life. For the first two decades of Cuban independence from Spain, sugar mills provided communities with the main means for social and economic development. At the same time, the production of sugar stratified social dynamics in Cuba. Recall that sugar cane needs to be harvested by agricultural workers and then has to be processed by a mill near the sugar cane fields. The mill extracts the raw sugar in order to send it to a refinery (often in a more industrialized economy) which then processes the raw sugar for the purpose of consumption.

"Sugar barons" and their families owned and ran large-scale sugar mill complexes (*centrales*) throughout Cuba. These elite mill owners created sugar mill towns, providing health care, education, electricity, radio stations, railroads, and social services to the hundreds of workers and their families. The wives of these "barons" usually provided charity to workers and their families. Since the Cuban state provided few such social and economic benefits, jobs in sugar mills were the most valued in Cuba. Many of these mill owners were fascinated with progress and efficiency, and competed to develop the most modern towns. Nevertheless, with this economic progress and social charity came repression. Sugar patriarchs considered their acts of philanthropy to be mechanisms of social control and worker appeasement. They did not hesitate to beat or exile workers thought to be rebellious or disruptive, and suppressed any worker movement which tried to organize.[358]

Sugar created transnational commercial ties between financial institutions in the US and Canada (namely, Chase National Bank, the National City Bank, Hayden, Stone & Co., and the Royal Bank of Canada) and some of the Cuban elite. The sugar mills in Cuba were often financed or owned by US businessmen and North American banks. The Cuban sugar mill elite had close personal ties with these US financiers; they were often educated or had business ventures in the US.[359]

[356] A classic text examining the central role that sugar played in forming Cuban life is Ortiz, *Cuban Counterpoint*.

[357] Pérez, Jr., *Between Reform and Revolution*, p. 225.

[358] McGillivray, *Blazing Cane*, chapters 4 and 5.

[359] See Ayala, *American Sugar Kingdom*, for an analysis of local relations of sugar production in Cuba within the context of the transnational organization of capital. On the

Many sugar mills received their raw sugar from surrounding cane farmers (*colonos*). *Colonos* were from a variety of backgrounds. Many were political bosses who were leaders in the 1895–8 war of independence against Spain. Moreover, amongst the *colonos* there were disparities in economic power. Some grew cane on their own land, some rented out their land to *subcolonos*, while others farmed on land rented from a *central*. *Colonos* had a tenuous relationship with the *centrales* and US financial interests. The *colonos* sometimes presented themselves to the government and business community as partners with the sugar mill corporation for the purpose of sugar export – the planters provided the labor and sugar, while the sugar mill provided the railroads, mills, and access to international markets. Other times, the *colonos* presented themselves as nationalist Cuban farmers who were the largest employers of Cuban labor and were oppressed by US interests and elite sugar mill owners. There were times when the *colonos* organized themselves, threatening to strike in order to negotiate better returns from the corporations. The *colonos* had to compete with large US-owned sugar mills, which purchased sugar cane farms and harvested cane using company workers (this was called *administración* sugar). Nevertheless, some of the more wealthy *colonos* developed some close personal and commercial ties with Cuban sugar mill owners and US financiers.[360] McGillivray outlines how the *colonos* formed an emerging middle class during the 1920s, which had obtained great economic and political power by the 1933 revolution in Cuba.[361]

Up until the 1920s, the *centrales* and *colonos* were the primary source of social and economic welfare for most people in Cuba. It would not be until Gerardo Machado y Morales became president in 1925 that the Cuban state would play a more active role in the social and economic life of Cubans.[362] Indeed, by the 1920s, a distinctive *Cuban* sugar interest was forming which represented a significant economic class with close ties to or overlapping with the Cuban political class. This coincided with an increase in Cuban nationalist rhetoric.[363] Thus, the Cuban state, starting with Machado's tenure, mostly represented the interests of the Cuban sugar mill owners and *colonos*.

transnational character of the sugar market in the context of the Chadbourne Agreement, see von Graevenitz, "Changing Visions."

360 Ayala, *American Sugar Kingdom*, pp. 121–47.

361 McGillivray, "'Dear President Machado'."

362 McGillivray, *Blazing Cane*, pp. 126, 145–6, 189.

363 deWilde, "Sugar."

Cuba's dependency on the US

The demarcation of "US interests" and "Cuban interests" was never very clear. What was complicated was that even though US financial interests intertwined with Cuban sugar interests, the rising Cuban *colonos* and elite sugar interests were often at odds with US political interests. Cubans had begun to diversify their economic investments and amass more wealth than before. Even though Cuban sugar planters and mill owners relied on US finance, they were at the mercy of US political decisions.

Cuba's relationship with the US, starting from its independence from Spain in 1902 until the 1958–9 revolution, was marked by various degrees and forms of imperial control.[364] From 1902 until 1934, the US maintained formal political and military influence over Cuba through the Platt Amendment. This was a provision introduced by a US Senator, incorporated into the Cuban constitution and further formalized through the 1903 Treaty of Relations. The treaty outlined the political relationship between the two countries and provided the circumstances in which the US might intervene in Cuban domestic and international politics. Accordingly, Cuba was sovereign to manage its political affairs, subject to the exceptions enumerated in the Platt Amendment for when the US might elect to intervene.[365] After the 1933 revolution, the US and Cuba signed a new treaty as part of Roosevelt's Latin American "Good Neighbor Policy"; the 1934 Treaty of Relations abrogated the Platt Amendment and reduced the US's right to a military presence in Cuba to maintaining a naval base in Guantánamo Bay.[366]

The US also held powerful economic influence over Cuba through various pieces of domestic sugar legislation and bilateral reciprocity trade treaties. In fact, Article I of the 1947 GATT has a provision that explicitly allows US preferences for Cuba as an exception to the most favored nation rule. From 1920 to 1933, especially during Machado's presidency, Cuban government officials and Cuban industry vigorously lobbied the US government to keep sugar tariffs low and preferential amounts high. Despite Cuban sugar's preferential access to the US market, the US government often set tariffs so high that these offset the benefits of the preferential rate for Cuban sugar – Cuban sugar producers

[364] Jenks, *Cuban Colony*, p. 271; Dominguez, *Cuba*.
[365] Jenks, *Cuban Colony*, pp. 75–103.
[366] Smith, *United States and Cuba*, pp. 149, 157.

were adversely affected because they could not compete with domestic sugar. The fluctuating price of sugar further frustrated Cuban sugar producers, and workers added considerable instability.[367] Some workers sang songs tinged with anger and irony, expressing their frustration with the US government's ability to dictate the fate of their lives with its domestic sugar quotas.[368]

Not only did US sugar laws and treaties destabilize Cubans' lives, but they also crippled Cuba's ability to industrialize and diversify its economy. These laws ensured that sugar continued to be Cuba's principal source of wealth. The 1903 Reciprocity Treaty granted Cuban agriculture a 20 percent preferential duty, and Cuba granted the US a 20 percent preferential duty on most items, with 24, 30, and 40 percent on selected categories. The 20 percent preferential duty for US goods was on products which already dominated the Cuban market, and therefore the reduction of the tariff was not expected to affect trade. The higher tariff reductions were for goods for which US officials anticipated competition from other industrialized countries.[369] Since the Reciprocity Treaty allowed cheap US manufactured goods to flood into Cuba, it made it very difficult for the nascent Cuban industry to develop.

In addition, the preferences granted to Cuban sugar were only for raw sugar. This meant that there was little incentive for refineries to be built in Cuba. In 1925, the Hershey Company established Cuba's first modern sugar refinery and began the first significant vertical integration of industry (from soil to supermarket). Hershey's, and bottlers of carbonated beverages such as Hires Root Beer, lobbied the US government for low duties on all Cuban sugar, since they wanted to build more refineries in Cuba to ensure access to cheap sugar.[370] Keep in mind that refined sugar generated a higher profit margin than raw sugar, and US refiners did not want to compete with Cuba-based refineries that were closer to cane fields. As such, US-based refiners successfully lobbied their government to ensure that only raw sugar was granted preferential access.[371] The US State Department considered the Reciprocity Treaty to be a way to stimulate the Cuban sugar economy (which was dominated by US-owned sugar mills) and ensure that the US had a monopsony on Cuban sugar.[372] Thus, the Cuban economy not only depended on sugar, but also on the US.

[367] *Ibid.*, pp. 42–71. [368] McGillivray, *Blazing Cane*, p. 1.
[369] Pérez, Jr., *Platt Amendment*, pp. 121–2.
[370] Dominguez, *Cuba*, pp. 21–2, 35; Smith, *United States and Cuba*, p. 30.
[371] McGillivray, *Blazing Cane*, pp. 75–7. [372] Pérez, Jr., *Platt Amendment*, p. 122.

Leland Hamilton Jenks, in his classic 1928 study of the US's economic imperial relationship with Cuba, links the emerging Cuban nationalist fervor of the 1920s with Cuba's role in the League. His analysis captures Cuba's relationship to the US through the League and is worth reproducing in detail:

> A host of imponderables assisted to build up Cuban consciousness of national personality. Cuba had signed the Versailles treaty and joined the League of Nations in 1920. And when the American Senate refused to endorse the diplomacy of President Wilson, *Cuba was left for the first time in an international position where she was not under the wing of the United States*. The benefits of the expanded international horizon were emphasized in 1922 when a Havana jurist, A.S. de Bustamante, was chosen one of the judges of the World Court. In 1923, another Cuban lawyer, Cosmé de la Torriente, served as president of the fourth assembly of the League. The rapidity with which Cubans have made their abilities recognized in the arena of world politics is further illustrated by the election of Cuba, for the year 1927–28, to a temporary seat on the Council of the League.[373]

Considering how central sugar was to every aspect of life in Cuba, the Cuban proposal for a sugar convention at the League can be understood as an attempt by the Cuban state to exert economic sovereignty in response to domination by US financiers and US-owned *centrales*.

Within five days of President Machado being overthrown on January 1, 1934, the US abrogated the Platt Amendment and started negotiating a new Reciprocity Treaty. Many Cubans thought that the 1933 revolution would change Cuban politics and economics. US laws, however, ensured that the Cuban economy remained dependent on sugar and the US. The new treaty had much the same effect as its 1903 predecessor and ensured that Cuba remained dependent on sugar until the 1950s.[374] The Reciprocity Treaty, as part of the New Deal, was coupled with the 1934 Jones-Costigan Act. The Jones-Costigan Act shifted US policy from regulating the import of trade through tariffs to regulation through import quotas. The combination of the Reciprocity Treaty and the Jones-Costigan Act allowed the US government to navigate between US international economic interests and competing interests in the domestic sugar industry.[375]

The Cuban economy was hurt by the way the Jones-Costigan Act set quotas. The act was based on previous years of production; in the past, Cuba had voluntarily reduced its production (through the 1931

[373] Jenks, *Cuban Colony*, p. 271. [374] McGillivray, *Blazing Cane*, pp. 223, 260.
[375] Smith, *United States and Cuba*, pp. 157–64.

Chadbourne Agreement) in an attempt to raise sugar prices and counter the sugar depression. As a result, it was locked into a quota that was far below 1925 levels.[376] The post-1933 Cuban elite agreed to the treaty and US sugar laws because they thought that they had to ensure, at least in the short-term, that Cuba had access to a stable sugar market.

The Cuban partial response to the US sugar laws and Reciprocity Treaty was the 1937 Sugar Coordination Act. To some Cubanist historians, this act epitomized the post-1933 empowerment of the *colonos*. The Sugar Coordination Act would be the cornerstone of the Cuban economic and political system until 1959. It regulated the production of sugar cane in favor of the *colonos*. The act provided a minimum quota for the grinding of cane from *colonos*, fixed the rent of the *colonos* at a very law rate, and linked the wages of workers to the price of sugar.[377] In response to the US, the interests of *colonos* and Cuban sugar mill owners were coalescing into a *Cuban* sugar producer interest.

The rise of a Cuban state

Cuba and the 1920 world sugar crises

Cuban delegates' decision to employ League doctrines of rationalization was not a simple importation of League ideas, nor a diplomatically opportunistic decision to piggyback on the League's prestige. The social, political, and economic conditions of Cuban sugar growing provide the context for what likely influenced Cuban delegates to employ and refine League economic discourse. Part of these conditions included Cuban sugar planters' transnational relationship with the US government and financiers. This was because the US domestic trade laws and US–Cuba trade treaties not only contravened League consensus, but also determinately affected the lives of many in Cuba.

During the First Word War, the same system of commodity control that was intended to ensure the supply of essential goods to Allied forces and war-ravaged Europe contributed to Cuba's economic boom. The US and British governments purchased Cuba's entire sugar crop at a controlled yet profitable price. As such, Allied Europe's primary source of imported sugar was Cuba, and Cuba's only export market was the Allied countries.[378] It is likely that the Cuban sugar producers' wartime

[376] Ayala, *American Sugar Kingdom*, pp. 239–340.
[377] Pollitt, "Cuban Sugar Economy," pp. 97, 98.
[378] Geerligs and Geerligs, *Cane Sugar*, p. 14; Rowe, *Studies*, p. 4.

experience, much like Salter, influenced their decision later to advocate for international sugar agreements based on theories of rationalization.

Many Cuban sugar mill owners did not like the arrangement of selling sugar at a price determined by others. They only agreed after the US government threatened Cuba with economic sanctions.[379] Nevertheless, demand for Cuban sugar increased during the war, and production almost doubled from 1914 to 1918. For many Cubans, this was a time of increased wealth, especially since Europe increasingly demanded imported sugar.[380]

The system of price control ended in November 1919. Even though Cuban sugar producers were not pleased by a system of price control during the war, they were impressed by the system in the last two years, since they benefited from stable prices.[381] After the wartime system of price control ended, the price of Cuban sugar fluctuated in New York from 7 cents to approximately 20 cents within a year. US and European consumers were experiencing a sugar famine, while US financiers and Cuban elites took advantage of this price fluctuation during 1919–20. Investors placed so much faith in speculation, and exchanged so much debt and credit with such frenzy, that Cuban journalists called this phenomenon the "dance of the millions."[382]

All this came crashing down in 1920, when the price of sugar throughout the world dropped rapidly. While Europe was recovering from the Great War and entering a period of economic development, Cuba was devastated by a world sugar crisis. During the planting season that coincided with the "dance of the millions," Cuban producers, after two decades of increasing demand, planted more cane than ever. They did not anticipate the sudden collapse of sugar prices that same year before the cane was ready to harvest.[383] Despite the crisis of 1920, the price of sugar remained at a sufficiently profitable level for Cuban sugar producers to recover gradually.[384]

Domestic Cuban banks, however, did not fare so well. During the Brussels International Financial Conference of 1920, Europe was looking to stabilize its currencies, in order to achieve improved economic conditions that would eventually rebuild Europe and increase world trade. Meanwhile, the Cuban financial crisis was far more dire. Domestic banks, all of which had lent money on sugar and mills, collapsed. North

[379] Jenks, *Cuban Colony*, pp. 196–205. [380] Rowe, *Studies*, pp. 5, 42.
[381] Jenks, *Cuban Colony*, p. 215. [382] *Ibid.*, pp. 206–28.
[383] Albert and Graves, "Introduction," pp. 1, 6. [384] Rowe, *Studies*, pp. 5, 42.

American banks remained the sole financiers on the island.[385] These foreign banks found themselves possessing considerable equity in mostly domestic-owned sugar mills that had run into difficulty. Foreign investment in Cuba had previously been from foreign private parties. Now, foreign banks, such as National City Bank and the Royal Bank of Canada, were the primary source of capital. The foreign banks' interests, which were already entangled with US Atlantic seaboard refineries importing raw Cuban sugar, and with private investors with capital in Cuba, now had a direct stake in Cuban sugar mills.[386] Thus, the crash after the "dance of the millions" probably made the wartime system of price control seem even more of an ideal and viable concept.

Competing Cuban Identities

Much like how League experts took from the war the idea of using rationalization for the purpose of economic development, the Cuban government experimented with domestic and international institutions to attempt to stabilize and control the price of sugar. The 1920 sugar crisis marked the beginnings of the Cuban state being used to affect the Cuban economy. This spurred two decades of debate in Cuba regarding the relationship between the state and the market in regard to sugar marketing policies.[387] Concerns were not only focused on the US, and people disagreed vehemently over what transnational ties Cuba should foster, and whether Cuba should look outward at all. Moreover, rapid technological changes made the harvesting and production of sugar significantly more efficient. This further deepened the presence of foreign corporations on the island, because these were one of the few entities with the necessary capital to invest in the new technologies (and purchase large amounts of land) for the purpose of mass-producing sugar for agricultural export.[388] This made the relationship between the burgeoning Cuban state and entrenched foreign corporations even more acute.

The building of the Cuban state coincided with often-violent contestations of Cuban identity. One result of the 1920–2 sugar crisis was the rise of racist attacks against West Indians by Cubans. Many in Cuba felt that cheap imported labor had caused the crisis. In Cuba during the 1920s and 1930s, ideas and movements such as radical nationalism, pan-hispanism, anti-imperialism, Afro-Cubanism, and labor activism contended with

[385] Jenks, *Cuban Colony*, pp. 229–45. [386] Rowe, *Studies*, pp. 11–13.
[387] Swerling, "Export Industry." [388] Dye, *Cuban Sugar*.

each other.[389] To some Cubanist historians, these two decades would significantly influence contemporary Cuban identity.[390] Cuban experiences were parallel to trends throughout the colonial world – the agricultural depression in the 1920s, which was further exacerbated by the Great Depression in the 1930s, caused social and political discontent, forming the basis for many anti-colonial national movements.[391]

In Cuba during the early 1920s, anti-imperialism and economic nationalism were popular themes. Also, a group of younger writers made the first tentative attempts to address class and race issues.[392] Nevertheless, much of the nationalist rhetoric of the time took racist stances against the influx of laborers from Haiti and Jamaica, who worked for cheaper wages. This vision of Cuba precluded an identity that extended beyond the island.[393] The "exclusionary aspirations" of the new nationalist mood met with resistance from the Cuban branches of the United Negro Improvement Association of Marcus Garvey, calling for black "racial pride," as well as the Cuban Communist party and elements of the growing labor movement emphasizing class alliances.[394]

The state responded with contradictory policies in an attempt to allay competing local demands. In response to sugar companies' demand for cheap labor, the Cuban government allowed for the increased import of West Indian labor; in response to some local workers and nationalists, the government financed much-publicized expulsions of West Indians.[395]

Another example of government involvement as a response to the crisis was the establishment of the first Cuban postwar sugar control agency, the Sugar Finance Committee. This agency took over the national sale of crops during 1920–2. Six of the seven-man committee were representatives from North American banks and US sugar mill owners in Cuba, with only one representative from larger Cuban planters.[396]

The composition of the Sugar Finance Committee exemplifies the complex relationship between Cuban national identity, US private interests, and US and Cuban government interests. The relationship amongst all these different groups was constantly contested and renegotiated during the rise of the Cuban state in the 1920s and early 1930s. Cuban mill

[389] Chomsky, "Barbados or Canada?," 453–9.
[390] Carr, "Identity"; Kapcia, *Havana*, pp. 61–118.
[391] Hobsbawm, *Age of Extremes*, pp. 106–7. [392] Chomsky, "Barbados or Canada?," 454.
[393] McLeod, "Undesirable Aliens"; Helg, "Aftermath"; Blanca G. Silverstrini, "National Spaces."
[394] Carr, "Identity," 84–5. [395] Chomsky, "Barbados or Canada?," 453.
[396] Swerling, *International Control*, p. 33–4.

owners and *colonos* had close ties to US financiers, but at the same time empowered the Cuban state in order to enhance their own economic sovereignty. In 1918–19, US-owned sugar mills accounted for 51.4 percent of the harvest. By 1927, US-owned sugar mills accounted for 62.5 percent of production, rising to 68.1 percent by 1934. Even though US-owned mills were outnumbered by Cuban-owned mills, their total production yield was higher because US owners had more access to capital, generating larger and more technologically advanced *centrales*.[397] The Cuban sugar and commercial elite often worked alongside US business interests and comprised most government positions, including the presidency.[398]

Cuba and US tariffs

One factor that galvanized different interests in Cuba was the reaction against depending economically on sugar exports and the US. Many Cubans argued against this dependency on one commodity, or called for socio-economic changes that would make the domestic sugar economy more equitable.[399] The contradictory streams of rising Cuban nationalism meant something different from the "nationalism" criticized from within the League. The League worked to overcome a nationalism that consisted of high tariffs and self-sufficiency, which would devastate most lives in export-dependent Cuba. Indeed, this type of nationalism, abhorred at the League, would be what Cuban delegates disliked about their relationship with the US.

Despite the 1903 and 1934 Reciprocity Treaty granting Cuban sugar preferential access to the US market, many Cubans argued that this was not reciprocity, because the US only made concessions on a few products, since Cuba was only capable of exporting a small number of products, whereas Cuba made concessions on a wide range of products. Cuban exporters, however, were pleased, because the treaty granted some preferential access to the US market and created a boom in sugar production. This preferential access meant that Cuban sugar competed with domestic cane and beet sugar, and with US colonial cane sugar from Hawaii, Puerto Rico, and the Philippines (which all received duty-free status). Because Cuban sugar was granted preferential, but not duty-free status, Cuban sugar producers had an advantage over other imported sugar in the US, but had to ensure that its cost of production was low enough to compete with domestic and US colonial sugar. This made it difficult for

[397] Dominguez, *Cuba*, p. 22. [398] Smith, *United States and Cuba*.

[399] See, e.g., Guerra, *Sugar and Society*.

sugar workers' wages to rise. Despite all these difficulties, Cuban sugar producers managed to practically displace full-duty sugar by 1912. This meant that until the 1930s, the vast majority of sugar consumed in the US was domestic, colonial duty-free, and Cuban preferential sugar.[400]

Farmers in the US missed out on the opulence of the roaring twenties, given that they were enduring a depression. As a result, the US government raised tariffs for agricultural products, including for Cuban sugar. As the agricultural depression continued, the 1922 Tariff Act (through the so-called "flexible provisions") allowed the president to adjust tariffs according to the cost of production for a foreign competitor. The purpose was to "equalize" the cost of production between US and foreign producers. This meant that if the Cuban cost of production decreased, and the president decided to increase the tariff accordingly, thereby stabilizing the US price of refined sugar, the US domestic sugar producer and the US treasury would benefit. If Cuban costs of production decreased, and the president decided to do nothing, the price of US refined sugar would decrease, thereby benefiting the US consumer, US refiners importing raw Cuban sugar, and US investors in Cuban sugar properties.[401] One complaint in Cuba was that this granted the US too much economic power over Cuba and stagnated the Cuban sugar industry – for all Cuban efforts to decrease production costs, usually by decreasing labor wages, the US had the ability to transfer those savings to US government coffers.[402] While US sugar tariffs fluctuated, Cuba sought other markets, with limited success. The other significant sugar consumer, the UK, had reduced its dependency on European sugar and established a trade policy that included colonial preference for cane sugar and subsidization of a domestic beet sugar industry.[403]

The Chadbourne Agreement

The prelude to international sugar rationalization

From 1925 to 1929, in an effort to raise sugar prices, the Cuban government devised a variety of administrative arrangements intended to restrict the production of sugar.[404] This was a difficult time for Cuba,

400 Wright, *Sugar*, pp. 64–5. 401 *Ibid.*, pp. 58–60, 237–43; Dalton, *Sugar*, pp. 60–1.

402 Guerra, *Sugar and Society*, pp. 107–14.

403 Timoshenko and Swerling, *World's Sugar*, pp. 200–34 (chapter prepared by R. J. Hammond).

404 Rowe, *Studies*, pp. 19–29.

which, along with the Dutch colony of Java, was the world's largest producer of sugar for export. Cuba initiated a policy to restrict sugar production for two purposes. First, it was an attempt to raise sugar prices in the US. Cuban sugar greatly benefited from a price rise because, thanks to the Reciprocity Treaty, Cuban sugar had supplanted all full-duty sugar purchased by the US. Second, it was an attempt to induce other countries to follow the same policy of restriction, in order to reduce world supply and achieve a balance between supply and demand.

The policy affected different components of the Cuban sugar industry in competing ways, and different groups rallied for or against restriction. By this time, North American sugar-refining companies and sugar-using industries (such as confectioners and soft-drink makers) purchased a number of *centrales* on the island; it was in their interest to maintain low sugar prices, since their profit derived from refined sugar, not sugar production; as the price of sugar went down, their profits would go up. Also opposed to the restriction of sugar production were the *centrales* owners and those *colonos* who had some advantage over smaller operations for various reasons (more capital, more fertile land, more modern machinery, cheaper immigrant labor force, etc.) and sold to markets that did not provide preference for Cuban sugar; these owners would benefit if the price drop eliminated the weakest mills. Those who supported restriction were the smaller *centrales* owners and those *colonos* who would face ruin from overproduction and hoped that restriction, as a last resort, would increase the price of sugar and save them from the dire conditions under which they were operating.

Laborers, whose wage rate was tied to the market value of sugar, were damned regardless of whether sugar production was restricted or not. With overproduction, laborers obtained more days of employment per year, but at a miserable wage. With restriction, they earned somewhat better pay, but worked fewer days.[405]

Cuba's policy of self-restriction did little to affect world prices and quell discontent. Between 1925 and 1927, the Machado government launched a devastating attack against the Cuban National Labor Confederation (CNOC) and the Communists. Labor leaders were deported or assassinated and their political parties were banned. Revolts broke out in Cuba in 1928, challenging the stability of Machado's power.[406] Cuba's sugar

[405] Guerra, *Sugar and Society*, pp. 158–61.

[406] Kindleberger, *Depression*, p.81 (Kindleberger states that these insurrections would "stimulate fifty revolutions in Latin America" that spread across the region until 1933).

economy was further affected by the US agricultural crisis of 1929 that preceded the oncoming Great Depression. The 1930 Smoot-Hawley Tariff Act, a response to the agricultural crisis, further strained sugar producers in Cuba; the US raised its tariffs and restricted Cuban access to the US. Cuban sugar producers, who had already been experiencing a sugar crisis when prices started to drop in 1925, were pummeled when the Great Depression vanquished any hope of recovery for the price of sugar in the world.[407]

Even with some semblance of government control over social discontent, the Cuban economy was collapsing, wages were declining, and politicians were joining the opposition. Beginning with the general strike in 1930, workers, most of them under Communist direction, waged a continuous battle against the Machado government, which was chased out in 1933.[408] Even before the 1933 revolution, many in Cuba considered that no amount of domestic policy could save Cuba and that relief would come from international stabilization measures that would rationalize the global production of sugar.[409] However, it took multiple attempts before a final, functioning agreement was reached in 1937.

The 1925 sugar crisis

As US tariffs fluctuated and rose, demands for the stabilization of tariffs at the League of Nations were acutely relevant for sugar producers in Cuba. US financiers joined with Cuban sugar producers to create international sugar agreements intended to stabilize and raise the price of sugar. This relationship, however, was never stable, especially as Cuban sugar producers tried to negotiate the presence of US capital on the island while at the same time trying to assert an increased degree of economic sovereignty.

Orestes Ferrara's experiences as Cuban ambassador to the US and, later, as Cuban delegate to the 1933 World Monetary and Economic Conference, exemplify this relationship. His frustrations with the US and proposals at the League illustrate how Cuba turned to the League to try to obtain more economic sovereignty from the US. On two separate occasions in 1927, Ferrara made requests to the US for some form of relief during a sugar depression, each of which was denied. He tried to convince the US government to increase the preferential duty for Cuban sugar from 20 to 40 percent, or, as a second-best option, to create

[407] Dalton, *Sugar*, pp. 62–8. [408] Dominguez, *Cuba*, p. 51.
[409] Guerra y Debén, "Evolution," pp. 171, 176; McAvoy, *Sugar Baron*, pp. 223–34.

a sliding scale preferential rate that adapted to the fluctuating price of sugar – a preferential rate that was high when the price was high, low when the price was low.[410] That same year, Ferrara informed the State Department that the Platt Amendment made Cuba appear less sovereign and independent; Ferrara (and later Machado) did not request to eliminate the legislation, but rather wanted to change the form, so that Cuba "would look better to the world."[411] Being refused, Cuban delegates turned to the League as a forum to attempt to stabilize the international price of sugar – and, in essence, to try to negotiate increased economic sovereignty from the US – by requesting the creation of an international sugar agreement at the 1927 World Economic Conference.[412]

Despite the fact that at the 1927 World Economic Conference there was no consensus as to what form an industrial agreement embodying "rationalization" would take, or even whether industrial agreements were desirable, attending Cuban experts proposed to devise an international sugar agreement to control world production.[413] The Cubans' determination, despite the lack of a sugar agreement, and their League colleagues' disagreement, is understandable in light of how acute the sugar crisis was in Cuba by this time.

In 1925, while most continental Europeans and North Americans were living through a period of prosperity, Cubans were experiencing a time of dissonance. A sugar crisis struck the world sugar producers in 1925, when the global rate of production far surpassed the rate of consumption. Cuba, which by this time accounted for 25 percent of the world's sugar production, was hardest hit only a few years after recovering from the 1920 collapse of prices. The sugar crisis of 1925 in Cuba ushered in President Gerardo Machado y Morales; his administration marked a time of state building and social unrest in Cuba and would culminate in riots, student revolts, and a military coup d'état.

Machado was also part of the nationalist fervor of the time, except that his was a "business nationalism."[414] This business nationalism characterized Cuban sugar producers' interests (which dominated the Cuban government) well past Machado and through Cuban history, until 1958. Machado politely but consistently attempted to gain increased political independence from the US, but made sure it was

410 Smith, *United States and Cuba*, pp. 49–50. 411 *Ibid.*, p. 120.

412 De Blanck to Secretary-General, September 12, 1927, LON, R460, 10/61898/52794.

413 Economic and Financial Section, *Report and Proceedings*, vol. I, p. 239.

414 Smith, *United States and Cuba*, p. 113.

not tarnished with anti-US sentiment and offence to US commercial interests; he still believed that the welfare of Cuba was interlaced with the interests of the US.[415]

During the first two years of Machado's administration, the state became active in national economic development and spent millions of dollars on public works projects. Machado's plan of national industrial development and economic diversification included government-sponsored agricultural credit and tariff support. For almost a decade, Cuban industrialists had been demanding some sort of tariff relief. In 1927, the Machado government responded and enacted the Customs-Tariff Law, which to some Cubanist historians was one of the most important pieces of economic legislation of the early republic. The Customs-Tariff Law was informed by a plan for agricultural diversification and industrial development. It reduced tariffs and duties on raw materials in an effort to promote local manufacturing activity, on crude oil to encourage the expansion of refining facilities, on cotton to encourage textiles, and on machinery and heavy equipment to stimulate the expansion of industrial facilities, and it provided a duty-exemption for sisal in order to promote local rope and cordage manufacturing.[416]

To be sure, Machado's economic development plan did not directly envision social welfare or improvement of the conditions of the poor and working class. Machado made it clear to US banks and financiers that he intended to maintain stability and contain the "radical" forces of social unrest, most notably the labor movement and Communist Party, in order to ensure that their investments in these public projects were secure (a promise which he kept by using violent repression). This was a development plan intended to benefit US financiers and Cuban entrepreneurs.[417] Machado also stood to gain personally from his program of public works because of investments in the Cuban Electric Company.[418]

Machado needed a vast amount of capital to execute his economic development plans. Foreign funds were a primary source of finance for public works. Machado's administration became extremely indebted to North American banks, especially Chase Bank.[419] Also, US private investment in sugar increased tenfold from 1906 to 1927. Since US sugar refiners had successfully lobbied the US government to keep refined

[415] McAvoy, *Sugar Baron*, p. 183; Aguilar, *Cuba 1933*, pp. 45–68.
[416] Pérez, Jr., *Cuba and the United States*, pp. 177–8. [417] *Ibid.*, pp. 178–9.
[418] McAvoy, *Sugar Baron*, p. 165. [419] Smith, *United States and Cuba*, pp. 122–9.

sugar tariffs, these investments primarily served to export raw sugar to the US.[420]

Although US financiers significantly influenced Cuba and its government, their sugar interests in the US Congress were subordinate to the interests of domestic producers and the US-colonial territories of Hawaii, Puerto Rico, and the Philippines.[421] Thus, Machado's and US commercial interests in Cuba aligned to become one and the same. As the president of the American Chamber of Commerce of Cuba stated in 1926: "If our commercial intention is to continue, we must identify ourselves with her [Cuba's] purposes and make common cause with her in favor of her nationalistic program."[422] Even though many Cuban mill owners feared the influence of US capital, the more the US increased its tariffs on Cuban sugar, the more Cuban-owned and US-owned mill interests united against this common economic impediment.[423]

The Cuban state, however, was not simply a proxy for US commercial interests in Cuba. From 1925 to 1933, many mills were forced to cease production because of the sugar depression. Since American-owned mills had easier access to capital and tended to be technologically superior, the vast majority of those mills that suspended operation were Cuban-owned. These mills were the economic and social core of life on the island, and directly and indirectly benefited their surrounding rural communities and provincial towns. Therefore, when mills closed down, not only was the livelihood of employees and suppliers arrested, but also entire communities degenerated.[424]

Up until the sugar crisis, forests were being cleared to make way for sugar fields and railroads at such a high rate that many in Cuba feared that the "health of the island" and the public interest were in danger. In 1926, Machado completely reversed a hundred years of indiscriminate cutting and burning of forests to clear fields for sugar cane. He prohibited the clearing of high woodlands, regardless of whether the land belonged to the government or to a private citizen.[425]

Machado also did not want to appear to his compatriots as a patsy for the Americans.[426] In an attempt to self-restrict sugar production, in 1926 the government passed legislation that called for a 10 percent

[420] Dominguez, *Cuba*, p. 21. [421] Pollitt, "Cuban Sugar Economy," p. 98.
[422] Quoted in Jenks, *Cuban Colony*, p. 390, n. 4. [423] Rowe, *Studies*, p. 15.
[424] Swerling, "Export Industry," 348.
[425] Funes Monzote, *Rainforest to Cane Field*, pp. 1, 256–7. [426] McAvoy, *Sugar Baron*, p. 185.

reduction in output for each mill. It also granted priority to sugar delivered from (Cuban) *colonos* over sugar from land owned by the mills themselves (which were owned by US financiers). Even though this legislation was limited in scope and only lasted two years, it is indicative of how the Cuban state was negotiating the interests of US capital and Cuban planters.[427] After the revolution of 1933, the Cuban state's balance of interests tipped even more in favor of Cuban producers over US capital.

Compared to the past, Machado's reign enacted a remarkably different role for the Cuban state. From 1914 to 1920, the government had no monetary power; neither the government nor any institution under its influence, such as a central bank, created money. The US dollar had free circulation in Cuba during this period, so the government could not alter the exchange rate. Also, Cuba had no banking legislation, which meant that the government had no effective control over regulating and inspecting banks or over the establishment of new banks. Accordingly, during the 1920s and most of the 1930s, foreign banks and balance of payments determined the volume of the money supply in Cuba.[428]

Since the Cuban government had little control over the foreign banks, it was left with experimenting with its trade policy to serve the domestic needs of ecónomic development. Cuban delegates were therefore eager to organize an international sugar agreement, regulating world production in sugar, at the 1927 World Economic Conference. While League delegates could not come to any sort of conceptual consensus regarding what definition of "rationalization" would best to ensure international economic stability and prosperity, the Cuban delegates presented a specific outline and advocated (though unsuccessfully) for an international sugar treaty that would control the price of sugar.[429]

The attempt to create an international sugar agreement in the late 1920s reflected the balancing act of Cuban "business nationalism." It was nationalist in that it was an agreement that provided control of sugar production to the Cuban government; it was business-friendly, since the majority of sugar produced in Cuba came out of US-owned mills. Saving the Cuban sugar industry would directly benefit US investors, US banks, the Cuban elite, and US Atlantic Seaboard refiners (who depended on Cuban raw sugar).

[427] Pollitt, "Cuban Sugar Economy," p. 100. [428] Dominguez, *Cuba*, p. 33.
[429] Economic and Financial Section, *Report and Proceedings*, vol. I, pp. 89, 237–8.

The League decides not to get involved

After Cuba raised the issue of a sugar agreement at the World Economic Conference, in May 1928 Belgium formally placed it on the Economic Consultative Committee's agenda.[430] In June 1928, the League Council, upon advice from the Economic Consultative Committee, adopted a resolution calling for the Economic Committee to study world sugar consumption and production patterns and conditions, and to determine whether international action was warranted. The result was an extensive survey of sugar-producing and -consuming countries.

Starting in the fall of 1928 and continuing into 1930, the Economic Committee researched the sugar problem through extensive expert consultation and national surveys.[431] During this process, Cuban delegates pushed hard to expand the mandate beyond a simple research endeavor and closer to reaching an agreement.[432]

In the meantime, delegates from Cuba, Colonel José Miguel Tarafa and Dr. Viriato Gutiérrez Valladon, toured throughout Europe during 1929–30, in an attempt to form an agreement amongst the world's sugar producers to reduce production. Rionda, the old sugar baron, had backed both Tarafa and Gutiérrez on their European tour. Rionda saw Tarafa off and must have passed along his faith in the 1902 Brussels Convention. On the ship back from Europe, Tarafa carefully studied a stabilization proposal by H. C. Prinsen Geerligs, entitled "Project of the Reconstruction of the Brussels Convention of 1902," which he brought back to Rionda.[433] Prinsen Geerligs was a preeminent Dutch sugar scientist, who not only provided one of the best studies of the 1902 Brussels Convention at the turn of the century,[434] but was one of the experts commissioned by the League to draft the influential memo in 1929 outlining the world's sugar situation.[435]

Tarafa and Gutiérrez's European tour was unsuccessful. One reason that the Cuban delegation failed was that Dutch-controlled Java refused to enter into an agreement; Java was the world's other largest sugar producer and had the lowest cost of production. Not until later, in 1930, when the world price of sugar dropped so low that even the Java

[430] "The Question of Sugar," May 12, 1928, LON, R2818, 10D/3761/3427; "Draft Resolution submitted by the Sugar Sub-Committee," May 16, 1928, LON, R2818, 10D/3965/3427.

[431] LON, E/Sugar/1–51; E/Sugar/P.V.1(1)–5(1).

[432] Note various documents in LON, R2820, 10D/7810/3427.

[433] McAvoy, *Sugar Baron*, p. 225. [434] Geerligs, *Sugar Industry*, pp. 378–80.

[435] Geerligs, "Production," p. 4.

producers were no longer making a profit, were they ready to negotiate an international agreement.[436]

While Tarafa and Gutiérrez were on their European tour, a very influential memo by three experts was published on cane sure production (Geerligs), beet sugar production (Licht), and sugar consumption (Mikusch).[437] Geerligs advocated (though not in this memo) for an agreement akin to the 1902 Brussels Convention that would address government measures which were thought to artificially increase production.[438] Licht and Mikusch were reluctant to regulate supply and suggested campaigns to increase sugar consumption. In the end, the Economic Committee decided not to convene an international conference and left the sugar industry to itself to resolve the crisis.[439]

The rationalization of the world sugar market

Cuban-owned mills had historically resented the more efficient and wealthy mills flush with US capital. The 1930 Smoot-Hawley Tariff, however, coalesced the interests of all mill owners in Cuba, regardless of nationality, against the high US tariffs excluding all sugar from Cuba. After Tarafa and Gutiérrez's unsuccessful European tour and the stalled efforts within the League, Cuban sugar mill owners selected Thomas Chadbourne, a Wall Street lawyer, to try to organize and stabilize world sugar production and prices.[440] Cuban sugar mill owners chose Chadbourne because New York banks could bring (if not drag) together, not only US beet interests, but also the sugar field owners of Puerto Rico, Hawaii, and the Philippines, as well as the European and Javanese producers. This was because their financial interests spanned the world, whereas Tarafa and Gutiérrez could only do so much, since they only represented Cuba. From the Cuban perspective, Java was the most feared competitor and less likely to negotiate because of the independent wealth of the Netherlands.[441] With the League's tepid response to the sugar depression of the 1920s and the Great Depression intensifying the sugar crisis, Chadbourne's task was made all the more urgent.

[436] Rowe, "Sugar," pp. 23–6. [437] Geerligs, Licht, and Mikusch, *Sugar*.

[438] "Note by the Secretariat, transmitting an article by Dr. Prinsen Geerligs on the subject of the finalization of an international sugar convention," E/Sugar/42 (October 16, 1929). Geerligs had provided his technical expertise in sugar during the negotiations of the Chadbourne Agreement; see McAvoy, *Sugar Baron*, pp. 234–5.

[439] Economic Committee, *World Sugar*.

[440] McAvoy, *Sugar Baron*, pp. 191, 225–6; Smith, *United States and Cuba*, pp. 53–71.

[441] McAvoy, *Sugar Baron*, p. 226; von Graevenitz, "Changing Visions."

In 1931, representatives from the sugar industries of the participating countries (Cuba, Java, Germany, Czechoslovakia, Poland, Hungary, and Belgium) signed the Chadbourne Agreement in Brussels. In fact, Chadbourne used similar ideas from what was previously an unwritten "gentleman's agreement" that he had helped to arrange that previous year between the sugar producers from the US, the US's "insular possessions" (i.e. Puerto Rico and the Philippines), and Cuba.[442] There were high hopes for the agreement. It was the first agreement to attempt to rationalize the international sugar market.[443] In honor of their accomplishments, the French appointed Chadbourne *Officier* of the Legion of Honor, and the Cubans granted Lucien Beauduin, the Belgian senator and president of the conference (and subsequent president of the International Sugar Council), the Grand Cross of the Order of Carlos Manuel de Céspedes of Cuba.[444]

To Chadbourne himself, the agreement provided the best mechanisms to stabilize the international price of sugar because it did not fix a set price, but instead was an industrial agreement that attempted to "restore the balance between production and consumption in a commodity the demand for which is relatively inelastic."[445] This, to him, constituted a "league of nations on sugar affairs."[446] According to Chadbourne, by organizing the world's sugar producers, the agreement overcame the perceived impossibility for "producers in any one nation by concerted action, much less by tariff barriers, to check that unbridled, catch-as-catch-can competition which drives industry into bankruptcy and workers into poverty and misery."[447]

The agreement exemplified the spirit of rapprochement, but not through the reduction or removal of tariffs. Nevertheless, to some, the Chadbourne Agreement (and the 1937 ISA)[448] *could* have the secondary ability of reducing high tariffs. The thinking was that if the price of sugar was stabilized at a rate that was fair to producers, then producers would be better off in commercial terms. Under such a scheme, producers would therefore have less of a political claim for their governments to

442 "Chadbourne Committee Meeting," *Weekly Statistical Sugar Trade Journal* (August 28, 1930) 427 (text of the "gentleman's agreement").

443 See, e.g., Cohen, "Law" (celebrating the Chadbourne Agreement because it was an example of rationalization); Mermin, "Sugar" (criticizing the Chadbourne Agreement because it was an example of rationalization).

444 von Graevenitz, "Changing Visions," 738. 445 Chadbourne, "Stabilization," 384.

446 McAvoy, *Sugar Baron*, p. 233. 447 Chadbourne, "Stabilization," 383.

448 Rowe, "Sugar," p. 28.

support them through tariffs.[449] This reflected the pattern of thinking at the League, that economic rationalization should be addressed first, before trying to implement freer trade policies.

The Chadbourne Agreement only anticipated disputes involving factual determinations of whether quotas were exceeded.[450] If national producer representatives could not agree that quotas were exceeded or if another dispute arose, then they had to resolve the matter between themselves, without employing any institutional support from the newly formed International Sugar Council.[451]

The Chadbourne Agreement provided two ways to increase the price of sugar: reducing the accumulation of surplus stocks and the production of sugar.[452] Despite the agreement, sugar stock remained in surplus in most countries. Many considered this to be a technical miscalculation and attributed the problem to the fact that the agreement did not anticipate that further stocks could be accumulated, even if producers conformed to the terms of the agreement.[453] Sugar producers generally honored the stipulated production quotas, thereby reducing sugar production.[454]

Some economists celebrated the fact that this was an agreement concluded by producers and not by government representatives. It was thought to avoid political complications and allow sugar producers to directly address the conditions of their own industry.[455] It was not that the national governments had no presence at the negotiations, nor that their role was not anticipated in the Chadbourne Agreement; rather, the sugar producers, in effect, represented the state. In most cases, the national producer organizations, like the Cuban Sugar Stabilization Institute, were government agencies empowered to represent the national sugar industry. Once the agreement was finalized, national governments enforced it, either through direct means, such as enacting laws (as was done in Cuba), or through indirect means, such as adjusting duties and export taxes.[456]

449 Geerligs and Geerligs, *Cane Sugar*, pp. 28–9.

450 Art. VIII (Establishing a board of arbitrators to resolve matters of fact regarding export quotas).

451 Dye and Sicotte, "Brinkmanship"; Wilk, "International Affairs," 870. 452 Art. II.

453 Swerling, *International Control*, p. 47. Surplus was calculated in the agreement based on consumption patterns in 1929, based on the assumption that consumption is fairly inelastic.

454 Geerligs and Geerligs, *Cane Sugar*, p. 35. 455 James, "International Control."

456 Wilk, "International Affairs," 871–3. The only exception was Belgium, which enacted no laws.

Power was delegated according to sugar production through the voting scheme. The agreement distributed power to the sugar producers by allocating votes in the International Sugar Council roughly along the lines of sugar production. Therefore, the significant number of votes went to the Cuban corporation (35 out of 90) and the Java corporation (30 out of 90).[457]

Implementation was delegated to national governments, and the International Sugar Council acted as a coordinating inter-industry agency, much like the First World War commodity regulating agencies. National producers were each allocated a number of votes, and a majority vote authorized Council decisions.[458] The Council's role was to supervise the operation of the Agreement. Since the Agreement provided the details of determining production and surplus quotas, the Council's role was monitoring, investigating, and advising in relation to sugar prices and quotas.[459]

Even though the Chadbourne Agreement was not under the auspices of the League, US financiers lobbied Salter and others to sponsor the agreement's negotiations. Norman Davis, a sugar magnate, who at one time had served as a US diplomat and Wilson's Assistant Secretary of Treasury and later Undersecretary of State, wrote to Salter in his personal capacity. He urged Salter to consider bringing the sugar producer negotiations under the auspices of the League.[460] Likewise, Charles C. Bauer, in his capacity as Financial Advisor to the League of Nations Association in the United States, and in his personal capacity, wrote to Manley O. Hudson, who was a member of the Legal Section of the League Secretariat at the time. Bauer relayed and endorsed Chadbourne's desire to bring the negotiations through the League.[461] US Financiers and Cuban sugar producers wanted to convene a conference following the "general lines of League experts" – meaning through doctrines of rationalization. They suggested that such a conference could set an

[457] Art. IV(d). [458] Art. IV(f). [459] Arts. I(e), IV(i), V.

[460] Davis to Salter, July 31, 1930, LON, R2822, 10D/21808/3427.

[461] Bauer to Hudson, August 8, 1930 and August 10, 1930, LON, R2822, 10D/21808/3427; de Bordes to Salter, August 9, 1930, LON, R2822, 10D/21808/3427. Chadbourne was a financial supporter of the League of Nations Association; see Sweetser to Salter, August 28, 1930, LON, R2822, 10D/21808/3427. The League of Nations Association was a national organization with semi-autonomous branches in various parts of the US. The association supported revision of the League Covenant and American membership. It waged an educational campaign to inform Americans of the League's activities and accomplishments, and generally tried to foster international cooperation, both politically and economically.

example for other commodities that had to be stabilized before the respective industries were ruined and further human suffering ensued. They did not think they needed formal government representatives, but they needed the League because its prestige and prowess would make it significantly easier to organize the world's sugar producers on a global scale. Moreover, US financiers were trying to work around the fact that the US government did not accept the Economic and Financial Section's invitation to participate in League consultations regarding the world sugar crisis.[462]

The fact that the request to League officials was brought by interests representing private sugar producers made it legally difficult for an intergovernmental organization to sponsor the conference. To Hudson, doyen of international law in the US and one of the principal jurists in the League, this request came from a "queer angle."[463] Nevertheless, the legal question of private actors and public international institutions was not the determinative reasoning.

Instead, the issue was principally framed as an economic question over the appropriate commercial policy.[464] Many of the principal decision-makers, such as Arthur Salter in the Economic and Financial Section and Arthur Sweetser in the Public Information Section, also took the request seriously. The fact that there was, in effect, significant state involvement during Chadbourne negotiations, albeit in the background, means that it would not have been difficult to frame the negotiations as intergovernmental to some degree.

The economic argument that influenced the decision within the League was that an international agreement on "the sugar question" could only be obtained if governments were committed to freer trade. In League doctrinal terms, what was going on was that political approaches of economic rapprochement through multilateral commercial treaties (and notions of freer trade) were favored over economic approaches of rapprochement (and notions of rationalization). The widely held view in Europe, especially in Belgium and the Netherlands, was that government intervention was the main culprit; their argument was that overproduction was caused by government stimulus in the form of subsidies and tariffs, and therefore government action was needed to solve the problem.

[462] de Bordes to Salter, August 11, 1930, LON, R2822, 10D/21808/3427.

[463] Handwritten note from Hudson to de Bordes, *c.* August 11, 1930, LON, R2822, 10D/21808/3427.

[464] Memo by Jan van Walre de Bordes, "The American Request for a Sugar Producers' Conference," August 22, 1930, LON, R2822, 10D/21808/3427.

Belgium had taken the lead, as the historical sponsor of the 1902 sugar treaty, to organize a conference of the world's sugar-producing nations; since this was overtly a state-led initiative, League officials held back on any intergovernmental conference organizing from their end.[465] The conference held in Belgium in December 1930 would be part of a series of conferences strengthening ties amongst European sugar beet growers, who were becoming more of a formal political block. Cane growers in Cuba and Java, who up until now had been rivals as the world's largest sugar producers, found themselves the joint target of European beet growers. European planters and politicians laid the blame for the world sugar crisis on overproduction by cane growers. In turn, European governments such as Germany rejected Javanese and Cuban producers' requests for a broad-based international agreement akin to the 1902 Brussels Convention, as well as Chadbourne's proposal for a global reduction in sugar production.[466]

Another important reason that the League did not sponsor the negotiations, separate from transnational sugar interests and intergovernmental politics, was that League officials thought there was a high chance that sugar producer negotiations would fail, as they had done in the past. The concern was that such a failure would degrade the League's tenuous reputation since, according to one member of the Economic and Financial Section, "we have already had too many League conferences during the last year which were more or less concealed failures."[467] It was thought that more direct government involvement in negotiations would increase the chances of a successful conference. The calculation was that it was in the League's interest to protect its reputation and only get involved in conferences that had a high chance of succeeding; success was measured in terms of whether an agreement was drafted and ratified by the states.

The World Monetary and Economic Conference and the Cuban Revolution, 1933

Despite the reduced production and occasional moderate rise in price, the Chadbourne Agreement was considered dead by the 1933 World

[465] Salter to Davis, August 9, 1930; Sweetser to Salter, August 13, 1930, LON, R2822, 10D/21808/3427.

[466] von Graevenitz, "Changing Visions," 733–4.

[467] de Bordes to Sweetser, August 14, 1930, LON, R2822, 10D/21808/3427.

Monetary and Economic Conference, and officially lapsed in 1935.[468] Few criticized the implementation of the Chadbourne Agreement, since the assumption was that it was economically sound in principle. At the 1933 World Monetary and Economic Conference, the Cuban delegation made a detailed proposal for a sugar agreement.[469] Their proposal stood in contrast to the League discussions, which remained at the level of generalities and focused on trying to find a conceptual consensus on "freer trade."

Cuban delegates at the 1933 World Monetary and Economic Conference stated that the sugar crisis continued, despite the Chadbourne Agreement, because the Great Depression significantly reduced consumption. They also argued that Chadbourne was successful because signatory producers decreased production according to the agreement, but non-Chadbourne countries (namely the US and its territories, and European countries) neutralized the benefits of production control when they raised their tariffs or subsidized their domestic industry, thereby increasing production.[470] In League parlance, Cuban delegates blamed non-Chadbourne countries for engaging in policies of "economic nationalism" or "self-sufficiency." The thinking was that Chadbourne producers had underestimated the extent to which European countries' high tariffs and subsidies would rejuvenate the postwar domestic beet sugar industry.[471] Cuba was hardest hit due to its dependency on the US market, and despite US investors' and Cuban sugar producers' intent, the Chadbourne Agreement did little to ameliorate the effects of the Smoot-Hawley Tariff. Cuban sugar lost nearly half its market share in the US from 1930 to 1933, while the share of domestic production in the US rose, along with duty-free sugar from the Philippines, Hawaii, and Puerto Rico.[472] The solution, according to the Chadbourne producers, was to expand the membership of the international sugar agreement to include more countries, in order to rationalize the entire world production, distribution, and consumption of sugar.[473]

One reason the Cuban delegates brought forth a detailed proposal could be because they had learned their lesson from the League platitudes

[468] Swerling, *International Control*, pp. 49–50.

[469] This proposal was seconded by the Chadbourne International Sugar Council. See League of Nations, *Journal*, 112 (June 28, 1933) and 116–17 (June 29, 1933).

[470] *Ibid*. For similar views, see Rowe, *Markets and Men*, pp. 83–5; Swerling, *International Control*, p. 48.

[471] James, "International Control," 493.

[472] Smith, *United States and Cuba*, p. 70.

[473] *Ibid*.; Wilk, "International Affairs," 871; Swerling, *International Control*, p. 50.

regarding the sugar crisis of the 1920s.[474] Moreover, a lot was at stake for Cuba to ensure a stable sugar market. The League conference spanned from June 12 to July 27, 1933, during which time the Cuban delegates were negotiating against the backdrop of peasant revolts, labor strikes, student protests, the rise of the military's political power, and US embassy intrigue.

The US government was concerned that Machado's diversified economic interests in Cuba would mean that he would not likely be amenable to allowing US imports to compete with his and his cronies' investments. They were also concerned with the rising political instability, and sent Ambassador Sumner Welles to Havana in May 1933 to mediate between the competing political forces. Washington DC also instructed Welles to negotiate a reciprocal agreement with Cuba, because it was thought that a new treaty would "not only revivify Cuba but will give us practical control of a market we have been steadily losing for the past ten years not only for our manufactured products but for our agricultural products in such categories as wheat, animal fats, meat products, rice and potatoes."[475] Philip Jessup was hired by several US companies in order to suggest how to go about establishing a new reciprocity treaty with Cuba that would allow for the importation of US goods. Jessup wrote:

> Cuba has been endeavoring to get away from being practically a one crop country. She has built up a number of industries which may or may not be suitable for permanent development. Some of these infant industries are owned or controlled by President Machado; Cuban interests in their maintenance might well therefore depend somewhat upon whether or not Machado remains in power.[476]

Many of the Cuban delegates to the League – such as Orestes Ferrara y Marino,[477] Oscar B. Cintas,[478] Viriato Gutiérrez Valladon,[479] and José

474 Geerligs and Geerligs, *Cane Sugar*, pp. 28, 40. (H. C. Prinsen Geerligs was involved in the expert meetings and concluded that "their effect was absolutely nil.")

475 Welles to Secretary of State, May 13, 1933, quoted from Pérez, Jr., *Platt Amendment*, p. 305.

476 Philip Jessup, "Confidential Memorandum on the Cuban Situation," *c.* early 1933, quoted from Pérez, Jr., *Platt Amendment*, p. 303. Jessup also used this experience to argue that multilateral trade treaties were too complicated and that the US should focus on negotiating a series of reciprocity treaties; see Jessup, "Negotiating."

477 Pérez, Jr., *Platt Amendment*, pp. 144, 229, 303; McAvoy, *Sugar Baron*, pp. 91, 96–7, 165. Ferrara, a Cuban jurist born in Italy, would write a monograph in English in support of Wilson's Fourteen Points and the League upon its formation; see Ferrara, *Lessons of the War*.

478 Pérez, Jr., *Platt Amendment*, pp. 310, 312–14; Aguilar, *Cuba 1933*, pp. 140–1.

479 McAvoy, *Sugar Baron*, pp. 150, 165, 196, 202.

Manuel Gómez Mena[480] – were commercially, personally, and politically close to Machado. Their commercial interests were directly linked to Machado and his economic diversification plans, and competed with US capital in Cuba. Moreover, Ferrara (who was the Cuban Secretary of State for Foreign Affairs and President of the delegation)[481] and Cintas (who was the Cuban ambassador to the US)[482] were hardly sympathetic to Ambassador Welles and had tried to directly negotiate more sovereignty with the US. Many delegates were personally threatened by the 1933 revolutions. For example, in February of that year, during student protests, Gutiérrez usually travelled well-guarded, in an armored car.[483] During popular protests, less than a month after the end of the World Monetary and Economic Conference, Ferrara's house was ransacked.[484]

These high stakes likely contributed to the Cuban delegates' insistence at the world conference that negotiations for a detailed sugar treaty between sugar producers and importers be conducted immediately.[485] The Cuban delegates' proposal embodied the League's economic doctrines. They proposed to rationalize the world sugar industry by halting the construction of new sugar factories and reducing the production of existing factories.[486] They also proposed a "freer trade" policy, which disallowed the increase of the tariff on duties above a certain rate.[487] The Cuban delegates, like in the 1902 Brussels Convention, also stipulated that no new subsidies be granted to the production or export of sugar in an effort to raise sugar prices.[488] While British delegates at the 1902 Brussels Convention intended to abolish European subsidies in order to increase West Indian sugar production, Cuban delegates at the 1933 World Monetary and Economic Conference looked to reduce subsidies in order to reduce world sugar production.[489]

Delegates at the World Monetary and Economic Conference could not come to an agreement because, amongst other reasons, the British and Indian delegates insisted on retaining the ability to dictate national

[480] *Ibid.*, pp. 183, 214–15, 225.

[481] Pérez, Jr., *Platt Amendment*, pp. 154–5; Aguilar, *Cuba 1933*, pp. 110–11, 148–9.

[482] Pérez, Jr., *Platt Amendment*, pp. 310, 312–14; Aguilar, *Cuba 1933*, pp. 140–1.

[483] McAvoy, *Sugar Baron*, pp. 241–8. [484] n.a., "Cuba."

[485] League of Nations, *Journal*, 112 (June 28, 1933) and 116–17 (June 29, 1933).

[486] Art. I; "Annex: Articles as Submitted by the Cuban Delegation," in League of Nations, *Journal*, 116–17 (June 29, 1933).

[487] Art. III. [488] Art. II.

[489] Gutiérrez had closely studied the 1902 Brussels Convention; see McAvoy, *Sugar Baron*, p. 225.

sugar policy.[490] The Cuban delegate withdrew his proposal, and it was left for the Chadbourne International Sugar Council and League Conference Bureau to continue work towards further negotiations.[491]

One month after the 1933 conference in London, social unrest in Cuba turned into revolution. This was a time of anti-imperialist protests, labor strikes, student uprisings, pro-US maneuvers, and military empowerment; these popular movements complicate historical determinations of what social changes were ushered in by the 1933 revolution.[492] On August 12, 1933, Cuban army officers forced President Machado to resign. Machado agreed and, by resigning, acquiesced to US Ambassador Welles's plans.[493] The post-1933 Cuban government was beleaguered by political instability, violent clashes, and frequent rotation of the presidency, an office which often relied on Batista's military support, until Batista himself became president in 1940.[494]

The Cuban political order in 1933–4 went through interrelated changes: a change in the form of US government control in Cuba, and an increase in the Cuban government's independence from the US. In the past, the US government had been concerned with the details of internal rule. After 1933, the US government's primary concern was the overall structure of the Cuban political system. They did not care too much who exactly was in charge of the Cuban state, and no longer mediated between rivals of power; they would only intervene when the underlying rules regarding US political and economic interests in Cuba were challenged.[495]

The role of US investors also changed. By 1933, US capital was losing some its previous influence in Cuba, while Cuban entrepreneurs' clout grew. After 1934, there was no report of any Cuban mill passing into foreign ownership.[496] Of course, US commercial interests in Cuba still had a significant presence, especially since most of the Cuban commercial and political elite (which were virtually one and the same) had financial interests or direct involvement as executives in US companies in Cuba.[497]

As always, Cuban politics involved a constant negotiation of power amongst the domestic Cuban elite, the US government, and US

[490] n.a., "Sugar at the World Economic Conference."
[491] League of Nations, *Journal*, 200 (July 20, 1933).
[492] McAvoy, *Sugar Baron*, pp. 245–58; Smith, *United States and Cuba*, pp. 144–64; Aguilar, *Cuba 1933*; Pérez, Jr., *Cuba and the United States*, pp. 178–201.
[493] Aguilar, *Cuba 1933*, p. 149. [494] Dominguez, *Cuba*, pp. 76–80. [495] *Ibid.*, p. 54.
[496] *Ibid.*, pp. 67–70; Pollitt, "Cuban Sugar Economy," p. 104. [497] McAvoy, *Sugar Baron*.

commercial interests. And, as before, this relationship was complicated by the fact that the interests were intermingled.[498] What differed after 1933 was that Cuban domestic interests and the Cuban state would increase in power and effectiveness over many aspects of the Cuban sugar industry (such as labor regulation and production quotas).[499] What remained consistent from before 1933 and afterwards, during the carousel of presidents, was that the Cuban state continued to regulate and control sugar, and increasingly did so in ways that benefited Cuban *colonos*.[500]

The 1937 International Sugar Conference

League and sugar diplomacy

Despite all the political instability in Cuba, the Great Depression, and the lackluster 1933 World Monetary and Economic Conference, the International Sugar Council remained a consistent institutional presence that paved the way for the 1937 ISA and all further sugar agreements. The formal function of the Council, according to the Chadbourne Agreement, was to monitor, investigate, and advise in relation to sugar prices and quotas. In practice, the Council was the conduit for sugar politics. First, it provided a forum for the world's major sugar producers, especially Cuba and Dutch-controlled Java, to negotiate production levels.[501] Second, it provided sugar producers with a forum in which to align their interests in relation to the major sugar-consuming countries such as the US and the UK. Thus, League and national officials spoke of "Chadbourne countries."

The Chadbourne Agreement was a political success, since it brought together the world's sugar cane competitors in Cuba and Java. Even though the sugar producers had put their house in order, they recognized that they needed the League's support if they wanted to work through the technical and political complications of rationalizing the world sugar market and to bring in sugar-consuming countries.

Starting in 1933, Cuban delegates pressed on the formal diplomatic front within the League for a sugar treaty that rationalized the world sugar market, while the staff of the International Sugar Council pursued

[498] Smith, *United States and Cuba*, pp. 144–86.
[499] Pollitt, "Cuban Sugar Economy," p. 101; Swerling, "Export Industry," 352–4.
[500] Pollitt, "Cuban Sugar Economy"; McGillivray, "'Dear President Machado."
[501] Pérez to Beauduin, June 14, 1934, LON, R4643, 10D/10924/6183.

more informal means. Lucien Beauduin, the Honorary President, Francis Powell, the Chairman, and Margaret Douglas Shufeldt, the Secretary, worked closely with Pietro Stoppani from the League Economic and Financial Section and Sydney Caine from the British Colonial Office.[502] Working with the League Secretariat, Shufeldt and Caine provided the logistical and informational backbone that made the 1937 conference possible.[503]

In fact, Shufeldt was the cornerstone in the lead-up to the 1937 ISA, as well as the International Sugar Council in all its permutations. She was described by an eminent international sugar diplomat as "an intellectual idealist of left sociopolitical orientation." As a British national, she had the full support of the British government. Between 1935 and 1937, the sugar institution no longer formally existed, since the Chadbourne Agreement had lapsed. Shufeldt was asked by the British government to stay on, informally, with her staff, on the now renamed International Sugar Committee, in order to provide assistance with regard to the proposed international sugar conference.[504] This was key, because even though significant talks about a sugar conference began at the 1933 World Monetary and Economic Conference, momentum for a world sugar conference took off when the British government took the lead in international sugar negotiations. This was because the UK remained a major consumer of sugar and still exercised significant influence in the world sugar market. Thus, Shufeldt and International Sugar Council officials, supported by Dutch and Cuban diplomats, worked with League and British officials to bring other countries, such as the US, USSR, and Japan, to the sugar conference.[505] The International Sugar Conference was eventually held in London, from April 5 to May 6, 1937.

[502] See extensive number of correspondences in R. 4643, 10D/6183/6183 and R. 4643, 10D/10260/6183; Shufeldt to Stoppani, January 11, 1936, R4376, 10A/16063/1250; Leith-Ross to Stoppani, February 5, 1937, R4444, 10A/27507/27507.

[503] Lloyd to Cummings, February 17, 1937, R4444, 10A/27507/27507; League of Nations, *International Sugar Conference*, p. 6.

[504] Shufeldt to Stoppani, May 12, 1936, LON, R4376, 10A/16063/1250; January 11, 1936, LON, R4376, 10A/16063/1250; Shufeldt to Stoppani, February 2, 1937, LON, R4444, 10A/27676/27507; Lloyd to Cummings, February 17, 1937, LON, R4444, 10A/27676/27507. She took on the lease for the ISC office in her personal capacity; see Khan, *Law*, p. 368.

[505] "Aide Memoire. Summary of Interview Which Mr. F. E. Powell, Dr. W. G. F. Jonegejan, and Senor Luis Marino Perez Had With Sir Phillip Cunliffe-Lister at the Colonial Office, London, on 20th December 1933," LON, R4643, 10D/6183/6183; see extensive correspondence in folder entitled "Principal Letters Exchanged with Officials of the American State Department and the Department of Agriculture, 15 January 1934,"

Shufeldt was one of the earliest employees of the League, starting out in 1920, working with Salter and at the First Assembly. It is very likely that this made it easier for her to develop close ties with League officials in general. More specifically, this probably also helped her to smooth relations between Stoppani and the British government, since the British government had (unsuccessfully) opposed his appointment as Director of the Economic Section in 1931.[506]

Shufeldt was not simply a front or mouthpiece for the British government.[507] As Secretary to the Chadbourne International Sugar Council, Shufeldt had to represent the interests of the world's major sugar producers; as the largest producer, Cuba had the most influence on the Council. Shufeldt had a very good relationship with the Cuban delegates, who, in turn, at the 1937 conference, recommended that she continue as Secretary of the reconstituted International Sugar Council.[508] She would continue to provide her expertise, experience, and institutional memory until after the Second World War. She remained as Secretary to the International Sugar Council until at least the late 1940s (now operating under the auspices of the UN system), thereby setting the foundations for all ISAs to come.[509]

Business nationalism and Cuban diplomacy

After the 1933 revolution, Cuban international sugar politics was still represented by the members of the same Cuban sugar political and commercial elite that had ruled during Machado's presidency. For example, Pérez remained Cuba's commercial attaché in London and acted as spokesperson for the Cuban Sugar Stabilization Institute (ICEA), the Cuban producer association created by the Cuban government and signatory to the Chadbourne Agreement.[510] The Cuban delegates still represented the business nationalism that negotiated

LON, R4643, 10D/6183/6183; Shufeldt to Baumont, May 12, 1936, LON, R4376, 10A/16063/1250.

506 Handwritten note on Shufeldt to Stoppani, January 25, 1933, LON, R4376, 10A/1250/1250. Stoppani served as Director of the Economic Section during 1931–9. On Stoppani and the British, see Clavin, *World Economy*, p. 34.

507 Later she served on the British Board of Trade and at the Ministry of Agriculture; HC Deb, February 23, 1943, vol. 387, col. 7.

508 League of Nations, *International Sugar Conference*, p. 67; "Closing Speech of the Cuban Delegate Mr. Aurelio Portuondo, at the Last Session of the International Sugar Conference Held in London," May 6, 1937, LON, R4444, 10A/27676/27507.

509 Viton, *Sugar Agreements*, pp. ix, 1–5, 9–10, 55, 81.

510 Parties to the Chadbourne Agreement, December 29, 1933, LON, R4643, 10D/6183/6183; Pérez to Beauduin, June 14, 1934, LON, R4643, 10D/10924/6183.

delicately between US capital and Cuban sugar growers.[511] This was the same elite that, during Machado's administration, was becoming less intertwined with US capital. The Cuban delegates to the 1937 International Sugar Conference were not necessarily "anti-American," nor were they willing to concede everything to US interests. The head of the delegation, José Manuel Gómez Mena, who had diverse business interests, such as real estate and banking, served on the Machado-era sugar control agency. The agency barely lasted a year and was marked by rivalry between Cuban and US interests.[512] Aureleio Portuondo Barceló, another prominent delegate, was active in the Cuban cane grower community. He was close to Machado and had decades of experience lobbying for Cuban interests in Washington.[513] As the Great Depression wore on and sugar prices remained low, these men, who were acutely aware of the role of sugar in Cuban life, personally felt the high stakes in achieving an international sugar agreement.

Cuban sugar producers were now intent on protecting their market share in the US and reducing the influence of US capital. Under Machado, some basic legislation (with little effect) was enacted to protect smaller Cuban mills. The ICEA was originally created for the purposes of the Chadbourne Agreement, and was used to strengthen the Cuban voice in the island's sugar industry. The ICEA had eighteen members: six represented the larger (mostly US-owned) mills, six the smaller (mostly Cuban-owned) mills, and six the (mostly Cuban) *colonos*.

After the revolution, the ICEA regulated the production and marketing of sugar in Cuba in a way that reduced the financial advantages enjoyed by US-owned mills with close ties to the US market. By 1937, the *colonos* had obtained many of their demands through the Sugar Coordination Law, which increased sugar growers' financial and commercial security.[514] With this increased clout, the Cuban delegation, all members of the ICEA, headed out to the International Sugar Conference.[515] Now that the *colonos* had more power within the Cuban state, and international political-legal conditions were clearer, the major sugar-producing and -consuming nations of the world would negotiate an agreement.

[511] The delegates included José Manuel Gómez Mena, Aureleio Portuondo Barceló, Arturo Mañas, Rafael Maria Angulo, and Edelberto Farrés; League of Nations, *International Sugar Conference*, p. 23.

[512] McAvoy, *Sugar Baron*, pp. 183, 214–15, 225.

[513] *Ibid.*, pp. 176, 185, 196, 259–60.

[514] Pollitt, "Cuban Sugar Economy," pp. 102–3.

[515] League of Nations, *International Sugar Conference*, p. 23.

When Portuondo made Cuba's opening speech at the International Sugar Conference, he emphasized the central role of sugar in Cuban life. This meant, according to Portuondo, that the sugar market had to be economically viable in order to prevent hardship and social unrest; he stated that by ensuring a stable world sugar market, the Cuban standard of living would improve, which would increase people's purchasing power and promote the growth of international trade.[516] Portuondo not only echoed the common sentiment at the conference, that a rationalized sugar market would lead to increased trade, but he was also speaking from personal experience. In September 1933, when collapsing sugar prices triggered political upheaval and social strife that would lead to revolution, Portuondo's family had to flee when rebels sacked their house.[517]

Editors at *The Economist*, impressed by the number of distinguished diplomats for the sugar conference, thought that there was more at stake than simply regulating the sugar trade: "What has brought these statesmen to London is the hope of initiating a decisive move towards freer trade."[518] Yet, while reducing tariffs was on the mind of some delegates, those who in the past had championed "freer trade," now conceded that the sugar crisis, which generated an "abnormal variation in price," warranted an attempt to rationalize sugar production first, in an effort to reduce incentives for protection.[519] Thus, as at the League world economic conferences, "freer trade" remained secondary to "rationalization."[520]

Participants included (1) countries that produced almost exclusively for export – Cuba, Java (represented by the Netherlands), Peru, Dominican Republic, Haiti; (2) exporters who also enjoyed a sizable internal market – for example, South Africa, Australia, Belgium, Brazil, Czechoslovakia, Hungary, Japan, Poland, Portugal, the USSR, and Yugoslavia; (3) countries largely self-sufficient in sugar – France, Germany, and India; and (4) countries requiring large imports – Canada, China, the US, and the UK, each of which also had some level of domestic production.[521]

Two obstacles had been removed which allowed the International Sugar Conference to proceed: disagreement between ex-Chadbourne countries regarding the division of the "free market" (discussed below)

[516] *Ibid.*, pp. 31–3. [517] McAvoy, *Sugar Baron*, p. 253. [518] n.a., "Now or Never."
[519] League of Nations, *International Sugar Conference*, pp. 35, 74, 82. [520] *Ibid.*, pp. 81–2.
[521] Swerling, *International Control*, p. 55.

and uncertainty as to the US sugar policy. The US clarified its sugar policy in 1934, when, as part of Roosevelt's New Deal, it passed the Jones-Costigan Act.[522] This legislation determined sugar policy in Cuba until the 1959 revolution.[523] It established quotas for how much sugar the US imported, essentially acting as a preferential trade treaty. US business interests in Cuba were quite satisfied with the several New Deal strategies that promised to provide the economic and political stability necessary to secure their capital in Cuba. Cuban sugar producers held that the new quota system diminished the place of Cuban sugar in the US market. The quota was based on average shares in the market between 1931 and 1933, a time when Cuba reduced its production according to the Chadbourne Agreement, and the US increased its domestic and colonial sugar production, displacing Cuban sugar's market share by almost half.[524]

The 1937 ISA

A Cuban institution

With the Chadbourne Agreement, US financiers prominently represented Cuban producers. But after the 1933 revolution, as reflected in domestic institutions and the 1937 ISA, the Cuban government continued to build the Cuban state through the political economy of sugar production, and to buttress the interests of Cuban *colonos* and mill owners. It is important to remember that the Cuban *colonos* and small mill owners were more acutely affected by sugar price fluctuations than US financiers, and as such had the most to gain from a stabilized international sugar market in which production was rationalized in step with consumption patterns. Also recall that the Cuban government had little control over capital in Cuba, leaving only trade policy as the principal policy tool to serve the domestic needs of economic development.

It is against this backdrop, then, that we can examine the text and, to some degree, the operation of the1937 ISA. The sugar treaty in fact connected Cuban sovereignty to international trade, since a state's formal voting representation was determined exclusively by the amount

522 Shufeldt to Stoppani, May 12, 1936, LON, R4376, 10A/16063/1250. This was the first of many "Sugar Acts" regulating the production, importation, and marketing of sugar in the US until 1974. See Alvarez and Polopolus, "Sugar Protection."

523 Alvarez, *Agricultural Sector*, p. 29.

524 Smith, *United States and Cuba*, pp. 70, 163–4; Pollitt, "Cuban Sugar Economy," p. 101.

of sugar it exported or imported.[525] Since Cuba was the largest producer of sugar, according to the treaty, this actually granted Cuba the greatest degree of international economic power. Thus, the trade treaty increased Cuba's economic sovereignty in relation to the US.

Most participating sugar-producing countries had domestic sugar control agencies akin to Cuba's ICEA. Under the Chadbourne Agreement, these domestic administrative bodies proved to be a successful means of enforcing international production quotas, but not prices.[526] The key issue that remained was how to control sugar prices through the regulation of production, export, and import. How sugar prices were to be controlled reflected the negotiation of power between sugar importers (consumers) and sugar exporters (producers). Fluctuating sugar prices were deleterious to all; however, rising prices provided an initial benefit to sugar producers, and decreasing prices provided an initial benefit to sugar consumers. The ISA, in effect, empowered sugar importers to use domestic measures to regulate the flow of sugar, while it empowered sugar exporters to use the treaty's international institution to regulate the export of sugar. Accordingly, Cuba gained the power to regulate the world sugar trade under the treaty, whereas the US reinforced its domestic power.

Many deemed the Chadbourne Agreement a failure because it did not achieve its purported ultimate goal of stabilizing and raising the price of sugar. But the Chadbourne Agreement's failures were usually attributed to problems of implementation, which suggests that there remained a conceptual consensus over the feasibility of a trade agreement built around ideas of rationalization.[527] What is telling about the assumptions is how negotiators and commentators characterized what was problematic about the Chadbourne Agreement, and how the 1937 ISA was thought to remedy the previous sugar agreement's shortcomings.[528] In other words, by understanding what needed to be "corrected," we can discern the economic and institutional assumptions underlying the consensus about the way in which rationalization was to be implemented through international trade agreements.

The 1937 ISA employed the same assumptions as Chadbourne, namely that an international agreement is necessary to enforce required production quotas calculated by experts. The 1937 ISA was thought to correct the failures of Chadbourne by devising more flexible quotas,

[525] Freeman, "Administrative Law," 979. [526] Swerling, *International Control*, p. 46.
[527] Rowe, *Markets and Men*, p. 82. [528] Wilk, "International Affairs," 864.

involving governments, and including consumer countries. So, the 1937 ISA is evidence of how claims are buttressed that the state is necessary to regulate commodities in an effort to increase prices. The agreement also shows how sugar was considered to be an "international" issue that needed to be regulated under the auspices of the League of Nations, in order to capture all the interests in the world in an effort to achieve rational compromise. The most central tenet of both sugar agreements was that the state was characterized according to its role in the international sugar market. In the Chadbourne Agreement, sugar producers were the signatories, but, in effect, they were supported and empowered by their national governments. The 1937 ISA was negotiated by national governments, and formal voting power was allocated according to the proportion of sugar exported or imported. In effect, on the one hand, the treaty further legitimized Cuba's dependency on the US for its sugar export, and on the other hand, it created opportunities for Cuba to export sugar elsewhere and increased its power in regulating the international sugar market.

Defining the free market

Central to the conference negotiations was the delimitation of what was called the "free market."[529] The world was divided between countries that were self-sufficient or exported to a preferential market and countries that exported to the "free market." The free market was defined as all remaining markets that were not self-sufficient or offered preferences.[530]

The treaty set out to establish the free market as the norm against the plethora of non-free markets. The reasoning, in light of the Chadbourne countries' frustration with non-Chadbourne countries in the past, was that countries exporting to the free market could only control and raise plunging sugar prices by reducing production. For this policy to be effective, however, importing/self-sufficient countries/exporters to preferential markets had to make some concessions that they would not increase production and export to the free market, thereby reducing the world price of sugar.[531] Or, in the words of the treaty, countries not exporting to the free market had to "contribute ... to the maintenance and if possible the expansion of the free market for sugar."[532]

[529] League of Nations, *International Sugar Conference*, pp. 26–7. [530] Art. 1(6).
[531] League of Nations, *International Sugar Conference*, p. 46. [532] Art. 8.

The intent was to limit the influence of the non-free market countries over free market countries, without disrupting the respective sugar markets. Free market countries were allowed to maintain their status quo, since no provisions were made to encourage or require countries to reduce existing tariffs or subsidies. As a concession to the US and the UK, the status quo of preferential/colonial arrangements was maintained as much as possible.[533]

Cuban sugar exports

The agreement reflected Cuban sugar producers' complicated relationship with the US – in the short-term, they wanted to maintain their preferential access to the US market, but they also wanted to reduce their dependency on the US. The ISA regulated the US preferential market, along with US access to the free market, but in a way that reflected existing US legislation. The result was that Cuban sugar's dependency on the US market was maintained and further legitimized.

Cuban sugar exported to the US as per the Jones-Costigan Act quotas was excluded from the ISA's definition of "exports to the free market."[534] This meant that Cuba's sugar exported to the US, like the US colonies, was dictated by US policy. The complicated relationship between US Atlantic Seaboard refiners and Cuban raw sugar exporters continued. Cuban sugar exported to the US, but then re-exported from the US to another country, was deemed to be an "export to a free market." According to the ISA, this meant that sugar exported by these US sugar refiners counted towards Cuba's allocated export quota and not the US net imports, thereby intermingling the US refining industry with Cuban sugar production in international sugar market calculations.[535]

Even though the US was Cuba's largest market for sugar, Cuban sugar producers wanted to use the ISA to increase the viability of exporting sugar to the free market. The agreement provided this opportunity to Cuba through the allocation of free market export quotas.[536] Thus,

[533] For example, the agreement allotted to the UK a baseline quantity of domestic production reflecting the quantity established by its domestic legislation (Art.11(a)). The Agreement also outlined the amount that the UK could import from its colonial empire (Art. 11(b)), Australia, and South Africa. (Arts. 12–14). The free market would supply the remainder of the UK's demand for sugar. It was stipulated that as UK and British Empire demand increased, free market exporters were to retain the proportion of the total which they had supplied in the year ending in August 31, 1937 (Art. 14(d)).

[534] Art. 6(a). [535] Arts. 6(a), 9(a). [536] Art. 19.

Cuba still had preferential access to the US, but opportunities in non-US markets also opened up.

The ensuing trade institution

The International Sugar Council was reconstituted to administer the agreement and provided with powers that were more expansive than under the Chadbourne Agreement. The Council had the general powers that were necessary to operate the complicated system of quotas, such as information gathering and advising.[537] It was also empowered to decide upon matters that were substantive to the agreement, such as determining and adjusting the annual quota for the free market,[538] and securing accessions from non-signatory governments.[539] Moreover, the Council had the function of interpreting provisions[540] and resolving disputes between members.[541] The dispute resolution system, under Article 44, was characterized as a "special meeting of the Council," which made a decision according to three-quarters of the votes cast. Its jurisdiction was to "decide whether any infringement of the Agreement has taken place, and if so, what measure shall be recommended to the Contracting Governments." To many national delegates in the Council, disputes were a matter of international arbitration, to be handled by international jurists.[542] Within the League, however, a commonly held opinion, much like for the Brussels Convention, was that disputes were best resolved by someone who knew a lot about international commodity markets.[543]

Cuba was granted considerable power to determine how the ISA was to operate. The Council constituted a delegation from each country.[544] Each country's delegation was allotted a number of votes, which roughly reflected the proportion of sugar a country imported or exported.[545] Exporting countries combined were allotted fifty-five votes, Cuba receiving the highest number (10), followed by the Netherlands (Java; 9). Importing countries combined were allotted forty-five votes, the US and the UK receiving the highest number (17 each). For most issues, a

[537] Arts. 3, 6, 7, 14, 15, 24, 33(f), 34. [538] Arts. 20, 21, 24, 32(c). [539] Art. 33(g).
[540] Arts. 28, 46. [541] Art. 44.
[542] Shufeldt to Stoppani, June 26, 1936, LON, R4440, 10A/30792/29954.
[543] Smets to Shufeldt, July 5, 1937, LON, R4440, 10A/30792/29954.
[544] Art. 31 (the provision stipulates that the delegation was to consist of not more than three "members" and three "advisers").
[545] Art. 37(a).

simple majority dictated the Council's decisions.[546] The ISA ensured that exporters would always retain voting power over importers by maintaining the 55-45 proportion if non-signatory countries acceded to the agreement.[547] So, even though Cuba had fewer votes than the US, its largest market, it had the most influence in the exporting country voting bloc. Cuba's power within the ISA, however, was tempered by the fact that the majority of its sugar still went to the US and was regulated by US laws. Nevertheless, this system still provided Cuba with the ability to affect sugar quotas (with the intent of regulating price) in the world free market, marking Cuban sugar producers' ambition to increase their economic sovereignty.

The Council could delegate most of its quota-determining powers to an Executive Committee.[548] The Executive Committee was to be composed of three representatives of governments of importing countries, three representatives of governments of cane sugar-producing countries, and three representatives of governments of beet sugar-producing countries. The composition roughly reflected the power dynamics established by the extent of sugar import or export, crystallizing exporters' power over importers, the difference of the needs between beet sugar growers and cane sugar growers, and the power of individual countries. The UK and the US were permanent importer representatives, while the third seat alternated annually between India and China. Cuba and the Netherlands were permanent cane sugar representatives, while the third seat rotated annually amongst Australia, Dominican Republic, Peru, South Africa, and Brazil. No beet sugar producer maintained a permanent seat, so membership rotated amongst Czechoslovakia, Germany, the USSR, France, Poland, Belgium, and Yugoslavia.[549] Indeed, within this matrix, Cuba and Dutch-controlled Java, which produced the largest amount of sugar in the world, were granted the most formal power.

546 Art. 38. Some notable exceptions include a three-fifths majority required to provide temporary adjustment to quotas (Art. 20), and a three-quarters majority required to resolve disputes (Art. 44(b)).

547 Art. 37(c).

548 Arts. 40–41. The Council could delegate any power to the Executive Committee except reducing quotas, allotting additional quotas, determining adherence conditions for non-signatories, determining treaty withdrawal conditions, and dispute resolution.

549 Art. 39.

Regulating the price of sugar

The Chadbourne Agreement was thought to be overly rigid, so the new agreement included more flexible elements. Even though the treaty addressed many technical issues regarding production and consumption, much was left open to interpretation. This was not necessarily a design flaw. Much like multilateral agreements after the Second World War, the treaty language was in more broad terms because the majority of delegates held a shared understanding about how a normal sugar market should operate.[550] At this point, the question was how to technically structure a rationalized sugar market. Future sugar agreements would become more detailed and creative in developing price-controlling mechanisms, as international sugar politics included more diverse interests, market prices continued to fluctuate, and commodity agreements became more prevalent. The first technical issue that delegates had to determine was what amount of sugar would be allocated to the free market. Disagreements regarding the details of export quota levels were almost acrimonious. The fact that debates over export quota levels almost caused the treaty negotiations to fail emphasizes that the politics of technical details was central to any such rationalization scheme.[551]

Under the chapter entitled "General Undertakings," Article 4 was the most detailed provision suggesting government action. This provision outlined what principles were to guide governments in times of rising sugar prices. If prices continued to be high, there was the fear that consumption of sugar would decrease. If consumption decreased too quickly, then producers would generate an excess of sugar, which in turn could cause sugar prices to drop quickly. The provision first reaffirmed each state's economic sovereignty:

> While recognizing that all Government measures relating to agrarian policy and to State assistance to the sugar industry are governed by the internal conditions of each country and in many cases require the approval of a Parliament.

The provision went on to provide that:

> the Contracting Governments *agree that it is desirable* that (a) If and when prices on the free market rise, *all necessary steps should be taken* to prevent the rise in world prices from leading on one hand to an increase of internal prices for consumers such as would be likely to check consumption, and on the other

[550] Lang, *Trade Law*. [551] League of Nations, *International Sugar Conference*, pp. 49–57.

hand to a rise of wholesale prices (beyond the level required to secure a fair return for growers and producers) to such a point to stimulate excess production not justified by the requirements of the market, thus defeating the object of the present Agreement.

The initial impression is that the language is not very binding – "the Contracting Governments agree that it is desirable." This language, however, must be understood in the mindset of ensuring that governments should react rationally to rising sugar prices. The opening phrase reaffirms state economic sovereignty, and outlines what needs to be done as if it were a proviso of sovereignty. Instead, it actually empowers states to take "*any necessary steps*" to react to the rising price of sugar. In other words, it restricts sovereignty in that it directs state action, but it also empowers states by allowing any means necessary. Moreover, Article 4's language indicates some imperative when contrasted with Article 5 (encouraging the consumption of sugar), which provides:

The Contracting Governments agree that, as far as possible, favourable considerations should be given to all proposals having for their object [principles encouraging the increase of sugar consumption].

The proceedings from the 1937 International Sugar Conference provide some context as to what was meant by "any necessary steps." The opening speech of the conference president, Ramsay MacDonald, identified one of the purposes of the conference as ensuring the following:

if and when prices on the free market rise to an economic level, they [signatory countries] will do what is possible to adjust protective duties, subsidies, etc., so as to prevent their internal prices rising to a point which would check consumption and stimulate new production and thus defeat the object for which we are working.[552]

Thus, one can imagine the US, in light of rising international sugar prices, raising tariffs and subsidizing the domestic production of sugar in order to reduce the price of sugar – thereby detrimentally affecting sugar producers such as Cuba, while still benefiting domestic producers *and* consumers. However, during the conference, the Report of the Committee on General Questions was unequivocal when addressing the adjustment of protective duties, subsidies, and so on, in the event of an increase in world sugar prices, despite the treaty's ambiguous language:

[552] *Ibid.*, p. 26.

It is above all things essential that the successful conclusion on an International Agreement should not aggravate the situation by proving a fresh stimulus to production through an improvement in selling-prices.[553]

So the treaty left it as a matter of interpretation as to what domestic measures would be deemed an appropriate "necessary step" to keep the rising price of sugar in check.

According to MacDonald, another purpose of the sugar treaty was to ensure that countries exporting to the free market "keep supplies at a level appropriate to the probable demand."[554] The exception to this principle of tempered production would apply if sugar prices dropped. The ISA, however, never explicitly outlined what was to be done if this were to happen. Instead, Article 21(a) empowered the Sugar Council to reduce export quotas "if, after a survey of the probable requirements of the market for the year in question, it decides such reduction is necessary." In effect, this allowed sugar exporters to coordinate production reduction in light of dropping sugar prices.[555]

The dispute settlement power enforcement mechanism of the Council's dispute settlement duty emphasized how the primary objective of the treaty was to regulate the production of sugar:

If the Council shall decide that it is desirable that the other Contracting Governments shall prohibit or restrict *the import of sugar from the country which has infringed the agreement*, the taking of such measure shall not be deemed to be contrary to any most-favoured nation rights which the offending Government may enjoy. [emphasis added][556]

This anticipated that any infringement would likely be by an exporting country. It left it unclear, though probably unlikely in light of Article 4's language, if the Council could deliberate on domestic measures affecting the import of sugar, such as subsidization or tariff levels. Indeed, since exporting countries had the most power in the Council, it probably would have been unacceptable to importing countries for it to determine whether its domestic laws infringed upon the ISA.

553 *Ibid.*, p. 75. 554 *Ibid.*, p. 26.

555 Article 21(a) applied to 1937 and 1938. For the years thereafter, Article 21(b) stipulated that the Council could recommend reduced production, but only if all countries entitled to a basic quota or participating in the reserve (i.e. sugar producers) consented to it.

556 Art. 44(a).

Conclusion

Not all signatory countries ratified the international sugar treaty. Nevertheless, signatory countries agreed to give effect to the treaty amongst themselves. The International Sugar Council operated in full for two years until the outbreak of Second World War (the ISA did not formally lapse until 1944).[557]

The 1937 ISA was the model for the next fifty years of international sugar agreements.[558] What made the 1937 ISA remarkable was that it crystallized a particular conception of the League doctrine of rationalization. In doing so, the sugar treaty was a space for postcolonial state-building for Cuba within the League. To Europeans, the League's economic conferences were a failure; to the Mandates, the League was domineering; but to the elites who ruled Cuba, the League was a place that allowed them to augment their development plans. The business nationalism of the Cuban elite and middle classes reflected the same posture held by many other local leaders in the colonial and postcolonial world during this time. The Cuban ruling elite was similar to nationalist leaders in the African continent such as Herbert Macaulay, Leopold Senghor, and J. H. Casely Hayford Samuel Ahuma, and to those in the Arab world such as Saad Zaghloul, Nuri as-Said, and Bishara al-Khoury, as well as to future revolutionaries in East Asia such as Ho Chi Minh. During the interwar period, they used law and politics to negotiate with imperialism in its various forms and did not yet clearly or completely develop an anti-imperialist policy.[559]

[557] Wilk, "International Affairs," 869; Stocking and Watkins, *Cartels*, pp. 43–9.

[558] Hagelberg and Hannah, "Quest," 24.

[559] Said, *Culture*, p. 196.

PART IV

The 1977 ISA and the implications of institutionalization

"But the important thing is to consider all the Houses that depend on ... [corporate] profits. And think of the enormous proportion of those profits dependent upon a single product – the spice. Imagine what would happen if something should reduce spice production."

"Whoever had stockpiled melange [spice] could make a killing," Paul said. "Others would be out in the cold."

Herbert, *Dune*, pp. 42–3

The objectives of this Agreement are to assure supplies of sugar to importing countries and markets for sugar to exporting countries at equitable and stable prices;

Article I, 1953 ISA

7 The postwar institutional landscape

Introduction

The League doctrines of rapprochement, rationalization, and freer trade continued to influence trade institutions after the League and Second World War came to an end. Yet the doctrines' effects and configurations had changed.

By the time the WTO was enacted, rationalization was no longer present in international trade policy. The official GATT interpretative guides,[560] the WTO Dispute Settlement Panel,[561] the Appellate Body,[562] and contemporary trade scholars[563] sometimes reference the League for purposes of GATT interpretation. When referring to the League, they ignore how rationalization was a dominant economic doctrine of the time. Instead, they reference the League's tariff policies and one (failed) League tariff treaty, without contextualizing freer trade within broader League economic discourse.[564]

Why, then, and when exactly did rationalization entirely fall out of the realm of free trade theories and policies? To be sure, it was not when the League ended. Part of the answer has to do with the life and death of ICAs within the context of Third World politics. In the 1930s, Cuban delegates delicately negotiated their neocolonial relationship with

[560] World Trade Organization, *GATT Law*, pp. 62, 279, 332–3, 597, 927, 1014.

[561] *US – Shrimp*, Panel Report, WT/DS58/R and Corr.1, adopted November 6, 1998, as modified by Appellate Body Report WT/DS58/AB/R, paras. 3.187–189; *US – Gambling*, Panel Report, WT/DS285/R, adopted April 20, 2005, as modified by Appellate Body Report WT/DS285/AB/R, paras. 3.278, 6.472.

[562] *US – Gasoline*, Appellate Body Report, WT/DS2/AB/R, adopted May 20, 1996, para. 65.

[563] See, e.g., Charnovitz, "World Trade Organization," 827.

[564] International Convention for the Abolition of Import and Export Prohibitions and Restrictions, Geneva, November 8, 1927, 97 LNTS 391.

the US, while trying to modernize their state, develop their economy, and regulate the world sugar market. After the Second World War, an increasing number of postcolonial Third World delegates also linked rationalization to development, but employed language in terms that vehemently challenged the First World. At the same time, freer trade was no longer the corollary to rationalization. Instead, it was deployed by the First World partly as a reaction against Third World development plans.

Despite the increasing antagonism between the Third World and the First World, the institutionalization of rapprochement was not entirely lost. The first attempt was to reconcile rationalization and freer trade through the ITO. Cuba again played a central role in constituting the international economic system. Havana was where the ITO Charter was finally negotiated and signed.[565] By 1950, however, the ITO was declared to be defunct before it began operation. Most developed countries then turned to the GATT as the principal treaty for the regulation of international trade.[566] Accordingly, postwar histories of international trade usually focus on the rise of the GATT after the demise of the ITO.

International trade, however, was comprised of more international institutions than the GATT. After 1950, ICAs, which employed doctrines of rationalization, were where agriculturalists from all over the world turned their attention to in order to address global market conditions. They were also where the Third World and the First World found political compromise. The 1977 ISA is an exemplary commodity agreement for its time and was one of the most sophisticated agreements of the postwar international trading order. But before I delve into the life and death of rationalization and postwar ICAs as exemplified by the 1977 ISA in the next chapter, we must better understand the broader institutional landscape of international trade law and policy of the time. To go from 1937 to 1977, we must take a moment in 1945–7 and examine the negotiations to create an ITO, the Charter that constituted the ITO, and the implications of the end of the ITO.

Even though the ITO died the moment it came into effect, it generated profound institutional and ideational aftershocks. It was here that rationalization was linked more to the Third World, and freer trade to

[565] *Final Act and Related Documents of the United Nations Conference on Trade and Employment*, March 24, 1948, E/Conf.2/78 [ITO Charter].

[566] See United States Department of State, "Future Administration of GATT." US President Harry S. Truman's decision not to submit the ITO Charter to Congress is commonly attributed as the formal "end of the ITO"; see Diebold, Jr., *End of the ITO*, p. 1.

the First World. And it was here that rapprochement, rationalization, and freer trade were redefined and realigned in a way that continued for about four decades.

During the interwar period, Salter and Keynes held the view that due to postwar economic crises, international rationalization would best address exceptional economic circumstances. To them, and to many others within the League and in government offices, certain economic and financial conditions needed to be met before a tariff-reducing policy of freer trade could be adopted. The ITO, however, institutionalized rationalization and freer trade as a concurrent compromise between policies of economic stability and development (rationalization) and growth (freer trade).

This tension between Third and First Worlds, as well as rationalization and freer trade, eventually fractured the ITO into the UNCTAD, ICAs, and the GATT. During the creation of UNCTAD, developing countries debated amongst each other and negotiated with developed countries as to what would be the nature of UNCTAD's relationship with the GATT.[567] The common account has been that developing countries attempted to use UNCTAD to do away with the GATT altogether. Focusing on the relationship between UNCTAD, ICAs, and the GATT, however, teaches us that developing countries, especially those whose economy depended on international trade, were not necessarily using UNCTAD to destroy the GATT. Tensions between developing and developed countries manifested themselves both between the GATT and UNCTAD and within the respective trade institutions.[568]

Since developing countries often depended on a small number of agricultural commodities and were disproportionately exposed to fluctuating world prices, they acutely needed stable commodity prices to maintain domestic social stability. But developing countries also wanted to change their economic structure; they wanted ICAs in order to increase capital flows into the economy in the short-term, in order to provide the time and resources necessary to subsidize industrial capacities. Thus, most developing countries navigated between at least two tactics as part of a long-term development strategy towards industrialization: they used UNCTAD to generate trade policies conducive to development and to continue to enhance and improve ICAs, and, at the same time, they participated in the GATT so that when they had the ability to competitively export manufactured goods, they would have

[567] Toye and Toye, *UN*, pp.193–8. [568] Rajagopal, *International Law*, pp. 73–94.

access to Western markets and reduce their dependence on primary commodities. As a result, developing and developed countries confronted each through the doctrine of rationalization within UNCTAD and through freer trade within the GATT, but found some compromise over both doctrines within ICAs.

Revisiting embedded liberalism

The common account of embedded liberalism

Embedded liberalism can be understood in two ways: it was a normative general framework that defined the appropriate scope and goals of domestic policy and international institutions for approximately forty years after the Second World War; it was also a description of the specific institutional arrangements constructed accordingly.[569] To Howse, embedded liberalism's success arose from the fact that it was a trade policy drawn from a political commitment shared amongst the majority of the world's influential policy-makers.[570]

In order to understand the 1977 ISA within this context, I first have to revisit and augment postwar accounts of embedded liberalism. This is because the common account does not make room to understand theoretically and historically what role ICAs played in postwar trade law and policy. By augmenting embedded liberalism, we can see that its trade policies were defined not only by the GATT, but also by earlier institutions like the ITO, and by later ones such as UNCTAD and ICAs. We can also appreciate how it made significant provision for development theories and demands.

Embedded liberalism had two interlinked trade goals. It was to ensure that domestic pressures would not lead states to raise trade barriers in such a way as to prompt a protectionist "race to the bottom," eventually leading to pervasive war and depression.[571] It also had to minimize social disruption in domestic industries caused by international functional differentiation and tariff level reduction.[572]

Drawing from Polanyi, Ruggie suggests that the policies were based on the premise that the market was embedded within the nation-state and that domestic stability was predicated on a particular political

[569] Steffek, *Embedded Liberalism*, p. 4. [570] Howse, "Politics to Technocracy," 97.

[571] With thanks to Robert Wai, who alerted me to how modern trade lawyers have always been and still are preoccupied with avoiding the twin specters of war and depression.

[572] Ruggie, "International Regimes," 399.

and social vision, committed to a progressive, welfare state. Embedded liberalism envisioned a state whose principal purpose was to ensure full employment, economic growth, and citizen welfare. The state was granted several functions that were thought to be required to achieve those goals. It redistributed wealth through fiscal policy and job creation. It was also expected to manage consumer demand and regulate the market. This was done through numerous administrative agencies that employed a variety of policy tools, such as controlling capital mobility, expanding public expenditure and developing social programs.

At the same time, embedded liberalism's compromise was "liberal" in that it avoided protectionist policies, attended to global conditions, and demanded multilateral negotiation.[573] It designed postwar international trade and financial institutions in a way that allowed states to manage their domestic economies with the aim of achieving social welfare and political stability, and to offset the risk of world war and depression from such domestic policies.

Within this shared political commitment and policy framework there was great difference of opinion over which domestic and international institutional arrangements were necessary to implement this vision.[574] Under the purview of embedded liberalism, industrialized countries were preoccupied with demarcating the line between state and market in domestic regulation. The US and UK implemented policies such as infrastructural investments, agricultural price supports and social expenditures; they differed in the extent to which Keynesian economics influenced government policy and the degree to which the state played an explicit role in socio-economic regulation.[575]

With respect to trade, the GATT prohibited quantitative restrictions, but allowed for exceptions that were deemed necessary to safeguard the balance of payments; these enumerated exceptions included payment difficulties that resulted from domestic policies designed to secure full employment and domestic price support programs for agriculture.[576] The GATT was also designed based on the assumption that countries were at significantly different levels of industrial development and that they held dramatically different viewpoints with respect to economic policies. To Jackson, such an "interface" system recognized the different economic systems and ameliorated the international tensions caused

[573] *Ibid.*, 393–5, 398. [574] Howse, "Politics to Technocracy," 97.
[575] Ruggie, "International Regimes," 394. [576] *Ibid.*, 397.

by those differences.[577] What significantly differed among countries was the form of regulation, but what was rarely challenged was the premise that regulation was necessary.[578]

Embedded liberalism, as the common account continues to tell us, was an attempt by industrialized countries to reconcile liberal multilateralism with the welfare state. The compromise and ensuing institutions of embedded liberalism were the result of conflicting and competing postwar objectives, mainly between the US and the UK.[579] The history of how these interests jostled, interacted, and were finally conciliated is well documented.[580] Suffice to say, there were great debates within the US and the UK, amongst scholars and industry leaders, as to what was to be done to secure an economically viable system of multilateral trade alongside the domestic needs of full employment and economic redistribution.

Augmenting understandings of embedded liberalism to include development concerns and institutional diversity

According to the account thus far, embedded liberalism only reflected and responded to the needs of industrialized countries.[581] Ruggie worried that developing countries were subject to liberal international institutions such as the IMF and the GATT, but did not have the domestic political and institutional capacity to nationally redistribute the benefits of liberal international economic institutions, or the ability to ameliorate the domestic unemployment caused by liberal international economic institutions.[582]

Ruggie and others regard embedded liberalism's exclusion of developing countries' interests to be problematic. Some have raised the concern that embedded liberalism is an account of the postwar international trade regime that silences important concerns by marginalized communities.[583] They have noted that development issues are lost in our previous and current understandings of international trade, and call for a new account of international trade that does not necessarily

577 Jackson, *Restructuring*, pp. 82–4. See also Howse, "Politics to Technocracy," 97.
578 Ruggie, "International Regimes," 393–4. 579 *Ibid.*, 393–4.
580 See, e.g., Gardner, *Diplomacy*; Brown, Jr., *Restoration*, pp. 146–52; Zeiler, *Free Trade*, pp. 20–58; Steil, *Bretton Woods*.
581 See, e.g., Steffek, *Embedded Liberalism*, p. 53; Harvey, *Brief History*, p. 11.
582 Ruggie, "International Regimes," 413–14; Ruggie, "Embedded Liberalism," pp. 93, 94.
583 Lang, "Embedded Liberalism," 100.

normatively reinvent embedded liberalism for today, but instead rethinks international trade.[584]

This call for a fundamental transformation of trade law is an excellent premise to have in mind when thinking about the future. Nonetheless, first we have to augment our historical understanding of embedded liberalism, which we can do with two points: the embedded liberal compromise was not only determined by the negotiation of interests within the global North, but also by tensions between the North and South; also, it had more room for development concerns than originally described.

Ruggie and others have focused on the notion that developing states did not have the *domestic* capacity to ensure full employment and redistribution. To Steffek, embedded liberalism was a division of labor between the national and international levels of policy-making. The purpose of international rules was only to establish and maintain a functioning world market; the function of domestic rules was to ensure that the market was embedded in a legitimate domestic social purpose.[585] In view of that, to Steffek, the GATT reflected embedded liberalism, and the ITO and, later, UNCTAD were beyond the purview of embedded liberalism because they prescribed goals such as full employment and wealth redistribution as a function of international institutions.

Recent discussions, however, emphasize that there is no one necessary institutional configuration of embedded liberalism. Rather, we should consider it to have been "a dynamic commitment to allowing countries to be different within a multilateral framework."[586] For example, Ruggie and others are trying to reconcile the compromises of embedded liberalism with contemporary structures of global governance. In doing so, they are looking to integrate a wider range of states, international institutions, and transnational social actors into working out how to maintain a multilateral world order along with domestic welfare concerns.[587]

Embedded liberalism's pervasiveness derived in part from its variety of policies and institutions, both domestic and international. Since embedded liberalism was not a predetermined plan regarding levels of social spending or tariff amounts, it allowed for diverse policy tools to

[584] *Ibid.*, 101; Dunoff, "Rethinking." [585] Steffek, *Embedded Liberalism*, pp. 4–5.
[586] Wolfe and Mendelsohn, "Embedded Liberalism," 262.
[587] See, e.g., Abdelal and Ruggie, "Principles."

implement its underlying purpose of reconciling a liberal trade regime with domestic economic welfare and stability.[588] As such, when states in the South created institutions around embedded liberalism policies, but within the context of meeting development needs, they turned to different policy instruments than those used by states in the North. Developing countries were not able to use domestic state institutions to achieve embedded liberalism's domestic policy goals of full employment and social stability. Therefore, they had to turn to international institutions.

According to Ruggie, the postwar international trade order focused on manufactured products and had little to do with regulating the flow of agricultural goods. This was because, "[a]part from oil, North–South raw material trade has posed few problems for industrialized countries, both because of their overall domination of world trade and because of the characteristics of the raw materials sector."[589] This account is not entirely complete, because countries in the South often depended on the export of agricultural products; during the 1960s and 1970s, many of these countries challenged the North's conception of an international trading system that excluded agriculture. This resulted in the formation of UNCTAD, which we will see institutionalized embedded liberalism's goals, but with an emphasis on developing countries' socio-economic conditions and geopolitical context. What is also significant is that the institutional make-up of embedded liberalism also included ICAs (such as the 1977 ISA). It is here that embedded liberalism regulated the international trade of agriculture, where North and South negotiated their interests, and where UNCTAD and GATT ideas met. ICAs institutionalized embedded liberalism in a most sophisticated way, yet until now their story has been excluded from the history of international trade.

To Ruggie, embedded liberalism "presupposed the existence of *national* economies, engaged in *external* transactions, conducted at *arm's length*, which governments could mediate at the *border* by tariffs and exchange rates, among other tools."[590] This may be true if we only look at how the GATT related to embedded liberalism's domestic goal of ensuring full employment and tempering social adjustment costs that open markets would inevitably produce. By including the ITO, UNCTAD, and ICAs in embedded liberalism's international institutional landscape, it becomes

[588] Ruggie, "International Regimes." [589] *Ibid.*, 403.
[590] Ruggie, "Embedded Liberalism," p. 94 [emphasis original].

clear that policy-makers in the North and South not only looked to domestic institutions, but also to international institutions to ensure that *global* market conditions, namely commodity prices, were regulated in such a way as to ensure the desired domestic socio-economic conditions in different countries.

The ITO and development concerns

The reason that development has been left out of today's understandings of the ITO is because the majority of these histories draw from a handful of texts that were written around the time of the US ratification debate. The authors were US officials who either participated at the highest level in the negotiations or were involved in developing the US's international commercial policies.[591] These texts remain the most comprehensive English-language analyses of the Havana Conference which led to the ITO. Only a few academic studies since have focused on the ITO[592] – and even those studies usually consider the ITO in light of Anglo-American compromises[593] or from the perspective of competing US interests.[594]

These early, influential, comprehensive accounts of the ITO were written to persuade the US intelligentsia to accept the Charter and as part of an effort to gain Congress's approval. It did not help the authors' cause to focus too much on the role of development, which had been an extremely contentious issue with US negotiators. The US officials who wrote comprehensive examinations of the ITO Charter, however, did still refer to the role of development and developing countries. Wilcox, who wrote one of the most authoritative accounts of the ITO Charter, stated that at Havana, "the most violent controversies at the conference

[591] See, e.g., Fulton and Javits, *International Trade Organisation*; Wilcox, *Charter*; Brown, Jr., *United States*. Influential texts after its demise include Diebold, Jr., *End of the ITO*.

[592] There have been some references to the ITO in contemporary arguments as a source for different ideas regarding how to structure the WTO or for historic interpretive value. See, e.g., Symposium, "International Trade"; Goldstein and Gowa, "US National Power"; George, "Alternative Finances"; Charnovitz and Wickham, "Non-governmental Organizations"; *Mexico – Taxes on Soft Drinks*, Panel Report, WT/DS308/R, adopted March 24, 2006, as modified by Appellate Body Report WT/DS308/AB/R, para. 8.176; *Mexico – Taxes on Soft Drinks*, Appellate Body Report, WT/DS308/AB/R, adopted March 24, 2006, para. 78, fn. 175.

[593] Gardner, *Diplomacy*; Hart (ed.), *Also Present*; Graz, *Aux Sources de l'OMC*.

[594] Dryden, *Trade Warriors*; Aaronson, *Trade*.

and the most protracted ones were those evoked by issues raised in the name of economic development."[595]

Nevertheless, these authors relegated the role of development to a secondary issue in regard to understanding the function and purpose of the ITO. They did not engage with the substance of development proposals. Instead, they discussed development only in terms of how developed countries used this concept to react against their counterparts from developing countries. Thus, the historical accounts written by US officials would themselves contribute significantly to the marginalization of the idea of development in contemporary histories of international trade institutions.

By closely reading how North American diplomats still mentioned development issues, along with referencing some of the ITO primary material, I think we can get a better sense of how development was a primary issue throughout the ITO negotiations, and appreciate what was at stake in the divide between "developed" and "underdeveloped" countries.[596] Those countries whose economies depended on exported foodstuffs and raw materials coalesced together as "underdeveloped countries." These were countries, primarily led by Australia, India, and Latin American states, who insisted that their infant industrial capacity needed to be protected in order to develop.[597] Underdeveloped countries considered international trade to be inextricable from development issues. The fact that Canada, a British settler colony that had some industrial capacity, self-identified as developed, and Australia, a British settler colony that had little industrial capacity at this time, self-identified as underdeveloped, highlights the fact that development was equated with industrialization.[598]

One of embedded liberalism's most significant accomplishments is that it expanded trade law and policy's purview. Since Ricardo developed

[595] Wilcox, *Charter*, pp. 48–9.

[596] All parties commonly used the term "underdeveloped" at the time. I use it throughout this chapter to indicate the countries which self-identified at the time as such, and not as a judgment of their socio-economic condition. I will use "underdeveloped" and "developing" interchangeably.

[597] Bidwell and Diebold, Jr., "United States," 191–2.

[598] See Wynia, "Opening." The Canadian delegate noted with some irony (but ignoring Canada's, albeit emerging, industrial capacity) that by this definition Canada would be an "underdeveloped country"; UN Conference in Trade and Employment, Heads of Delegations Summary Record of Meeting, Havana, Cuba, December 24, 1947 (E/CONF.2/23), p. 4.

his doctrine of comparative advantage in 1817,[599] the issue of employment was not discussed in free trade debates. In ideational terms, this was because everyone assumed, as a model, a world of full employment. Trade law and policy, up until that point, had been a discourse that was almost entirely preoccupied with, and, in effect, privileged, commodities and capital. The ITO created space within trade discourse to debate labor. This was a different institutional context than the Brussels Convention and the 1937 ISA, where the labor unrest and shortages that created the political impetus behind the respective treaties were barely given a mention in the official records of these treaties; when workers were mentioned, it was usually in racist terms, or they were characterized as imperial subjects governed by the mother country.

Nonetheless, how labor was going to be defined in the particular context of "trade and employment" was a matter of contention. The consensus was that all states wanted to ensure full employment for their citizens. The debate was over the meaning of "full employment." The stakes are most clearly articulated by the Colombian delegate in his speech during a discussion of convening an international conference on trade. He begins with his critique:

> For the United States, full employment is to be achieved by the expansion of world trade within a system of economic freedom. For us, the words "full employment" have a special and quite different meaning. What, indeed, can it mean to us that all our workers are employed so long as they work in the least productive branches of economic life for wages ten times lower than those of other nations? And how can we ensure stability in this "full employment" if we are limited to producing a single commodity which is exposed, as coffee is, to such violent fluctuations of price and volume of consumption on the international market?

He then provides a proposal that was pervasive in the then-burgeoning Third World:

> We are of the opinion that full employment in reasonable conditions is inseparable from the attainment of two fundamental objectives: variety of production, and increase in manufacturing industries which, through their ability to command higher wages than those which are normally attained in extracting industries, can raise the standard of living and shape a mentally and morally superior working class. The [United Nations Economic and Social Council] should ask itself if such an evolution can be assured by depriving young industries of all protection, and if it is not more natural that a policy of trade freedom

[599] Ricardo, *Economy and Taxation.*

should be developed in harmony with the peculiar conditions prevailing in industrially backward countries.[600]

The Colombian delegate's comments also highlight that the question of trade and employment was not only a question of domestic stability, but also one of development. His comments emphasize that the aims of embedded liberalism manifested in different social, political, and economic contexts for developing countries and thereby demanded different policy tools and institutional arrangements. What is also remarkable is that, unlike import substitution industrialization (ISI), which was a popular development policy at the time (discussed below), the Colombian delegate considered *avant la lettre* international trade to be a central feature of a development plan that included industrialization and economic diversification.

Indeed, debates over development were central to the creation of the ITO throughout every stage of negotiations.[601] In November 1945, the US Department of State provided early blueprints for a postwar international trade organization in a publication entitled *Proposals for Expansion of World Trade and Employment*.[602] Even though this text was published by the US, it was the product of Anglo-American discussions and negotiations.[603] One month after it was published, the US invited a number of other nations to convene an international conference on trade and employment.[604] In January 1946, this invitation was taken to the newly created United Nations Economic and Social Council (ECOSOC). Formally, ECOSOC assumed and continued the "non-political" work of the League, which included the economic and financial functions.[605] One of the first topics at ECOSOC was the US resolution calling for the convening of an "International Conference on Trade and Employment."[606]

Pursuant to the ECOSOC resolution, nineteen countries were invited to form a preparatory committee to set the stage for an international

600 United Nations Economic and Social Council, *Official Records*, p. 76.

601 Toye, "Multilateralism." 602 United States Department of State, *Proposals*.

603 Howson and Moggridge (eds.), *Wartime Diaries*, pp. 221–48; United States Department of State, "Joint Statement."

604 United States Department of State, "Trade Negotiation." The countries invited were Australia, Belgium-Luxembourg, Brazil, Canada, China, Cuba, Czechoslovakia, France, India, the Netherlands, New Zealand, South Africa, the USSR, and the UK. The USSR did not participate in any ITO negotiations or conferences.

605 *Non-political Functions and Activities of the League of Nations*, ESC Res. 12(I), UN ESCOR, 1st Sess. (1946) 133.

606 United Nations Economic and Social Council, *Official Records*, pp. 63–84.

trade conference.[607] The Preparatory Committee held three meetings: the First Session was in London, from October to November 1946;[608] a meeting of the Drafting Committee of the Preparatory Committee was held at Lake Success, New York, from January to February 1947;[609] and the Second Session was held in Geneva, from April to October 1947.[610] After the Preparatory Committee finalized the penultimate draft of the ITO charter in Geneva,[611] the whole process opened up to all potential member countries. The ultimate conference was the United Nations Conference on Trade and Employment that was held in Havana, Cuba, from November 1947 to March 1948. Fifty-six nations attended – Havana's geographic location between the global North and South reflected the tensions between developed and developing countries that would define the ITO Charter.[612]

At first, development was not on the agenda. The moment the US presented a draft resolution regarding an international trade conference at ECOSOC, underdeveloped country representatives expressed their skepticism towards the developed countries' proposals during ITO negotiations, and expressed concern that their needs were not being met[613] – forewarning the institutional fracture that was to follow. They stated at

607 *The Calling of an International Conference on Trade and Employment*, ESC Res. 13(I), UN ESCOR, 1st Sess., UN Doc. E/22 (1946) 133. The countries invited were Australia, Belgium, Luxemburg, Brazil, Canada, Chile, China, Cuba, Czechoslovakia, France, India, Lebanon, the Netherlands, New Zealand, Norway, South Africa, the USSR, the UK, and the US.

608 *Report of the First Session of the Preparatory Committee of the United Nations Conference on Trade and Employment*, E/PC/T/33, UN ESCOR (1946) [London Draft].

609 *Report of the Drafting Committee of the Preparatory Committee of the United Nations Conference on Trade and Employment*, E/PC/T/34, UN ESCOR (March 5, 1947) [New York Draft].

610 *Report of the Second Session of the Preparatory Committee of the United Nations Conference on Trade and Employment*, E/PC/T/186, UN ESCOR (August 22, 1947) [Geneva Draft]. Colombia, Denmark, Mexico, Peru, Poland, and Syria sent observers to the First Session. Colombia and Mexico sent observers to the Drafting Committee. The following countries sent observers to the Second Session, in addition to those that were represented at the First Session: Afghanistan, Argentina, Ecuador, Egypt, Greece, Iran, Saudi Arabia, Siam, Sweden, Turkey, Uruguay, Venezuela, and Yugoslavia.

611 *Ibid.*

612 *Ibid.*, p. 81; *Interim Report of the Second Session of the Preparatory Committee of the United Nations Conference on Trade and Employment*, E/PC/T/117 Rev.1, UN ESCOR (July 9, 1947), p. 8. According to the conference records, Havana was deemed a desirable location for the conference because it was in the western hemisphere and because Lake Success, which was the United Nations' temporary headquarters at the time, was deemed not to have the logistical capacity for such a large and complicated conference as was expected.

613 Geneva Draft; Wilcox, *Charter*, pp. 31–2; UN ESCOR, *United Nations Conference on Trade and Development*, UN Doc. E/Conf.2/23 (December 24, 1947); UN ESCOR, *United Nations Conference on Trade and Development*, UN Doc. E/Conf.2/36 (February 4, 1948).

the outset of the Havana conference that the lack of including development issues in the working ITO Charter draft was not simply a shortcoming of institutional design, but actually created a bias against them.[614] Their wariness stemmed from a concern that industrialized countries, as in the colonial past, were seeking cheap access to the raw materials of commodity-dependent postcolonial countries.[615]

Before the Preparatory Committee first met in London, the US published the *Suggested Charter for an International Trade Organization of the United Nations*.[616] This draft was immediately controversial and negotiations in London almost broke down when underdeveloped countries, represented by Australia, India, China, Lebanon, Brazil, and Chile, accused the US of ignoring their concerns regarding development and their demands to have the freedom to utilize import quotas to promote industrialization. Until London, neither the US nor the UK took seriously the industrialization programs announced by underdeveloped countries.[617] The controversy was resolved when the US agreed to include a chapter on economic development, which framed development demands as an exception and provided the details of how and when such an exception applied.[618] Thus, a "London Draft" of the ITO Charter was produced.[619] The London Draft was discussed in Geneva at the Second Session of the Preparatory Committee. Here, India led the battle by underdeveloped countries in their demands to remove preapproval for the use of import quotas and other restrictions. Even though underdeveloped countries were unsuccessful in removing prior permissions, they managed to shorten the approval process in order to reduce the chance of "obstructionist delays."[620]

Issues regarding developing countries and development also influenced the 1945 negotiations in Bretton Woods, New Hampshire, for embedded liberalism's other international institutions - the IMF and the World Bank.[621] We see some evidence of this in statements made by Harry Dexter White, who led the US negotiators at Bretton Woods and was one of the architects of the international institutions that defined embedded liberalism. Drawing on his experience with Latin America, White proposed that the International Bank for Reconstruction and Development (later known as the World Bank) help stabilize the

[614] Wilcox, *Charter*, pp. 47–9. [615] Scott, "Developing Countries."
[616] United States Department of State, *Suggested Charter for an International Trade Organization of the United Nations*.
[617] Gardner, *Diplomacy*, p. 365. [618] Wilcox, *Charter*, p. 42. [619] London Draft.
[620] Wilcox, *Charter*, p. 45. [621] Helleiner, "Bretton Woods," 964; Pahuja, *Decolonising*.

prices of primary commodities through an "International Commodity Stabilization Corporation."[622] White espoused a generally liberal disposition towards trade policy and wanted the gradual and negotiated reduction of tariffs.[623]

Nevertheless, in his Stabilization Fund proposal, White included some room for poorer countries' concerns regarding development. White's words provide exemplary insight into how embedded liberalism allowed for development ideas, and are therefore worth reproducing at some length:

> The belief that reduction in all import duties increases trade and yields a higher standard of living for all countries under all circumstances and in all stages of their economic evolution assumes that countries are utilizing virtually all their capital and labor; that a country chiefly agricultural in its economy has as many economic, political and social advantages as a country whose economy is chiefly industrial, or as a country which has a balanced economy . . . These assumptions, essential to the belief that "Free Trade" policy is ideal, are not valid. They are unreal and unsound. "Free Trade" policy grossly underestimates the extent to which a country can virtually lift itself by its bootstraps in one generation from a lower to a higher standard of living, from a backward agricultural to an advanced industrial country, provided always it is willing to pay the price. The view further overlooks the very important fact that political relationships among countries being what they are, vital considerations exist in the shaping of the economic structure of a country other than of producing goods with the least labor.[624]

White's point is that because developing countries rely on agriculture, international trade policies must take into account global political imbalances between agriculturally dependent countries at the periphery and industrialized countries at the center. White also suggests that in order for the Third World developing states to develop, they must overcome great obstacles and industrialize. The US State Department, however, would later remove commodity stabilization from the Bank's final functions.[625]

The ITO and embedded liberalism continue League doctrines

At a theoretical level, embedded liberalism's policies and institutions took League economic doctrines as their premise and similarly defined

[622] Helleiner, "Bretton Woods," 958.
[623] Horsefield (ed.), *International Monetary Fund*, vol. III, p. 70. [624] *Ibid.*
[625] Helleiner, "Bretton Woods," 960.

them. Jacob Viner, the renowned trade economist, captured the prevailing liberal trade beliefs at the time of the ITO:

Only the traditional free trader can deal with the problem of the desirable level of trade barriers as a clear-cut question of principle. He wants the reciprocal reduction of trade barriers carried as far as governments can be persuaded to carry it, even to the point of total elimination of tariffs, subject to a few debatable exceptions such as protection of infant industries and those which are strategically important.

Viner continues:

The free trader objects to trade barriers both as obstacles to international specialization of production in accordance with comparative national advantages for production, and as sources of international friction. But there are few free traders in the present-day world, no one pays any attention to their views, and no person in authority anywhere advocates free trade. The practical issue turns on *whether existing trade barriers should be reduced*, and, if so, how much; and *on these points there is perhaps nearly as much division of opinion within countries as between countries.*[626]

The debates that led to the ITO were not doctrinaire discussions of "free trade," but rather, as during the time of the League of Nations, it was about "freer trade." ITO delegates argued over how low and how quickly tariffs were to be reduced, if at all, and over exceptions to reducing tariffs.[627] Moreover, like the League, the ITO recognized exceptions to freer trade in which infant industries could be rationally buttressed to develop one's economy and possibly create a comparative advantage (and for strategically sensitive areas).

In fact, US drafters of the ITO Charter's commercial provisions turned to late League publications, such as *Commercial Policy in the Interwar Period: International Proposals and National Policies*, for guidance and inspiration.[628] The perspective in this publication essentially ignored rationalization and prioritized freer trade and the reduction of tariffs as the principal issue of international commercial policy. Drafters also looked to the 1927 International Convention for the Abolition of Import and Export Prohibitions and Restrictions – this treaty never came into

626 Viner, "Conflicts," 613 [emphasis added].

627 International Trade Organization, Hearings Before the Committee on Finance, Part I, US Senate, 80th Congress, 1st Session (1947), p. 3; Bronz, "Charter," 1093.

628 League of Nations, *Commercial Policy*; League of Nations, *Better Economic World*. See Wilcox, *Charter*, pp. 23, 162; Brown, Jr., *United States*, pp. 3–4, 29–46; Irwin, Mavroidis, and Sykes, *GATT*, pp. 5–6.

operation, but trade diplomats and jurists looked to it as an intellectual precedent and as a case study to understand why such a treaty had failed.[629]

Chapter IV of the ITO Charter defined "freer trade" through the MFN principle, which carried over into the GATT.[630] The chapter's principal purpose was to outline the boundaries between the domestic and international markets, and the state and the market. Delegates negotiated the degree to which the ITO Charter would allow for government market regulation and what preferences would be allowed as exceptions to the MFN principle.[631]

In the spirit of ensuring domestic stability, the negotiations were framed in terms of answering the question of what forms of domestic regulation would be allowed as exceptions to principles of freer trade. More specifically, delegates worked out exceptions to prohibitions against quantitative restrictions and increasing tariffs. It was through these exceptions that agriculture was separated from industry. Domestic agricultural price control was carved out of Chapter IV of the ITO Charter as an exception to the rule prohibiting quantitative restrictions (i.e. quotas, import or export licenses, and the like).[632]

Rationalization was defined through Chapter VI as a short-term plan to stabilize the price of and stimulate the export of primary commodities through ICAs.[633] Charter drafters relied on late League publications such as *Industrialization and Foreign Trade*,[634] as well as experiences from the 1933 International Wheat Agreement and the 1937 International Sugar Agreement.[635] They also most likely drew from the many League expert memos on the subject.

[629] Bidwell, *Commercial Policy*. [630] Art. 17.

[631] Exceptions included imperial and post-imperial preferences for the UK, the US, Portugal, France, Belgium, and the Netherlands (Article 16.2(a)–(d)); and preferences for enumerated countries forming regional blocs in the Levant and Latin America (Article 16(e)).

[632] Art. 20. There were other exceptions to quantitative measures, such as controls that avoided a serious decline in monetary reserves and maintained a country's balance of payments (Art. 21), and plans for postwar economic recovery for approved countries held to be in a transition period (Art. 23).

[633] See also Ch. IV, Art. 28.

[634] Economic, Financial and Transit Department, *Industrialization*.

[635] See Toye and Toye, *UN*, pp. 46, 48, 214. Also, amongst Albert Viton's papers regarding ISAs of the 1940s and 1950s is a copy of the 1937 ISA and documents pertaining to voting scheme negotiations of the 1937 ISAs. Viton was not at the 1937 ISA negotiations, suggesting that he may have referred to these during the 1940s and 1950 ISA negotiations: International Sugar Conference, London, April 1937, Negotiating

This was part of embedded liberalism's long-term goal to diversify and industrialize different economies, which can be found in Chapter III of the ITO Charter entitled "Economic Development and Reconstruction." In this context, the purpose of multilateralism was to facilitate global industrialization by ensuring an increased flow of capital, materials, technology, and technical skills to different countries.[636] All this development and industrialization was proposed in order to ensure that the following goals were met:

1. to assure just and equitable treatment for the enterprise, skills, capital, arts and technology brought from one Member country to another;
2. to formulate and promote the adoption of a general agreement or statement of principles regarding the conduct, practices and treatment of foreign investment;
3. to enlarge to the greatest possible extent the benefits to Members.[637]

Thus the Charter devised a framework that attempted to reconcile several dynamics. First, it addressed equity in regard to the global distribution of skills and knowledge. Second, it acknowledged that foreign investment plays a part in domestic economies, but that at the same time it needs to be regulated (the only explicit reference to a way of promoting foreign investment is through treaties devised to avoid international double taxation).[638] Finally, it included a notion of wide-scale welfare enhancement; it left it open as to whether an economic policy of redistribution or growth (or what mix of the two) was the best means to achieve this goal.

Chapter III also legitimized government subsidization for the purpose of development. But countries had to receive prior approval through multilateral negotiations in order for this sort of government assistance to comply with the Charter. The first provision of Article 13, like the exceptions to MFN in Chapter IV, highlights how the ITO institutionalized embedded liberalism's compromise between domestic and international concerns. It also treats the relationship between industry and agriculture as a central feature of development:

Committee, "Suggested Basis for Voting, Proposal submitted by M. du Toit" (Union of South Africa) (April 28, 1937) CONF./SUGAR/NEG.24; "Suggested Basis for Voting, Proposal submitted by Dr. Hartmand (Netherlands)" (April 28, 1937) CONF./SUGAR/NEG.26; "Suggested Basis for Voting, Proposal submitted by Dr. Sachs (Poland)" (April 28, 1937) CONF./SUGAR/NEG.27; "Report by Negotiating Committee" (April 19, 1937) CONF./SUGAR/NEG.20, AVP, Box 1, Folder 2.

[636] Arts. 10–12. [637] Art. 11.2. [638] Art. 11.2(a)(ii).

The Members recognize that special governmental assistance may be required to promote the establishment, development or reconstruction of particular industries or branches of agriculture, and that in appropriate circumstances the grant of such assistance in the form of protective measures is justified. At the same time they recognize that an unwise use of such measures would impose undue burdens on their own economies and unwarranted restrictions on international trade, and might increase unnecessarily the difficulties of adjustment for the economics of other countries.

The ITO and embedded liberalism reconfigure League doctrines

Through the ITO, embedded liberalism changed the configuration of rationalization and freer trade, from a relationship of exception and rule to one of opposition. This oppositional stance was the result of assumptions regarding the global political economy, and how the ITO defined and institutionalized the relationship between the Third and First Worlds based on those general assumptions. To US commentators, "freer trade," as defined in Chapter IV of the ITO Charter, was the key provision of the ITO Charter.[639] This perspective, taken up by most First World countries, coincided with the fact that they all depended on the export of manufactured goods and were home to most of the world's industrialists. The MFN principle was key to driving down high tariffs set against manufactured goods, thereby opening up markets for industrialists.

The Third World turned to rationalization as the predominant trade doctrine. Frequent commodity price fluctuations harmed most people in underdeveloped countries, since their well-being depended on the sale of primary commodities. As a result, underdeveloped countries were more politically sensitive to primary commodity prices than developed countries. Accordingly, developing countries employed embedded liberalism to stabilize commodity prices in the short-term, by devising a plan through the ITO Charter to stimulate the export of primary commodities through ICAs.[640]

Even though the Third World countries had a propensity for rationalization, and the same could be said for the First World and freer trade, nothing in theories of free trade demanded that the two sides had to be oppositional. On its face, the ITO Charter appeared to follow this same

639 Gardner, *Diplomacy*, pp. 101–9, 269–86; United States Department of State, *Havana Charter*, pp. 3–5.

640 Ch. IV, Art. 28; Ch. VI.

pattern of freer trade as the norm and rationalization as the exception. The ITO's demise, however, is indicative of how tenuous the compromise was that led to this form of norm-exception. In fact, the confrontation between developed and developing countries, and their respective conceptions of trade, threatened to scuttle ITO multilateral negotiations at every step. The ITO institutionalized the tension between the Third and First Worlds in a way that created some distance between them, which set the foundations for future conflict.

This is evidenced in several instances. For example, the ITO Charter split deserving countries into categories. Some were places in which "resources are as yet relatively undeveloped," and others were countries "devastated by war."[641] With such language, the ITO Charter distinguished undeveloped countries (which were, for the most part, former colonies, existing colonies, or non-settler colonial states) as separate but related to war-torn countries (which meant, for the most part, countries on the European continent or nearby islands or peninsulas). Thus, postcolonial development and postwar reconstruction split apart like buds on the same stem of embedded liberalism.

Another example is over the issue of quantitative restrictions, which was the most contentious and was consistently a cause for nearly ending ITO negotiations. One reason that embedded liberalism made some allowance for quantitative restrictions under exceptional circumstances was because the British wanted to ensure that it remained a legitimate and viable domestic policy tool.[642] Keynes was a major influence over the inclusion of quantitative restrictions. He carried his views from the time of the League to his views on post-Second World War trade institutions. Keynes was a harsh critic of trade liberalization proposals from different parts of the US and UK governments, and was more sympathetic to policies that allowed for quantitative restriction after the Second World War. He went so far as to characterize quantitative restrictions as the norm and not the exception.[643]

Indeed, Keynes unwittingly supported the position held by developing countries. Developing countries, working within the purview of embedded liberalism, wanted the freedom to impose quantitative restrictions for the purpose of development. Accordingly, they wanted

[641] Art. 8. [642] Gardner, *Diplomacy*, pp. 165–87.

[643] Keynes, "Raw Materials," vol. XXVII, p. 112; "Minute from John Maynard Keynes to Sir Richard Hopkins" (February 23, 1942), in Moggridge (ed.), *Collected Writings*, vol. XXVII, p. 106.

to grant the ITO power to review such measures after the fact and order discontinuance, rather than the power to disallow such measures in advance.[644]

While Cuban delegates had used rationalization in the interwar period to increase their country's economic sovereignty and conclude an international sugar agreement, at that time they made sure to frame their position as part of European interests and as part of the postwar reconstruction effort. Now, underdeveloped countries came together as a political bloc, which would later become the G-77 or Third World, and used this same rationalization discourse, despite US and European interests. Former colonial subjects were less willing to negotiate with former imperial overlords and explored different ways to obtain post-colonial restitution and redistribution through international economic structures.

There are several other reasons why the conceptions of trade within the League co-existed without threatening the institution's existence, but were so contentious as to contribute to the end of the ITO. First, rationalization lost some of its credibility after the Second World War. The success of the government control of goods in the First World War contributed to rationalization's viability. Similar methods were employed by the Allies in Second World War, whereby national representatives of different sectors were organized into a transnational network through a government-regulated board.[645] The UK, however, could no longer rely on its colonies to secure the supply of goods; this made it more difficult to rationally control the supply of primary commodities. Second, the UK entered into a Lend-Lease Agreement with the US. This agreement was a different system than the regulatory boards and left the UK heavily in debt to the US for wartime supplies. Addressing this debt was one of the US and UK's first orders of business for recovering the world economy; this had the effect of pushing the idea of rationalization to the side. Third, the US had more international power and influence after the Second World War, and state-led rationalization had always been an unpopular idea in the US State Department.[646] Finally, former colonies were now independent states and could wield unprecedented political power. These newly independent states also decided that if they organized as much as possible as a

[644] Wilcox, *Charter*, pp. 42, 45, 48–9. [645] Roll, *Food Board.*
[646] Gardner, *Diplomacy*, pp. 165–78, 101–9.

bloc, then they could harness this power to govern the world economy in a particular way that benefited poorer nations.

So when ITO delegates from the First World wanted to express their frustrations with the Third World within the terms of free trade debates of the time, they did so by denigrating rationalization. First, they emphasized all instances in which the League "failed" to liberalize trade. What they rarely mentioned was that ICAs were one of the few economic agreements that were successfully signed, ratified, and operationalized under the auspices of the League. US (and some UK) negotiators found rationalization on an international level not just exceptional, but antithetical to their conception of what the ITO's form, function, and purpose should be.[647] According to William Taylor Phillips, Acting Chief, Division of International Resources, Department of State, the US only begrudgingly included ICAs in the ITO Charter:

> The attempt here in this chapter [addressing intergovernmental commodity agreements] is to admit that there probably will be agreements. We are not trying to encourage such arrangements nor to prohibit them, but we feel that whatever agreements are entered into should follow the specific rules of the game, the most important of which is the requirement that consuming interests should have an equal voice in determinations with the production interests.[648]

By acknowledging that ICAs, a form favored by the Third World, were here to stay, Phillips implicitly acknowledged the rising power of the Third World, especially in regard to agricultural trade. By calling for an equal voice for "consumer interests," he was asking for a renegotiation of the trade rules in a way that granted the industrial core more power than it currently had in the majority number of ICAs.

But for most of the ITO negotiations, the US actively tried to exclude international rationalization conceptions of trade. According to Wilcox, who represented the US throughout these talks, developing countries were caught up with a "fetish of industrialization," which threatened any consensus on a multilateral trade agreement. To emphasize why views from developing countries were misguided, he summarized the problem as follows:

> In backward areas throughout the world, there is an insistent demand that standards of living be improved and an irrational belief that this improvement

[647] Wilcox, *Charter*, pp. 30–2, 44–9, 140–2, 152.

[648] United States Department of State, *Suggested Charter for an International Trade Organization of the United Nations*, p. 476.

is to be obtained only though a rapid industrialization of their economies. Almost everywhere it is the view that this industrialization cannot be achieved unless severe restrictions are imposed on trade.[649]

To Wilcox and some other North Atlantic delegates, the whole premise of drafting international rules that encouraged domestic industrialization was foolish and not worth engaging with; this had the effect of discounting demands made by underdeveloped countries.[650] To the US diplomats, the goal of economic development was legitimate in principle, but international economic rationalization was a misguided idea that frustrated Anglo-American plans. The Northern argument in response to development needs was that the Charter would *indirectly* contribute to industrialization. The thinking was that markets would be more open, thereby making it easier to earn funds to finance new industries.[651]

The underdeveloped countries were unified in their general criticism of US proposals for not addressing their economic development needs.[652] Many feared that the US wanted to reduce tariffs in order to flood the world with manufactured goods and prevent others from building competing factories.[653] Latin American delegates, who were treated as extremists by the US, demanded a series of policies intended to redistribute the wealth between rich and poor nations and reduce global economic inequality;[654] these demands were precursors to those made under the New International Economic Order (NIEO) put forward through UNCTAD in the 1970s.

The fracture of the ITO

From the beginning, there was hostility towards the ITO from various US interests. And even before the ITO was deemed to be over, some US industrialists and policy-makers argued that the US should shelve the ITO Charter and focus on the GATT, since it contained the most important provisions.[655] When the ITO fell through, these people were pleased. The

649 Wilcox, *Charter*, p. 30. Wilcox also wrote: "Some of the proposals advanced in the name of economic development must be seen to be believed" (p. 142).

650 Wilgress, *Internationalism*, pp. 79–104.

651 Wilcox, *Charter*, p. 141; Edminster, "International Trade," 312–14.

652 See, e.g., UN ESCOR, *United Nations Conference on Trade and Development*, UN Doc. E/Conf.2/23 (December 24, 1947); UN ESCOR, *United Nations Conference on Trade and Development*, UN Doc. E/Conf.2/36 (February 4, 1948).

653 Bidwell and Diebold, Jr., "United States," p. 198.

654 Wilcox, *Charter*, p. 32.

655 *Ibid.*, p. 199.

end of the ITO is well documented. But what is often forgotten or ignored is that with the end of the ITO, two trade institutions emerged with "a kind of independent existence" – the GATT *and* the Interim Co-ordinating Committee for International Commodity Arrangements (ICCICA).[656]

During ITO negotiations, various committees were set up to focus on different policies – Committee II was charged to address "general commercial policy" (i.e. manufactured product tariffs), and Committee IV was charged to address "inter-governmental commodity arrangements."[657] According to the Preparatory Committee, because negotiated tariff schedules "cannot easily be held in abeyance pending action by the International Conference on Trade and Employment and the adoption of the Charter by national legislature," tariff negotiations would lead to a separate GATT in order "to safeguard the value of tariff concessions."[658] Thus, the Preparatory Committee expected the GATT to "be legally independent of the Charter and [to] be brought into force as soon as possible after its signature and publication," while still conforming "in every way to the principles laid down in the Charter and . . . not contain any provision which would prevent the operation of any provision of the Charter."[659]

Thus, while delegates continued to negotiate the ITO, the GATT was signed and came into force two months before the ITO Charter was signed.[660] When the ITO Charter was not ratified, the GATT stood as an independent international legal treaty. The end of the ITO, however, was not the end of trying to cover ICAs under a multilateral umbrella. In 1947, ECOSOC was granted provisional status with regard to regulating the international trade in commodities, much like the GATT was originally granted provisional status with regard to international tariffs. This was actually at the behest of Western industrialized countries, since it allowed them to maintain the principles and concessions they received from the ITO Charter negotiations regarding commodity trade.[661]

ECOSOC continued to apply the principles established by the ITO Charter: ICAs would be adopted only to deal with severe market disruption; their aim would be price stabilization and not price increases; and importing and exporting countries would have equal voting power.[662]

656 Diebold, Jr., *End of the ITO*, pp. 26–7. 657 London Draft, p. 3. 658 *Ibid.*, pp. 50–1.
659 *Ibid.* 660 Jackson, *Law of GATT*, p. 45.
661 Finlayson and Zacher, "International Trade," 739.
662 United Nations Economic and Social Council, Interim Co-ordinating Committee for International Commodity Arrangements, March 28, 1947, Res. 30 (IV).

ECOSOC also set up the ICCICA in order to implement and coordinate efforts to conclude commodity agreements according to these principles. A number of ICAs, for commodities such as sugar, coffee, tin, and wheat, were concluded under the direction of the ICCICA.[663]

Even without the ITO, ICAs and the GATT were joined in a legal relationship through ECOSOC that, in theory, remains today.[664] Despite this connection between the GATT and ECOSOC (and the ICCICA), during the 1950s, delegates from developed countries more or less succeeded in directing trade issues away from ECOSOC because of the belief that the GATT should be the sole forum to discuss international trade.[665]

Embedded liberalism fragments into UNCTAD and the GATT

UNCTAD

In the 1960s, developing countries began coalescing their interests as the G-77 within the UN.[666] The General Assembly declared the 1960s to be the "development decade," and trade was considered to be the primary instrument for development.[667] In this spirit, UNCTAD was created and came into effect in 1964.[668]

UNCTAD inherited the functions performed by the ICCICA.[669] This meant that UNCTAD was the primary international institution responsible for negotiating and coordinating international commodity policy. Raúl Prebisch, UNCTAD's first and most famous Secretary-General (1964–9), took this mandate very seriously, especially in the context of the development decade. In his first UNCTAD report, Prebisch emphasized the importance of analyzing the international trade in primary commodities with a view to determining how it affected lives in

[663] Maizels, *Commodities*, p. 104; Rowe, *Primary Commodities*, pp. 155–63.

[664] Because the 1947 GATT was drafted to be in compliance with the ITO, it allows for international commodity agreements as long as they conform to ECOSOC Resolution 30(IV) (GATT Art. XX(h) and the interpretive note in Annex I).

[665] Finlayson and Zacher, "International Trade," 739. [666] Sauvant, *Group of 77*.

[667] United Nations General Assembly, International Trade as the Primary Instrument for Economic Development, December 19, 1962, Res. 1707 (XVI); United Nations General Assembly, United Nations Development Decade, December 19, 1961, Res. 1710 (XVI).

[668] United Nations General Assembly, United Nations Conference on Trade and Development, November 11, 1963, Res. 1897 (XVIII).

[669] United Nations General Assembly, Establishment of the United Nations Conference on Trade and Development as an Organ of the General Assembly, December 30, 1964, Res. 1995 (XIX), para. 23(a).

developing countries.[670] To Prebisch, UNCTAD would clarify ideas that were still vague and confusing at the Havana ITO Conference. UNCTAD looked to Chapter VI of the ITO Charter and the ICAs of the 1930s (which included sugar, wheat, rubber, tin, and tea) and used these historical moments to provide legitimacy to the idea of ICAs.[671] To Thomas Franck, Prebisch had such a profound sense of global institutions and rules that he described him as the Grotius of the late twentieth century.[672]

In 1974, NIEO was put forward during the leadership of UNCTAD's Secretary-General Gamani Corea (1974–84).[673] NIEO was an attempt to represent Third World interests by focusing on institutional issues that created or structured the economic disparity between developed and developing countries. NIEO's plan of action included the creation of new international legal instruments, such as, in 1974, the Charter of Economic Rights and Duties of States and the United Nations Centre on Transnational Corporations. In the late 1970s and early 1980s, when the idea of a "knowledge economy" was just sprouting, developing countries in UNESCO put forward ideas for a New World Information and Communication Order, in which the principal goal was to ensure that global telecommunications served the poorest countries. While these resolutions and declarations were never formalized in a treaty or accepted through universal customary practice, they continued to frame global political economic ideas and institutions in development terms, and influenced the language of diplomatic negotiation and institutional operations.

Many considered NIEO to be the Third World's response to the First World's interests, as institutionalized through the IMF, the World Bank, and the GATT. "North–South" dialogue and debate was a predominant political and intellectual theme.[674] The regulation of primary commodities was the first thing on the list of the NIEO Programme of Action.[675] The thinking was that Third World countries would export primary

[670] Prebisch, *New Trade Policy*; Prebisch, *Global Strategy*.

[671] Toye and Toye, *UN*, pp. 41–2, 214. [672] Franck, "Book Review," 401.

[673] *Ibid.*, 39. Corea had also represented what was then known as Ceylon at the ITO Havana Conference. There he was the draft Charter's key critic from developing countries and argued for ICAs that represented the interests of producers.

[674] See, e.g., Sauvant and Hasenpflug (eds.), *New International Economic Order*; Bhagwati (ed.), *New International Economic Order*.

[675] United Nations General Assembly, Declaration for the Establishment of a New International Economic Order, May 1, 1974, Res. 3201 (S-VII); United Nations General Assembly, Programme for Action on the Establishment of a New International Economic Order, May 1, 1974, Res. 3202 (S-VI).

commodities as they had for decades, but now with the added purpose of generating capital to invest in industry, thereby improving countries' ability to create economic growth and reduce their reliance on imported manufactured goods. As such, stabilizing and increasing the price of commodities via ICAs was central to the project of development. One of UNCTAD's most important institutional mechanisms, the Integrated Programme for Commodities, was created in 1976 as a unifying institutional framework for all ICAs.[676]

NIEO and the Integrated Programme for Commodities coincided with the GATT Tokyo Round of negotiations (1973–9). By the Tokyo Round, not only had GATT membership increased by just under 60 percent from the Kennedy Round (1964–7), but for the first time, developing countries constituted the majority of the GATT, making up a little over 66 percent of the 102 participating countries. Developing countries used UNCTAD as a forum to organize their interests for negotiations in the Tokyo Round.[677] Meanwhile, amongst the large number of experts and scholars in developed and developing countries that examined ICAs, there was a consensus that a general structure was needed to organize ICAs (despite each commodity's unique context), with little confidence that the GATT was the appropriate forum.

It would be erroneous, however, to think that UNCTAD represented a homogeneous bloc interest of "developing countries." Developing countries found themselves in a wide range of economic, political, and geographic conditions that were not necessarily a cohesive whole. Corea, however, suggests why the disparate interests in the developing countries might come together:

> You have NICs [newly industrialized countries], the least developed countries, and the landlocked countries. But again I feel that this does not negate the logic of the developing countries coming together. There is one important reason, and that is that in multilateral negotiations, despite their differences, the only strength they have comes from the strength of their numbers .... Despite the allusions to the differences among developing countries, which come a lot from the North, the North itself does not recognize that much differentiation when they talk of developed countries.[678]

Thus, the formation of "developing countries" as a bloc through UNCTAD (and international politics in general) can be understood as a

676 United Nations Conference on Trade and Development, Integrated Programme for Commodities, May 5, 1976, Res. 93 (IV).

677 Johnston, "Tokyo Round." 678 Weiss *et al.* (eds.), *UN Voices*, p. 200.

political project in response to the dominating power of developed countries.[679] We will see, however, that in relation to the 1977 ISA, international trade political interests were divided in even more complex ways – countries would add to the developed and developing dynamic and organize their interests between importers and exporters, as well as between large exporters and small exporters, and between large importers and small importers.

UNCTAD was not only a site for developing countries to oppose the GATT; it was also a site of contestation and compromise between developed and developing countries. Developed countries also played a role within UNCTAD (and ICAs) and actively tried to shape its policies in their own interests.[680] One reason that developed countries participated in UNCTAD was to temper developing countries' international policies.[681] Additionally, Adlai Stevenson, the US ambassador to the UN, suggested that the US stop its opposition and accept some of the less developed countries' demands for the creation of UNCTAD. His fear was that embittered developing countries would play into Soviet hands.[682] The result was that developed countries would restrain developing countries' policies within UNCTAD, ranging from the formation of UNCTAD's founding principles to proposals for the Integrated Programme for Commodities and the Common Fund for Commodities.[683]

Politics was not the only reason that developed countries participated in UNCTAD. The other was functional. Until the 1991 "Dunkel Draft,"

[679] Cf. Prashad, *Darker Nations*. [680] Klein, "Agreements."

[681] The US was at first very reluctant to create UNCTAD, but was forced to play an active role. The G-77 adopted a clever tactic around Western opposition to the creation of UNCTAD. It was not going to be a specialized UN agency, which by definition would have meant countries could refuse to join. Instead, it was a subsidiary body under the UN General Assembly, according to Article XXII of the UN Charter, thereby creating a system of one nation, one vote. This also meant that Western countries had to pay for UNCTAD, whether they liked it or not. By this formula, developed country governments thought it would be more prudent to try to temper developing country proposals through UNCTAD as much as possible, rather than trying to oppose it. Prashad, *Darker Nations*, p. 194.

[682] Robertson, "UNCTAD," pp. 258, 268. George Ball, Under Secretary of State for Economic and Agricultural Affairs, however, made a firm distinction between international mechanisms that addressed the volatility of commodity prices and those mechanisms that permanently raised them above the long-run average market price. Ball conceded that US agriculture would support the latter, but that Congress would not ratify them. Toye and Toye, *UN*, p. 197.

[683] Robertson, "UNCTAD," pp. 268–9; United Nations Conference on Trade and Development, *UNCTAD*, p. 15; Brown, *Political and Social Economy*, pp. 90–1.

the GATT was usually only applied to trade in manufactured products, and rarely employed in relation to trade in unprocessed agriculture.[684] If developed countries wanted to shape trade law and policy in agriculture, then UNCTAD and ICAs provided the most popular international fora.

GATT

The same tension present between developed and developing countries within UNCTAD also existed within the GATT, where the power dynamic was reversed. Developing countries organized within the GATT against developed countries to reform the GATT's international economic policies, which they thought were anti-development.[685] Several GATT cases and provisions examined below mark how developing countries attempted to reform international trade by negotiating changes within the GATT and using existing GATT structures.

The conflict between developed and developing countries during the Havana ITO conference carried into GATT Article XVIII. This provision allowed for deviation from GATT rules for the purpose of subsidizing an infant industry. Under the provision's original language in 1947, prior consent of GATT Contracting Parties was necessary for such a deviation. A 1955 GATT Review Session changed the language that maintained the consent requirement, but characterized a developing country's decision to support a particular industry in a more positive light.[686]

Soon after that GATT session, the Contracting Parties commissioned a panel of experts to examine past and (then) present trends in international trade in an effort to understand why international trade flows between industrial areas and non-industrial areas decreased in the mid-1950s, and why trade did not improve socio-economic conditions in less-developed countries as rapidly as it did in developed countries.[687] The Haberler Report, as the expert report was commonly known, would later lay the groundwork for GATT provisions addressing the needs of developing countries.[688]

[684] McMahon, "Uruguay Round," pp. 411–17.

[685] Ismail, "Developing Countries in GATT." [686] Jackson, *Law of GATT*, pp. 638–40.

[687] Haberler *et al.*, *Trends*; GATT, Declaration on Promotion of the Trade of Less-developed Countries, November 30, 1961, BISD 10S/26; GATT, Meeting of Ministers, Measures for the Expansion of Trade of Developing Countries as a Means of Furthering their Economic Development, May 21, 1963, MIN (63)7, BISD 12S/36.

[688] Jackson, *Law of GATT*, pp. 640–63.

By 1965, developing countries now constituted a majority in the GATT, and they introduced a new section known as Part IV.[689] This section was important because it provided the foundations for special and differential treatment for developing countries in the GATT (and, later, in the WTO). Not only did Part IV carve out some exceptional space for developing countries within the GATT, but it also expanded what little room the GATT allowed for ICAs.[690] In effect, Part IV brought into the GATT some rationalization policies.

Another example of developing countries' concerted activity through the GATT is when, in 1961, Uruguay filed a legal complaint, under Article XXIII of the GATT, against fifteen developed countries.[691] These countries constituted the entire developed country membership of the GATT at the time. Uruguay listed in its complaint 576 restrictions against its exports in the fifteen developed country markets, and argued that these restrictions seriously reduced its exports. To some commentators, this case represented Uruguay's dramatic use of "showpiece litigation,"[692] while to others, it evidenced developing countries' active participation within the GATT.[693]

ICAs: rapprochement between South–North, agriculture–industry, and US–UK

Despite the US State Department's hostility to the idea of ICAs, the US executive government could not take a principled position against ICAs as such. First, this was because of the compromise between the US and the UK which generated embedded liberalism; the British insisted on not eliminating ICAs as a viable idea worth investigating.[694] To Keynes, the international regulation of agriculture presented the strongest argument for quantitative restrictions.[695] This was also because domestic agricultural policy within the US and the UK was actually consistent with theories of rationalization and ICAs. In the 1940s, US and UK

[689] Part IV comprises Arts. XXXVI and XXXVII of the GATT. See General Agreement on Tariffs and Trade, *Developing Countries*, on the introduction of Part IV into the GATT.

[690] Art. XXXVI.4.

[691] *Uruguay – Recourse to Article XXIII*, Panel Report, adopted November 16, 1962, BISD 11S/95.

[692] Hudec, *Developing Countries*, pp. 46–7.

[693] Ismail, "Developing Countries in GATT," 57.

[694] Penrose, *Economic Planning*, pp. 63–86, 114.

[695] John Maynard Keynes, "Letter to Sir Arnold Overton" (February 3, 1943), in Moggridge (ed.), *Collected Writings*, vol. XXVI, p. 261.

agriculturalists in government wanted as much freedom as possible to use quantitative restrictions.[696] Within the US government, members of the Department of Agriculture were strong advocates of ICAs and were at odds with the many at the State Department.[697] This made US ITO negotiators, who were from the State Department, uncomfortable, because they were instructed to support ICAs, which contravened their conception of a liberalizing trade regime.[698] This also highlights the fact that during ITO negotiations, the US usually characterized itself as an industrialized country, whose interests were as a consumer of primary commodities; this relegated US domestic agricultural interests as secondary to industrial and consumers interests within the US.

Not surprisingly, during ITO negotiations, the US generally presented the narrowest role for ICAs, sometimes in response to underdeveloped countries, and at other times in response to the UK.[699] US negotiators imagined ICAs as public agreements amongst countries, intended to stabilize the price and supply of a primary commodity in exceptional times of commodity surplus, with shared representation by consuming and producing countries.[700] They were clear that they did not envision ICAs as mechanisms intended to shift domestic resources and manpower from unproductive industries into new and more industrious occupations. In other words, to the US, ICAs were not to be used as mechanisms for domestic market regulation or development. Rather, they held that the purpose of ICAs was to respond to primary commodities' unique world price inelasticity and to ensure long-term price stability.[701] Later, the US was the principal instigator of the 1983 International Coffee Agreement, because it suited US foreign policy to provide stability for the coffee trade in Latin America.[702] Thus, international market regulation was demarcated from domestic economic policy.

Various Latin American countries tried unsuccessfully to amend US proposals. They sought to exempt ICAs from requirements of prior approval, allow for ICAs without consumer representation, and establish formulas for a minimum price.[703] To them, ICAs were a legitimate form of domestic and international market regulation. Unlike the US,

[696] Penrose, *Economic Planning*, pp. 108–10.
[697] Bidwell and Diebold, Jr., "United States," p. 221.
[698] Wilcox, *Charter*, pp. 35, 114–15; Mason, *World Trade*, pp. 247–50, 263–4.
[699] Brown, Jr., *United States*, pp. 119–25.
[700] International Trade Organization, Hearings, pp. 18–19. [701] *Ibid.*, pp. 480–4.
[702] Weiss *et al.* (eds.), *UN Voices*, p. 106. [703] Wilcox, *Charter*, p. 120.

Latin Americans imagined domestic and international markets to be inseparable.

The result was that the ITO Charter allowed for ICAs, but only under specific conditions and with prior approval by the ITO. Primary commodities were deemed to be affected by "special difficulties" (i.e. disruptive price fluctuation and inelastic demand),[704] which therefore necessitated "special treatment" in international trade through ICAs.[705] Chapter VI of the Charter outlined how ICAs were to be created – for example, by listing general principles that would govern ICAs, providing the particular conditions for which an ICA was allowed, and the substantive requirements for the content of ICAs.[706] Chapter VI of the ITO, as an instrument of commodity regulation, was unique for two reasons. First, it established a multilateral framework to govern all commodities within one institution. Second, it granted countries whose interests were mainly as consumers equal voting power with producer countries.[707] Even though the US set legal boundaries around the use of ICAs, these boundaries were the starting point for UNCTAD's attempt to organize all international commodities, against US wishes, approximately three decades later.

[704] *Ibid.*, p. 114. [705] Art. 55. [706] Arts. 60, 62, 63. [707] Art. 63(a).

8 The 1977 ISA as an exemplar of postwar ICAs

Introduction

At the end of ITO negotiations, there were only two major ICAs that the ITO had to approve. They were the 1937 ISA (which was, in effect, defunct by this time) and the 1949 Wheat Agreement.[708] ICAs were still a provisional idea and the ITO was thought by some to "create a framework for international experimentation in a field in which competition has been particularly unmerciful in the past."[709] During ITO negotiations and the institutional aftermath, the Third World, transnational agriculturalists, and Keynesian economists succeeded in ensuring that ICAs and rationalization remained an important feature of trade law and policy until the 1980s. The contest was over how to enmesh ICAs within a broader landscape of international institutions, and how to distribute power amongst the multitude of global interests.

For example, after the Second World War, the Food and Agriculture Organization (FAO), under the leadership of James Boyd Orr, called for the creation of agricultural ICAs under its purview and competed with the proposal to grant the ITO such power. The FAO proposed to create a World Food Board, whose purpose would be to rationally organize world food production and distribution in order to eliminate hunger. Part of this entailed organizing agricultural ICAs and setting up a comprehensive system of a buffer stock, surplus disposal, and relief operation. US and British diplomats reacted against this idea and insisted that these discussions be held under the ITO. The FAO was granted an advisory role during negotiations and then relegated, through the Charter (Art. 67), to only providing studies of ICAs.[710]

[708] Brown, Jr., *United States*, p. 354. [709] Bronz, "Charter," 1113.
[710] Wilcox, *Charter*, p. 42; Staples, *Development*, pp. 84–96; Shaw, *Security*, pp. 15–36.

There are also some examples of trying to embed ICAs within the GATT. In 1955, in a failed attempt, Contracting Parties tried to bring ICAs under the auspices of the GATT through the Special Agreement on Commodity Arrangements; they tried to do the same during the Kennedy Round.[711] The International Dairy Arrangement, a Western-friendly ICA, was successfully negotiated as part of the GATT Tokyo Round, and would later be renewed and incorporated into the WTO.[712]

During the time of the 1977 ISA, however, the consensus was that UNCTAD would house most ICAs. UNCTAD, from its inception, was part of a larger Third World agenda. The Third World "launched and defended" UNCTAD for "tactical purposes as a commodity conference."[713] Their plan was to control as much as possible the sector that had the most immediate impact on their daily life. The relationship between UNCTAD and ICAs was further complicated by the fact that ICAs and their respective secretariats had their own institutional histories, predating UNCTAD. Thus, it was always a matter of political negotiation as to what it meant for ICAs to be part of UNCTAD.

The 1977 ISA came into effect on January 1, 1978 and provides insight into some of the more important global social, economic, and political issues, at a time when ICAs were at the apex of their popularity. In order to understand how the 1977 ISA was created and what its demise meant, I continue my institutional account of embedded liberalism within the context of Third World politics. The sugar treaty comprised three political dynamics. First, it emerged at a time when Third World–First World relations were the most charged. Within this setting, the sugar treaty provides insight into what was at stake and what were the assumed differences between the Third World and First World. The 1977 ISA also

711 Curzon, "Tariffs and Trade," p. 248.

712 Geneva, April 6, 1979, GATT Doc. MTN/DP/8. This International Dairy Agreement was extended several times. In 1994, it was extended and placed under the auspices of the WTO Secretariat. See International Dairy Agreement, Marrakesh, April 15, 1994, Agreement Establishing the World Trade Organization, Annex 4C, 1867 UNTS 410. The International Dairy Council operated under ambiguous terms in relation to the WTO (Art. VII.1(a)): "An International Dairy Council shall be established within the framework of the World Trade Organization." The International Dairy Agreement terminated in 1997 and was not renewed again.

713 Robertson, "UNCTAD," p. 270. Robertson also noted that even though UNCTAD would present itself primarily as an international organization addressing primary commodities, "By the autumn of 1962 everyone accepted that it would inevitably have to consider virtually all fields of trade and finance." See also Dell, "Origins," p. 10.

provides an excellent example of how an ICA was negotiated within the purview of embedded liberalism as a compromise between the Third and First Worlds; it was one answer to the question of how an international institution was to complement domestic welfare and development demands. Finally, it was through ICAs that any attempt of rapprochement could be institutionalized. It was here where countries negotiated multiple configurations of interests as between developed/developing countries, exporters/importers, and large/small sugar producers and consumers.

While Third World–First World dynamics help to explain some important aspects of the 1977 ISA, the more complete account must also include an examination of different perspectives from within the Third World. People committed to a collective Third World project argued amongst each other and (at times) worked out some compromises. The main point of contention was between two different development agendas associated with ICAs. The different perspectives of two famous Latin American development economists provide a rough sketch of ideational debates amongst different Third World intellectuals and policy-makers. Raúl Prebisch would argue – through what was later called the Prebisch-Singer hypothesis – that the enduring factor shaping multilateral trade institutions over the last century had been the tension between interests in core and peripheral countries.[714] Core countries are those whose economy primarily relies upon the manufacturing of goods, whereas peripheral countries are those whose economy relies on the production of primary products. One result of this global functional differentiation, Prebisch suggested, is that core countries have significant influence over the social and economic conditions through which primary products are produced within and exported from peripheral countries. Another result is that, measured over a long period of time, gains from manufacturing grew at a continuous rate, whereas there was a steady decline in returns on primary commodities. Thus, Prebisch described the global inequality of wealth in terms of national economic outputs.

Celso Furtado, who worked closely with Prebisch in the Economic Commission for Latin America (ECLA) and in the formation of UNCTAD, however, preferred to frame patterns of global wealth distribution and development as the product of the lasting impact of imperial and

[714] Singer, "Distribution"; Prebisch, *Economic Development*.

colonial structures.[715] This framed the problem of development in a way that had to remedy the contemporary political and economic effects of imperial history, as well as remaining imperial structures. His ideas were popular amongst Marxist dependency theorists and world-systems theorists.

All the different perspectives that defined the Third World project made some principal provision for ICAs. One position sought to implement development policies, which were built upon the Prebisch-Singer hypothesis, within the parameters of embedded liberalism. It imagined the landscape of international trade institutions to consist of a mix of domestic and international institutions. Thus, it preferred the structure and politics of ICAs, loosely held together by UNCTAD through general principles. While another position, drawing from certain dependency theories and world-systems analysis, sought to empower one multilateral institution (namely UNCTAD) to manage the world's commodities. Thus, under this agenda, UNCTAD would be put forward as the principal source of international trade law and policy. This would be articulated in international instruments, such as the General Assembly's 1974 NIEO. Because this agenda demanded a global redistribution of wealth from rich to poor countries, most scholars and policy-makers from the First World treated NIEO as a radical threat from the Third Word.

ICAs, in general, have a rich history and were not strictly a matter of technically configuring and calibrating commodity markets in an effort to create stability. To the leading jurists of ICAs, these trade agreements also reflected and affected some of the key global policy debates of the time.[716] Sugar treaties are an excellent case study of the international politics and economics of ICAs because they would be one of the more popular commodity agreements after the Second World War. In the absence of the ITO Charter, governments continued to negotiate freestanding commodity agreements. The first set of these independent ICAs was signed in 1953 and regulated sugar, tin, and wheat. According to one agriculturalist, the tin agreement was only tacitly supported by tin importers; the wheat agreement was actually opposed by wheat importers; but the sugar agreement "received a considerable acclaim"

[715] Cypher and Dietz, *Economic Development*, pp. 187–9.

[716] Khan, *Law*; Chimni, *Agreements*. Some of today's eminent jurists wrote some of their earliest pieces on ICAs. See, e.g., Kennedy, "Cartel Bogey"; Sands, "Book Review."

from all parties involved – even the Anglo-Americans and Soviets found common ground.[717]

Situating the 1977 ISA within the ideational history of ICAs

Postwar trade and development policies

After the ITO's demise, developing countries focused on multilateral institutions, such as ICAs, in order to implement the development policies of embedded liberalism. For us to understand why a large number of developing countries would eventually use ICAs as a means for development in the late 1960s and 1970s, it is necessary first to outline the general assumptions and goals of development policies immediately after the Second World War. By the 1950s, developing countries were frustrated with fluctuating commodity prices and their dependence on industrialized countries for manufactured goods. They also had claims against the meager economic returns from exporting primary commodity products, which were hardly much better than the socio-economic trade benefits received for much of their colonial history in the nineteenth and early twentieth century. Thus, in the 1950s and early 1960s, many developing countries, with some support from the World Bank and IMF, turned to import substitution industrialization (ISI) policies.[718]

Development economists assumed that economies were national. The national economy was understood to be a cycle of inputs in the form of labor, technology, and capital used to produce outputs in the form of income. Development meant modernization, and modernization meant that the Global South had to industrialize in order to reproduce the Global North's economic achievements. The thinking was that ISI would decrease international hindrances to a country's socio-economic development by reducing the dependence on agriculture and imported manufactured products; it would enhance development by industrializing the domestic economy.[719] Nonetheless, developing countries still turned to (new) international mechanisms, such as the Resolution on Permanent Sovereignty over Natural Resources, to enhance the state's ability to establish a manufacturing base and industrialize the agricultural sector.[720]

717 Swerling, "Sugar Agreement." 718 Faundez, "Economic Law," p. 10.

719 Kennedy, "'Rule of Law'," pp. 95, 98.

720 United Nations General Assembly, Permanent Sovereignty over Natural Resources, December 14, 1962, Res. 1803 (XVII). Many thanks to Julio Faundez for reminding me of this point.

The experiences of Latin America,[721] the Arab world,[722] and the south Asian subcontinent[723] provide a representative sample of ISI policies that were internationally prevalent in the 1950s and early 1960s. ISI's purpose was to establish firms within a domestic economy that would produce manufactured goods that would be locally consumed and replace imported goods. ISI was considered to be inward-looking, because infant industries would be subsidized for the purpose of domestic consumption and not for export. It was a policy that emphasized autarky often at the expense of economic growth and efficiency. Even if manufacturers wanted to export their goods, the high cost of production under ISI often made it prohibitive to do so.

ISI was possible to implement through a wide variety of policy instruments. During its heyday, much of the international pressure was not necessarily against ISI as such, but rather against certain policy instruments such as quotas and multiple exchange rates, thereby pushing ISI countries to rely more on raising tariffs. Moreover, different countries relied on different sources of capital. This was capital that would be used to import the technology and know-how necessary to industrialize. Latin American countries, for example, often relied on multinational corporations and foreign capital, whereas Egypt had a nationally centralized system of capital control.

With all this variety of policy tools and capital regulation in hand, ISI policy-makers were indiscriminate in deciding which specific industries they concentrated on. That is, government officials and technocrats rarely publicly justified which industries were favored, nor did they necessarily advance industries that might have had a comparative advantage. They did, however, favor industry over agriculture, shifting resources from the historical rural communities and agricultural sectors to the burgeoning urbanized and manufacturing sectors. This meant that ISI policies often made developing countries' agricultural products less competitive to export to the international market.

Even though ISI policies neglected stimulating traditional exports, during the 1950s and 1960s, Latin American countries still mostly exported primary commodities. In the early 1960s, some countries,

[721] See, e.g., Díaz Alejandro, "Argentine State"; Baer, "Import Substitution"; Bulmer-Thomas, *Economic History*, pp. 269–312.

[722] See, e.g., Girgis, *Industrialization*.

[723] See, e.g., Lewis, *Pakistan*; Krueger, *Benefits and Costs*; Dutt, *India*, pp. 98–123.

such as Argentina, Colombia, and Mexico, were not able to attract enough capital to counterbalance the decline in export receipts; later efforts to try to stimulate trade in primary commodities were too little too late. This generated perverse results in some countries where ISI policies led to more dependency on industrial countries for capital than ever before.

As a result, one major criticism of ISI was that it ignored the potential benefits of using international trade to develop socio-economically. Others criticized the increased inequality that ISI created between traditional rural sectors and emerging urban manufacturing sectors. These criticisms, along with external shocks, such as industrialized countries de-linking from gold and adopting floating currencies, the sudden rise in the price of commodities, and the OPEC-driven oil price spike, changed countries' development policies in the late 1960s and 1970s. More and more advisors argued that developing countries should stimulate commodity exports while attempting to diversify exports. Prebisch and the ECLA, who were ISI's more famous advocates in the 1950s and 1960s, would become more critical of ISI policies in the mid-1960s and 1970s.[724]

This led developing countries, the ECLA, and development economists to shift their development prescriptions towards the more export-oriented or "outward-looking" development policies, which married international trade policies with domestic industrialization and diversification.[725] These policies still held modernization theory assumptions that informed ISI policies. Also like ISI, these outward-looking policies assumed that the national economy was an enormous cycle of inputs and outputs.[726] The fundamental difference was that now the economy was thought of in more international terms and the market was treated as global.

Again, this new development theory manifested through a variety of different policies. Export promotion policies attempted to encourage the export of goods produced through ISI policies; export substitution policies sought to shift resources out of protected sectors; and primary-export development policies aimed to exploit the rise in world commodity prices.[727] It was during this outward-looking moment that ICAs would play a prominent role in development policies.

[724] Toye and Toye, *UN*, pp. 138–40, 147, 159. [725] Maizels, *Industrial Growth*.
[726] Kennedy, "'Rule of Law'," p. 98. [727] Bulmer-Thomas, *Economic History*, p. 315.

The life of ICAs

In the few instances that contemporary international trade law texts do mention ICAs, it is only as a minor point, treated as an anomaly within the history of trade. Since the declaration of the death of ICAs in the mid-1990s, the 2000s has seen some renewed interest in their history.[728] The purpose of these recent examinations of ICAs' record is to explore different mechanisms that regulate international trade in primary commodities and to discuss the role of government in regulating the market, often within a broader scope of investigating the relationship between trade and development.

ICAs first gained some popularity during the League of Nations, and in the 1930s there were a small number of systemic studies of ICAs (apart from the expert memoranda commissioned by the League).[729] What I mean by systemic studies are the examinations of ICAs whose purpose is to discern general patterns and principles of institutional structure, world affairs, and economic theory. One of these studies concluded with one of the earliest calls for a sort of "international economic law" (though the term was not used), to establish common rules to resolve trade disputes between producing and consuming countries.[730] It was not until the final years of the Second World War that systemic ICA studies first became popular.[731] It was in these studies that scholars and commentators from different disciplines (law, economics, politics, diplomacy) debated with each other about the relationships amongst international law, international trade, and economic development.

Part of the frustration of examining ICAs systemically, and determining whether they were "successful," stemmed from the fact that ICAs took several general forms. International buffer-stock schemes involved the creation of an international agency to buy and maintain surpluses or an international system to coordinate nationally held stocks. Trade quota schemes involved establishing permissible price ranges, whereby

[728] Maizels, "Economic Dependence," p. 169; Chrispeels (ed.), *Organisations in Transition*; Viton, *Sugar Agreements*; Crespo, "Trade Regimes"; Gilbert, "Agreements," in Gaisford and Kerr (eds.). While my notes in this section are not exhaustive, I have tried my best to capture the (mostly forgotten) literature of the time.

[729] Rowe, *Artificial Control*; Rowe, *Markets and Men*.

[730] Wallace and Edminster, *International Control*, pp. 332–43.

[731] International Labour Office, *Commodity Control*; Tsou and Black, "Commodity Arrangements"; Hexner, *Cartels*; Koch, "Cartels"; Knorr, "Instability"; Davis, "Experience"; Engle, "Cartels"; Knorr, "Problem"; Davis, *Commodity Agreements*; Cale and Zaglits, "Intergovernmental Agreements"; Amzalak, "Le café et le sucre."

producing countries were allotted quotas in times of surplus, while consuming countries were allotted quotas in times of shortage. Purchase contract schemes regulated long-term agreements between producers and consumers that set the price and quantities of trade.

The working premise of systemic studies of ICAs was that severe fluctuations of commodity prices are detrimental to almost all countries. Hence, studies centered on what the role of government should be in relation to the market and examined the different mechanisms employed by different ICAs to stabilize commodity prices. Most of these studies were acutely sensitive to the fact that many developing countries depended on a small number of primary commodities and were particularly vulnerable to fluctuating world prices.

It was difficult to gauge the success of ICAs in general in light of the unique contexts of each commodity and the different mechanisms used by different agreements. It was also difficult to determine if individual ICAs succeeded or failed for several reasons. Often agreements' objectives (beyond price stabilization) were ambiguous. Also, some agreements were not well funded or did not have enough members to achieve any objective. One commentator concludes the following:

> Overall, the agreements appear to only have marginal effect on reducing price variability, which was their declared objective, but when given adequate resources, they do appear to have raised prices over and above those which would otherwise have prevailed.[732]

Historical systemic reviews of ICAs regularly mentioned the international institutional environment of time. The focus in the mid-1940s was on the relationship of ICAs to the ITO, FAO, and ECOSOC. In the 1960s, ICAs were discussed against the failed Havana Charter and in light of institutions such as the GATT, IMF, FAO, and the Commission on International Commodity Trade (coordinating UN organs and the GATT); during this time, there was increased interest in ICAs implementing agencies' structures and policies.[733] Some legal scholars considered the ICAs and their respective implementing agencies as forming a particular sort of international institution, with legal personality, quasi-judicial functions, and norm-generating capabilities.[734]

[732] Burger, Gilbert, and Smit, "Regulation," pp. 17, 37.

[733] Krumme, "Agreements"; Walker, "International Law"; Baranyai and Mills, *Agreements*; Symposium, "Agreements"; Haviland, *Agreements*; Rowe, *Primary Commodities*; Lowenfeld, "Controls."

[734] Alexandrowicz, *Agencies*, pp. 252–78.

Table 8.1 Objectives and instruments of select ICAs from the mid-1970s to early 1980s[735]

	Sugar	Cocoa	Coffee	Natural rubber	Tin
A. Price and earnings objectives					
1. Price stability	✓	✓	✓	✓	✓
2. Earnings stability and growth	✓	✓	✓		✓
B. Long-term development objectives					
1. Market access and supply reliability	✓	✓	✓	✓	
2. Diversification and industrialization	✓	✓			
3. Competitiveness of natural products			✓	✓	✓
4. Market structure and marketing, distribution, and transportation	✓			✓	
5. Increased consumption	✓	✓	✓	✓	✓
C. Other objectives					
1. Alleviation of serious economic difficulties		✓	✓	✓	✓
2. Prevention of unemployment or underemployment			✓		✓
D. Price and earnings policy instruments					
1. Buffer stock		✓		✓	✓
2. Export quotas	✓		✓		✓

Source: Maizels, *Commodities*, p. 130

The 1970s and very early 1980s marked the highpoint of ICA studies, in terms of vigor and quantity. By this time, no one could discuss "global interdependence" and commodities without prioritizing the issue of

[735] Sugar: 1977 International Sugar Agreement. This agreement also provided for holding of national stocks under the control of the International Sugar Organization. The 1984 ISA contained no price stabilization provisions. Cocoa: 1980 International Cocoa Agreement; earlier agreements provided for a combination of buffer stock and export quotas. Coffee: 1976 and 1983 International Coffee Agreements. Rubber: 1979

development.[736] Table 8.1 highlights the variety of purposes and mechanisms in select ICAs of the time. The industrial core focused more on ensuring stable commodity prices, whereas the agricultural periphery wanted stable and "remunerative" prices. Many ICAs made explicit provision for alleviating domestic economic hardships, such as the prevention of unemployment or underemployment. Those that did not have these explicit purposes, such as the sugar agreement, took domestic development concerns very seriously and allowed for special and differential treatment for developing countries.

Underlying the ongoing debates as to whether ICAs effectively regulated commodity prices was the assumption that the range of objectives that ICAs served mattered.[737] The continuing concern of political scientists and jurists was how to organize all ICAs within or alongside multilateral institutional structures.[738] Economists tried to determine which were the best mechanisms to stabilize commodity prices - for example, buffer stocks or export quotas.[739] In light of commodity price fluctuations and the end of the Bretton-Woods monetary system, during the mid-1970s, editors of the *Journal of International Economics* felt it necessary to revisit Keynes's ideas regarding the international control of primary commodities; they wanted to understand how commodities were inextricably part of the "international economic order," which included monetary and trade policies.[740]

International sugar agreements

The postwar history of sugar agreements spans the life of ICAs. Agreements were signed in 1953,[741] 1958,[742] 1968,[743] and

International Natural Rubber Agreement. Tin: 1975 and 1980 International Tin Agreements.

736 World Economic Interdependence and Trade in Commodities, Cd 6061 (1975).

737 Hager, "Agreements"; Helleiner, *Development*, pp. 52–65; Law, *Agreements*; Gariepy, "Agreements"; North-South Institute, *Commodity Trade*; Goreux, "Stabilization."

738 Fawcett, "Function of Law"; Brown, *Primary Commodity Control*; Johnston, *Law and Policy*; Reynolds, *Common Fund*; Franck, "Minimum Standards"; Rangarajan, *Commodity Conflict: Political Economy*; McNicol, *Agreements*; Nappi, *Market Controls*; Brown, *Political and Social Economy*; Goodwin and Mayall (eds.), *Commodity Regime*; Ernst, *Agreements*; Khan, *Law*; Chimni, *Agreements*.

739 Herrmann, Burger, and Smit, *Policy*; Gariepy, "Agreements"; Newberry and Stiglitz, *Theory*.

740 n.a., "Editor's Note."

741 International Sugar Agreement for the Regulation of the Production and Marketing of Sugar, 1953, London, October 16, 1953, 258 UNTS 153.

742 International Sugar Agreement, 1958, London, December 1, 1958, 385 UNTS 137.

743 International Sugar Agreement, 1968, New York, December 3, 1968, 654 UNTS 3.

1977.[744] All four agreements[745] relied upon a mix of export quotas, target prices, and stocks to stabilize the price of sugar. Moreover, all the agreements made some attempt to benefit developing countries.[746] The 1977 ISA did continue certain sugar treaty trends, but it was also unique in its level of sophistication.

The 1953 ISA is commonly referred to as the "First International Sugar Agreement."[747] Nonetheless, the 1937 ISA was "the direct lineal ancestor" of all post-Second World War sugar agreements – this agreement included sugar exporters and importers, and divided votes based on production and import amounts; its enumerated purpose was to stabilize the world price of sugar, using a system of production quotas.[748] All subsequent agreements were the result of additions or modifications to the interwar sugar treaty. Postwar ISAs also followed the requirements set out in the ITO Charter (and still reflected in the GATT), to ensure that the total number of votes for importing and exporting countries, acting as proxies for producers and consumers, would be equal.[749] The 1953 ISA established the International Sugar Council that was deemed to accept the "records, assets and liabilities" of the 1937 International Sugar Council.[750] The subsequent ISAs would follow suit, by renewing or replacing the subsequent agreement and its respective International Sugar Council.[751]

Table 8.2 summarizes some of the main regulatory features of the 1937 and postwar sugar agreements. They all relied on export quotas to regulate price, and at least some make reference to supply commitments. Early sugar agreements had general language regarding supply commitments and domestic stocks; by 1977, this language was operationalized through international mechanisms. Moreover (as discussed further below), they all recognized the interconnectedness between the free market and preferential markets (or "special arrangements").

The 1953 and 1958 sugar treaties are the most comparable to the 1937 ISA, in terms of shared principle and purpose. These treaties used similar mechanisms, such as export quotas, to stabilize the price of sugar. After

[744] International Sugar Agreement 1977, New York, October 28, 1977, 1064 UNTS 219.

[745] A 1973 ISA entered into force, but parties could not agree to economic provisions which regulated the price of sugar, making the treaty practically irrelevant to most sugar-related interests. International Sugar Agreement, Geneva, October 13, 1973, 906 UNTS 69.

[746] Abbott, *Sugar*, p. 199. [747] See, e.g., Burger, Gilbert, and Smit, "Regulation," p. 21.

[748] Hagelberg and Hannah, "Quest," 24.

[749] *Ibid.*, 25. Votes would still be delegated to each country in proportion to their level of sugar export or import.

[750] 1953 ISA: Art. 27(5).

[751] 1958 ISA: Arts. 27(5), 46; 1968 ISA: Art. 3(1); 1977 ISA: Art. 3(1).

Table 8.2 Summary of main regulatory features of international sugar agreements, 1937–77

	1937	1953	1958	1968	1977
Export quotas	✓	✓	✓	✓	✓
Hardship Fund providing increased emergency quotas for developing countries				✓	✓
Exemptions for preferential markets	✓	✓	✓	✓	✓
Supply commitment language	✓	✓	✓	✓	✓
Supply commitment mechanisms				✓	✓
Limit to imports from non-members		✓	✓	✓	✓
Provision for domestic stocks	✓	✓	✓	✓	✓
International regulation of domestically held stocks for purpose of price control					✓
Price range (US cents per lb)	"Reasonable prices"	3.25–4.35	3.15–4.00	3.25–5.25	11.00–23.00

Source: Respective ISAs
Note: Price range for 1978: 11.00–21.00, subject to revision every year. In April 1980, range was increased to 12.00–22.00, and in November 1980, to 13.00–23.00.

the 1958 ISA, however, there would be shift in the function and purpose of ISAs. Once again, Havana and its relationship to sugar would embody broader geopolitical power struggles. The 1958 ISA took effect on January 1, 1959, which was also the day Batista fled Cuba, while Fidel Castro and his small band took over the island. Castro's attainment of power would prelude a change in international sugar politics. Sugar treaties subsequent to the 1958 ISA, like Castro and sugar-dependent Cuba, would be part of the rising wave of the Third World. For example, the 1968 ISA introduced a special fund for developing countries.

The 1968 ISA was the result of the close personal and institutional working relationship amongst Ernest Jones-Parry, Executive Director of the International Sugar Council, Raúl Prebisch, Secretary-General of UNCTAD, and Albert Viton, Senior Director of the FAO.[752] This relationship, however, was not always easy, since each man and respective institution held a different view of the role of ICAs in development plans. Viton was acutely concerned with development issues, yet had very little patience for "Third World" rhetoric; he sympathized with North Atlantic perspectives, and perceived ICAs as about stabilizing commodity prices, primarily through setting quotas and prices.[753] Jones-Parry presented a draft ISA in 1965, which Prebisch regarded as representing the "spirit of UNCTAD."[754] This was because this draft (and the ensuing 1968 ISA) was one of the first treaties to widen "the terms of reference" of ICAs, from issues pertaining to a particular commodity to a program of stimulating economic development in developing countries.[755] Prebisch believed that this agreement was one of his personal successes during his tenure at UNCTAD.[756]

Nevertheless, there was tension between the International Sugar Council and UNCTAD. The council's institutional politics involved navigating between sugar importer and exporter interests. At times, the International Sugar Council derided UNCTAD's approach to political economy as utopian. UNCTAD was driven by its desire to instigate political economic changes on a global scale and saw the international sugar trade as part of this larger plan – this did not always coincide with

752 International Sugar Organization, "Statement by Dr. Prebisch to the Council on 27 January 1969," Press Summary 69(1) (February 20, 1969), AVP, Box 1, Folder 1.

753 Viton, *Sugar Agreements*, p. 122. 754 *Ibid.*, p. 124.

755 Hagelberg and Hannah, "Quest," 26.

756 International Sugar Organization, "Statement by Dr. Prebisch," pp. 7–8 (Prebisch also used the opportunity of presenting the 1968 ISA to discuss his resignation); Toye and Toye, *UN*, p. 209.

the International Sugar Council's interests.[757] According to UNCTAD's official history, even though the 1968 ISA was thought to be an important treaty, since it was part of UNCTAD's policies of the time and UNCTAD considered sugar to be a "core" commodity, the sugar treaty "was more the culmination of a long series of consultations dating back to 1966 than the result of the resolution adopted at UNCTAD II [calling for a sugar treaty]."[758] The negotiation amongst FAO, UNCTAD, and the International Sugar Council's different perspectives would continue from the 1960s into the 1970s.

The law and politics of the 1977 ISA

Sugar as a global exemplar

The 1977 ISA was considered be a "state-of-the-art" ICA, due to its technical innovation, regulatory breadth, and wide-ranging membership.[759] Like previous sugar treaties, the ISA 1977 created the International Sugar Organization (ISO), which was the international institution intended to regulate sugar trade. The ISO mainly functioned through the International Sugar Council, the Executive Committee, and the Executive Director.[760] The International Sugar Council was made up of representatives from member countries, with the power to determine quantitative restrictions,[761] interpret provisions,[762] and resolve disputes.[763] Much like the 1937 ISA, sugar exporting and importing capacity determined power within the sugar organization. Exporters and importers were each allocated 1,000 votes as a bloc. Each year, those 1,000 votes would be divided amongst the individual exporters and importers, determined by export and import levels.[764]

[757] Viton, *Sugar Agreements*, p. 133. Viton suggests that personality clashes amongst the three may also have contributed to some of the tension.

[758] United Nations Conference on Trade and Development, *UNCTAD*, p. 61.

[759] Mahler, "Political Economy," 719; Khan, *Law*, p. 142; Abbott, *Sugar*, p. 195.

[760] Art. 3. [761] Art. 19(1). [762] Art. 8. [763] Art. 70.

[764] Art. 11(5). The 1,000 exporter votes would be distributed pro rata, weighted according to the following factors: (1) basic export tonnages (50%); (2) total net exports to the free market (18%); (3) total net exports under special arrangements (7%); (4) total production (25%) (Art. 11(4)). Of the 1,000 importer votes, 900 would be allocated based on the average net imports from the free market of the highest three out of four preceding years; the remaining 100 votes would be distributed pro rata, based on the proportion of imports under special arrangements for the preceding year, as compared to total imports under special arrangements of all importing members for the preceding year.

What was unique about the 1977 ISA compared to previous sugar agreements was that not only did it include traditional importer–exporter politics, but it was also the meeting point for policies from the GATT and UNCTAD, and as such was one important site for North–South dialogues of the time. The GATT Panel had few problems with the 1977 ISA, and treated it as matter of fact when describing the international sugar market.[765] Likewise, the ISO accepted that the GATT was an uncontroversial multilateral trade organization.[766] In practice, the ISA and the GATT were not divided by fundamental intellectual differences, and there was no anxiety associated with any sort of fragmentation of international trade law. Instead, the two trade treaties were distinguished by their different functions. The GATT was like the 1902 Brussels Sugar Convention in that it was used by large sugar exporters to try to reduce domestic subsidies granted to European sugar producers through direct subsidies and high tariffs; the 1977 ISA was like the 1937 ISA in that it was used by sugar exporters and importers to regulate sugar production in an effort to stabilize the price of sugar.

In alignment with UNCTAD and NIEO, the 1977 ISA provided exceptions and leeway, which were intended mostly to benefit smaller developing countries that depended on sugar exports and were the most

[765] *EC – Sugar Exports* (Australia), Panel Report, L/4833, adopted November 6, 1979, BISD 26S/290, paras. 3.21, 4.15, 4.16, Conclusions para. (e); *EC – Sugar Exports* (Brazil), Panel Report, L/5011, adopted November 10, 1980, BISD 27S/69, paras. 4.17, 4.31, Conclusions para. (g).

[766] UNCTAD, UN Sugar Conference, Note by the Chairman on the Consultations Held in London, July 20–29, 1977, TD/SUGAR.9/EX/R.4 (August 8, 1977), p. 7. The International Sugar Organization Executive Director and Conference Chair, Ernest Jones-Parry, contemplated the following relationship between the GATT and the ISO:

"Suggestions were made that developed importing countries should give serious consideration to the effects that tariff and non-tariff barriers on imports of sugar had on sugar exports by developing exporting countries. What was required was the introduction of measures to remove obstacles to increased imports from free market exporting countries by stimulating sugar consumption and discouraging protected production as well as the manufacture of substitute sweeteners.

"Whilst it is recognized that this matter was being discussed in the context of the multilateral trade negotiations by GATT, it was urged that it also be included among the topics to be considered by the resumed Conference."

See also ISO, ISC, Report of the Proceedings of the Eighth Session (November 19–20, 1979), ISC-Report-8 (January 11, 1980), pp. 5–6; ISO, ISC, Exports of Sugar by the European Economic Community – Resolution by the Council, C(79)29 (November 20, 1979), p. 2; ISO, ISC, Exports of Sugar by the European Economic Community (Draft Resolution), C(79)28 (November 19, 1979), with handwritten notes by Albert Viton, AVP, Box 9, Folder 8.

vulnerable to price fluctuations.[767] Unlike when special and differential treatment for developing countries was brought into the GATT, this did not agitate developed countries and was not a controversial idea during ISA negotiations. While sugar agreements that followed the 1958 ISA were part of the rise of the Third World, by 1968 there were also signs that importing countries were regaining some ground. For example, a new supply commitment mechanism that benefited importers was introduced into the sugar agreement.[768]

The 1977 ISA was negotiated with an aim of creating a sugar treaty that was as flexible and proactive as possible. The concern was that previous agreements were too reflective of short-term market conditions, which included the status quo of sugar production and consumption patterns; they wanted the new agreement to be forward-looking enough to adequately respond to changes in the market.[769] Sugar agreements had traditionally focused on regulating the disequilibrium between supply and demand, usually by reducing sugar production levels. ISAs rarely survived radical changes in the sugar market, such as production or consumption level shifts or technological innovations.[770] Other flexibilities were negotiated in order not only to respond to market changes, but also to allow for the increase of quotas in light of domestic sugar shortages, or the development needs of small sugar producers.[771]

As with other sugar treaties, the most tense negotiations involved allocations of annual quotas to sugar exporters through what was called "basic export tonnages" (BETs), in order to stabilize the world price of sugar. The theory was that in times of high prices, BET allocations would be raised, thereby increasing supply and reducing the price. While in times of low prices, BETs would be decreased, thereby reducing supply

[767] Brazil Statement [n.d., likely circulated at the beginning of negotiations in April 1977], AVP, Box 8, Folder 16; UNCTAD, Economic Committee, Report by Chairman of Working Group I, TD/SUGAR.9/EX/C.I/R.10 (September 30, 1977).

[768] 1968 ISA: Art. 30. Khan, *Law*, pp. 139–41.

[769] ISO, Statement by the USSR Representative, Mr. V. N. Polejaev, at the Meeting of the Advisory Group of the International Sugar Council (London, April 7, 1976), Conc. C-Report-5 Annex (April 9, 1976), AVP, Box 8, Folder 5; n.a., "Notes and Comments" (May 1975).

[770] Khan, *Law*, p. 138.

[771] See UNCTAD, *Preparation of an International Agreement Embodying International Measures Considered Desirable; Basic export tonnages; Proposals submitted by the Chairman of the Conference*, TD/SUGAR.9/EX/R.6 (September 30, 1977); n.a. (March 7, 1975) 26 *Commodities Bulletin*, 9; Viton, *Sugar Agreements*, p. 230.

and increasing the price. This is where the highest stakes of sugar trade politics were negotiated, since a country's domestic quota was dictated by BET allocations.

It would too simple to think that only large exporters (Australia, Brazil, and Cuba) and large importers (the US, Japan, the USSR, and Canada) differed as to how to calculate BETs. Amongst the three largest exporters, there were significantly varying views as to how to calculate BETs.[772] There were also tensions between small and larger exporters, regardless of whether they were developed or developing.[773] Nevertheless, development still played a role, and Cuba, in line with global South politics, argued (albeit without success) that the degree of dependence on sugar should be included as a factor of quota determination.[774] In light of declining sugar prices, what was clear to everyone was that current production amounts had to be severely cut.[775]

The 1977 ISA's other advanced feature was its price regulation system. Looking at Table 8.3, we see that the 1977 sugar treaty had the broadest price range for any sugar treaty. Policy-makers thought that such an ambitious range would allow for the scope and flexibility needed to regulate more than supply–demand disequilibrium and

772 *Brazil Statement* [n.d., April 1977?, likely circulated during conference] (preferred BETs to be expressed as percentages and not tonnages, i.e. a global quota would be determined and divided into market shares); *Cuba Statement*, [n.d., April 1977?, likely circulated during conference]; *Statement by Mr. Marcelo Fernandez Font, Minister of Foreign Trade of Cuba, the United Nations Sugar Conference, 1977 (non-official translation)* (April 20, 1977) (Cuba preferred BETs to be expressed in quantities). Even though one conference Working Group Chairman characterized this as a technical issue, the ensuing difference was more than one of calculation, since each proposed method would benefit the respective exporter; *Working Group I; [Personal] Progress Report of Chairman* (May 12, 1977). AVP, Box 8, Folder 16.

773 Developing exporting members were defined to be all exporting members in Latin America, including the Greater Caribbean area; Africa, except South Africa; Asia; Oceania, except Australia; and Romania. No importing countries were designated as developing at the time of drafting the Agreement, but provision was made in Annex III for a review of whether new importer members were developing countries upon their membership. Least developed countries were enumerated in Annex IV, according to UN designation. And although developing countries were defined in the Agreement (Annex III) to include all Latin American countries, including the Greater Caribbean areas, smaller developing country exporters did not always look favorably upon the larger exporters, such as Brazil and Cuba.

774 Viton, *Sugar Agreements*, pp. 211–12.

775 UNCTAD, *Preparation of an International Agreement Embodying International Measures Considered Desirable; Basic export tonnages; Proposals submitted by the Chairman of the Conference*, TD/SUGAR.9/EX/R.5 (September 9, 1977), p. 1.

Table 8.3 Price range of postwar ICA (US cents/lb)

ISA	Minimum price	Maximum price
1953	3.25	4.35
1958	3.15	4.00
1968	3.25	5.25
1977	11.00	21.00

Source: ISA 1953, Art. 20; ISA 1958, Art. 21; ISA 1968, Art. 48; ISA 1977, Art. 44

respond to major changes in the market.[776] The price-regulating scheme was innovative because it included a complex system of quotas and stock release that allowed for relatively adaptable responses to rising and dropping sugar prices.[777]

The free market as constituted by an international institution

In 1974, the world sugar industries, and especially the sugar producers, were quite disappointed with the 1973 ISA, since it did not have any economic provisions. This meant that the international sugar market had no mechanisms to control the price of sugar. This disappointment quickly dissipated when sugar peaked at an annual average of US 29.7 cents per pound. But when prices suddenly dropped, in 1976, to US 8.2 cents per pound, a price estimated to be below the cost of production in most places, many thought that international sugar treaty negotiations would be inevitable.[778]

Going into the 1977 ISA negotiations, sugar experts were optimistic, since they that thought political conditions, and not just economic necessity, were ripe for a successful and effective sugar treaty. The US, which was the largest sugar consumer in the world, and the EEC, which was emerging as the largest sugar producer, were invited to participate. Experts were also encouraged by the fact that important "structural" changes had taken place in the world sugar market, namely, the repeal of the US Sugar Act in 1974, the end of the Commonwealth Sugar Agreement, the end of the African and Malagasy Sugar Agreement, and the signing of the EEC Lomé Convention in 1975.[779]

[776] Khan, *Law*, pp. 138–9. Nevertheless, the price of sugar was often significantly below or above the ISA price range; see Raffaelli, *Rise and Demise*, p. 120.

[777] Arts. 41, 44, 57. [778] n.a., "Sugar in the Year 1976." [779] Smith, "Structure."

To appreciate why these were thought to be significant changes, it is necessary to understand that ever since the 1937 ISA, the world sugar market was divided between "special arrangements" and the "free market." Special arrangements were either multilateral or bilateral treaties that granted preferential market access for certain sugar exporters, often at a price higher than the world market.[780] The free market was then characterized as "residual," both because it was whatever sugar was exported after domestic consumption and special arrangement exports, and because it constituted the minority amount of sugar produced in the world.

During the 1970s, many equated support for the ISA with support for the free market and liberal trade.[781] Some even suggested that ever since 1937, ISAs were an effort to prevent protectionism.[782] In 1954, sugar exported to the free market was 19 percent of sugar produced in the world; in 1961, it was 24 percent; and in 1975, it would go down to 16 percent.[783] Thus, special arrangements were the political norm, but the legal and economic exception. The end of the US Sugar Act marked the first time since the 1930s that US domestic sugar would not be regulated by high tariffs and price controls and, as such, the first time that the US would be included in the world "free market" of sugar.

The common question at the time was not whether regulation was desirable or not. Rather, it was a matter of what sort of regulation was best, and the ensuing debates were then a question of what was meant by "best," and best for whom? The minority view held that the ideal market was an "unregulated" sphere of economic exchange.[784] The more popular definition of the "free market" of the time allowed for international price regulation when prices were so high or low as to cause socio-economic hardship in parts of the sugar sector.

Since the 1930s, Cuba, like many of the large sugar exporters, had been sensitive to the fact that special arrangement markets affected

[780] Smith, "Commonwealth," pp. 49, 53.

[781] UNCTAD, UN Sugar Conference, Economic Committee, Report by the Chairman of Working Group V, TD/SUGAR.9/EX/C.I/R.8 (September 27, 1977); UNCTAD, UN Sugar Conference, Economic Committee, Report by the Chairman of Working Group V, TD/SUGAR.9/EX/C.I/R.8 Add. 1 (September 27, 1977); UNCTAD, UN Sugar Conference, Economic Committee, Report by the Chairman of Working Group V, TD/SUGAR.9/EX/C.I/R.8 TD/SUGAR.9/EX/C.1/CRP.32 (May 18, 1977).

[782] Smith, "Commonwealth," p. 59.

[783] Hagelberg, "International Sugar Agreements," 8.

[784] n.a. (March 7, 1975) 26 *Commodities Bulletin*, 8.

free market prices.[785] But there were different proposals over how to structure the relationship between the free market and special arrangements. To some economists, specialized markets destabilized the price of sugar, and they wanted to restrict them as much as possible, if not do away with them entirely.[786] Exporters with favorable terms in special arrangements wanted to preserve those arrangements and depended on the free market to export their surplus sugar. Developing countries that depended on the global export of sugar advocated for ISAs that regulated special arrangements *and* the free market, since price stability in both were interlinked.

Buffer stock politics

The 1977 ISA was the only sugar agreement to use buffer stocks as a mechanism to stabilize the global price of sugar. To some, the sugar treaty's buffer stock system was influenced and inspired by UNCTAD's Common Fund for Commodities proposal, which was negotiated in the context of the NIEO Integrated Programme for Commodities around the same time.[787] Others have suggested that the 1977 ISA negotiations were not only about sugar in the context of developed and developing countries, but also that they determined the future of UNCTAD's ambitious commodity program.[788] The 1977 ISA was negotiated at UNCTAD facilities, lending further credence to the characterization of the sugar agreement as an UNCTAD/NIEO treaty. Besides, this was the first ICA that explicitly referenced UNCTAD's Integrated Programme for Commodities.[789]

It is, however, unfounded to assume that UNCTAD influenced the inclusion of buffer stocks into the 1977 ISA. Buffer stocks were not a new idea to ICAs in general. They were part of agreements for other commodities, such as tin, cocoa, and natural rubber. Moreover, the negotiation record does not entirely support the idea of buffer sugar stocks originating from UNCTAD proposals.[790] Nor did all the sugar negotiators (such as developing countries who were large exporters) originally want to include a reference to the Common Fund for Commodities.[791]

[785] *Address by the Chief of the Cuban Delegation, Raul Leon Torras, First Deputy of Foreign Trade*, [n.d. 1968?, likely circulated during conference], AVP, Box 1, Folder 1.

[786] n.a., "Notes and Comments" (February 1975); Harris, "British Sugar."

[787] n.a., "Sugar in the Year 1976," 225; Goldberg, "Prospects," 599.

[788] Hagelberg, "International Sugar Agreements," 10. [789] Arts. 1, 55.

[790] Brown, *Primary Commodity Control*, p. 179; n.a., "Notes and Comments" (January 1978).

[791] India proposed late into negotiations that when the Common Fund was established, that the International Sugar Council "*shall consider* the relationship between the

Scholars at the time were actually divided as to how much the 1977 ISA reflected the "spirit of UNCTAD" – that is, using international law and institutions to redistribute global wealth and power to benefit the poorer Third World.[792] While UNCTAD may have provided some intellectual legitimacy to the general idea of internationally regulated buffer stocks, delegates negotiated over and designed the 1977 ISA in order to stabilize the price of sugar to meet domestic welfare and development needs (aligning with embedded liberalism), and not to redistribute global wealth (as NIEO demanded). UNCTAD's buffer stock proposal had different implications than that created by the 1977 ISA. The 1977 ISA established a system of sugar stockpiles that would be held by national governments, but financed and regulated through an international institution (the ISO). Along different lines, UNCTAD proposed a global program of internationally held, financed, and regulated stocks. Thus, under the UNCTAD proposal, the international institution itself held more power over decisions than did individual countries.

Not only did the ISA buffer proposal differ from the Common Fund for Commodities, but during negotiations there were actually different conceptions of what sort of buffer stocks governments wanted, and for what reasons. The EEC made one of the first calls for a sugar agreement which principally regulated the price of sugar through buffer stocks.[793] One sugar economist at the time caught a peculiar congruity between the 1977 ISA negotiations and UNCTAD:

Agreement and the Common Fund, with a view to enabling appropriate advantage to be taken of the financial arrangements with the Common Fund." India brought forward this idea on behalf of several Asian exporters, who were reacting against proposals for a buffer stock under the proposed sugar treaty that only contemplated preventing the "the rise of prices beyond an agreed level coupled with a quota mechanism to bring about a better balance between supply and demand." UNCTAD, UN Sugar Conference, Economic Committee, Working Group I, Article VII; Relationship with a Common Fund; Proposal by India, TD/SUGAR.9/EX/C.I/WG.I/CRP.12 (September 12, 1977) [emphasis added]. To these Asian countries, only focusing on the supply and demand of one commodity would still adversely affect resource and development plans of developing countries; "Statement made by the Indian Delegation on behalf of Philippines, Indonesia, Thailand and India on 23rd September, 1977," AVP, Box 8, Folder 12. The final language of the 1977 ISA in Article 55, however, was less binding that the original proposal.

792 Khan, "Sugar Agreement"; *contra* Brown, *Political and Social Economy*, p. 179.

793 Sir Guy Sauzier, representing Mauritius, also wanted a sugar agreement whose principal price control mechanism was buffer stocks. Mauritius is a small African island, which, at the time, depended on sugar and had very few resources to diversify its economy, whether with other primary commodities or through attempts at industrialization. Its only hope was to expand its sugar production capacities for the

It is interesting that both the US and EEC proposals were closer to NIEO commodity agreement strategy in their emphasis on buffer stocks, than the draft prepared by the mainly developing country ISA membership.[794]

A buffer stock allowed for more production, since excess sugar could be stored for future export. Under such a system, sugar prices were regulated by controlling sugar *distribution*. This was different than a quota system, which determined sugar *production* in advance and was most often used to curtail the amount of sugar made. Large sugar exporters preferred a system that did not create incentive for others to increase their production levels, for not only did it create more competition, but it also made it more difficult to ensure stable, if not higher, prices of sugar.

The EEC proposal led to some of the most vigorous disagreements during negotiations. The EEC isolated itself from negotiations from the beginning, by consistently rejecting export quotas as outdated and insisting on a buffer stock-only ISA.[795] Some even thought that the EEC's stubborn position regarding a buffer stock-only sugar agreement was disingenuous, because the EEC was planning to continue to expand its sugar production and never intended to participate in the treaty.[796]

The EEC officially noted its surprise that other countries reacted against their proposals, and referenced other ICAs that used buffer stocks, as well as UNCTAD plans to buttress the legitimacy of their position.[797] This reference to UNCTAD is misleading at best, and insincere at worst. Even

purposes of export. Sauzier's proposal had one significant difference from that of the EEC – it contemplated an internationally financed scheme, which meant more control by the ISC over the international regulation of nationally held stock than in the EEC's nationally financed stock plan. ISO, Executive Director, "A Possible Approach to a New International Sugar Agreement," by Sir Guy Sauzier, C.B.E., ISO Memo 76(18) (March 25, 1976), AVP, Box 8, Folder 5. Sauzier, however, distinguished his proposal for an "intervention stock" from a "buffer stock," even though the two terms were commonly used interchangeably. But it was never clear what that distinction is. Sauzier never mentions UNCTAD and it is possible that he wanted to distance his proposal from UNCTAD.

794 Harris, "Policy Attitudes," 363.

795 Albert Viton, handwritten notes from the International Sugar Council Preparatory Committee meeting, January 30[?] – February 4, 1977, AVP, Box 8, Folder 15; ISO, Preparatory Committee, Draft Agenda for the First Meeting of the Preparatory Committee, Prep.C/Agenda (77)1 (January 4, 1977), AVP, Box 8, Folder 15. Viton's notes during the ISA Preparatory Committee right before the 1977 ISA negotiations meeting indicate that the EEC delegate characterized the previous system of quotas as outdated and not reflective of current realities akin to the Bourbon. The Australian and Cuban members responded that the EEC itself was the Bourbon.

796 Gilbert, "Agreements: Obituary," 5.

797 UNCTAD, UN Sugar Conference, Economic Committee, Report by the Chairman of Working Group I, TD/SUGAR.9/EX/C.I/R.3 (May 24, 1977). See also Comité Européen des

though both the EEC and UNCTAD had proposed buffer stocks as a means of stabilizing commodity (in this case, sugar) prices, the implications and character of the two schemes were significantly different.

The UNCTAD proposal for buffer stocks was for an internationally controlled, held, and financed system of buffer stocks to be used to regulate the price of multiple commodities; whereas the EEC proposed a sugar buffer stock system that was to be nationally held and financed, and only internationally "coordinated."[798] In sum, a call for an ISA that primarily relied on a buffer stock scheme, regardless of whether the purpose was to ensure the welfare of a developing country or to provide a market for a subsidized sugar industry, was an argument that benefited sugar producers who wanted to expand sugar production and compete with more established exporters, such as Cuba, Australia, and Brazil.

In 1975, Jones-Parry and the International Sugar Council Secretariat also proposed that the 1977 ISA should employ a buffer stock.[799] At first, the vast majority of International Sugar Council members supported a traditional type of sugar agreement, which only relied on export quotas, and there was little support for Jones-Parry's idea.[800] Jones-Parry presented his plan as a technical necessity to ensure a flexible treaty that was most responsive to changes in the market. In effect, he managed to find the common ground amongst the different interests. He suggested

Fabricants de Sucre, "Some Thoughts on the Negotiation of a New International Sugar Agreement" (September 6, 1977), AVP, Box 8, Folder 5. The Confédération Internationale des Betteraviers Européens and Comité Européen des Fabricants de Sucre, respectively representing European sugar beet growers and sugar refiners, supported (if not determined) the EEC policy, and also referenced UNCTAD's Common Fund as precedent to the idea of buffer stocks.

798 For the EEC's proposal, see ISO, Consultative Committee, "New International Sugar Agreement (Outline of EEC Approach)," Con.C/18 (November 15, 1976), AVP, Box 8, Folder 10; UNCTAD, UN Sugar Conference, Economic Committee, Chapters X–XII of the draft Agreement, Proposal by the European Economic Community, TD/SUGAR.9/EX/C.I/CRP.14 (May 6, 1977); UNCTAD, UN Sugar Conference, Economic Committee, Report by the Chairman of Working Group I, TD/SUGAR.9/EX/C.I/R.3 (May 24, 1977).

799 n.a. (March 7, 1975) 26 *Commodities Bulletin*, 10–11.

800 The anticipated difficulties for such a scheme would be determining the minimum price, determining the price at which the stock manager had the discretion to release stock into the market, and the cost and logistics of actually holding and maintaining stock. Some major sugar producers were averse to the idea because it was institutionally complex and financially costly. See, e.g., Memorandum by Albert Viton, "Recent Discussion of the International Sugar Council on a New International Agreement" (June 10, 1975, likely an internal FAO memo), AVP, Box 8, Folder 2; n.a., "Notes and Comments" (April 1975).

that the new sugar agreement be devised to protect minimum sugar prices. The argument was that a new sugar agreement would be the most flexible if it included both a system of quotas and a buffer stock – the stock protected a floor price and quotas ensured that sugar stock would not pile up. Moreover, Jones-Parry emphasized that such a system would stabilize sugar prices, thereby underwriting developed exporter expansion, and safeguarding developing exporter interests. Importer needs would also be met, since sugar supplies would be maintained.[801] The fact that major exporters such as Cuba and Australia, going into the 1977 sugar negotiations, were actually willing to contemplate a price-regulating system primarily based on quotas, but with some provision for buffer stocks, suggests that one of the reasons that Jones-Parry's idea was eventually taken up was for the technical reasons he put forward.[802]

In Polanyian terms, UNCTAD imagined sugar as embedded within a global primary commodities market, which thereby demanded international institutional regulation. The EEC made little provision for multilateralism and imagined sugar as embedded within a domestic/regional agriculture market, regulated by regional institutions which would potentially benefit by some sort of international coordination; while the International Sugar Council Secretariat proposed a buffer stock that was internationally financed and controlled, but nationally held. It adhered to embedded liberalism's sensibility in that it was a multilateral system that found political compromise amongst the different types of sugar producers and consumers, and that addressed domestic welfare and development concerns – which is probably why it was the scheme that was eventually adopted. This scheme not only provided market stability, but also included sugar regulation flexibility, by creating exceptions and special funds through a "Hardship Reserve" for developing small exporters.[803]

The final price mechanism included a series of quotas that would be imposed according to the price of sugar. Different mechanisms were triggered, depending on whether the price of sugar was increasing or

801 n.a., "Notes and Comments" (April 1975).

802 See Australian memo, "The Possible Use of Stocks as a Short Term Market Regulating Device in Export Quota Type I.S.A." (January 1977), [probably circulated at the ISC Preparatory Committee meeting], AVP, Box 8, Folder 15.

803 UNCTAD, *Preparation of an International Agreement Embodying International Measures Considered Desirable; Basic export tonnages; Proposals submitted by the Chairman of the Conference*, TD/SUGAR.9/EX/R.6 (September 30, 1977), pp. 1–2.

decreasing. Generally, when the price of sugar dropped to below US 14 cents per pound, then the global export quota would be reduced and the stock would be replenished. When the price of sugar rose to 13 cents, the global quota would be increased. When sugar was between 15 and 18 cents, there were to be no quota restrictions or reserve stock intervention. When the price of sugar rose to 19 cents, one-third of the buffer stock would be released. At 20 cents, another third would be released, and the final third of the stock would be released if the price reached 21 cents. If the price rose above 21 cents, no price-regulating mechanisms would apply.

The remaining question was how to finance the buffer stock. The US had opposed the EEC's proposal, which some interpreted as a principled position against any buffer stock system. But as the world's largest importer, it was also worried about sugar shortages. Two days after the US made its opening statement at the 1977 conference, it proposed a mandatory stock stabilization fund, "which turned the Conference upside down … for which delegations were in no way prepared."[804]

The final negotiated scheme, proposed by the US, was a reserve stock which set aside a certain amount of sugar that would be financed through a system of fees paid by importers and exporters, paid to the ISO or its agents. These fees would constitute a Sugar Stabilization Fund for the purpose of administering the financial operation of the scheme.[805] Not only did this scheme broadly align with Jones-Parry's proposal, but it also provided importers with the strongest assurance of supplies they had ever had.[806] The twist was that the US's proposal for a Sugar Stabilization Fund seemed similar to UNCTAD's Common Fund idea. The significant difference, however, was that the US's proposal was

[804] Viton, *Sugar Agreements*, p. 200; UNCTAD, UN Sugar Conference, "Note by the Chairman," p. 2. Like the 1968 ISA, the US proposed that the new treaty would have a minimum stock of 2 million tonnes. What was unique about the US's proposal was that the fund would be financed by importers and exporters, and that there would be an additional "special stock" of 2 million tonnes "that would attract financial assistance." This division of stocks was an idea which many found difficult to understand, and the US created further confusion when it did not specify how the special stock would be financed.

[805] UNCTAD, UN Sugar Conference, "Note by the Chairman," pp. 2–3. The final scheme was a special stock of 2.5 million tonnes, which was distributed and held by each exporting country, pro rata, according to their BET (Art. 46(3)).

[806] Khan, *Law*, p. 141.

intended to protect importers' interests, whereas UNCTAD's Common Fund was an attempt to protect exporters' interests.

Many characterized the 1977 ISA as inadequate because the EEC did not sign the agreement, and thus the agreement was not as complete as possible in regulating the world sugar market.[807] If this was a failure, it was political, not functional. It is important to remember that the price of sugar in 1977 was quite low and sugar producers were barely breaking even; thus the negotiators' priority was to reduce sugar production through BET levels and quota reductions, in order to increase the price of sugar. So the fact that the EEC never signed the 1977 ISA, increased its sugar production, and expanded its trade suggests that its main priority was production expansion, not price stabilization.[808] Many states resented the fact that the EEC was obstinate throughout negotiations, and questioned whether it entered talks in good faith. When the 1977 ISA was signed, members immediately reduced the production of sugar by approximately 2.2 million tonnes in 1978, and again in 1979, in an attempt to control plummeting sugar prices.[809] EEC sugar producers did not have to worry about low prices because they were heavily subsidized. Many thought that the EEC's decision not to sign the sugar treaty allowed it to reap the potential benefits of the treaty (a stable world sugar market) without having to adhere to international market regulation or treaty costs, allowing it to become the world's largest sugar producer.[810]

Another political frustration surrounding the ISA had to do with the US's slow ratification. Even though the US was structuring its domestic sugar policies around a successful ISA, the Senate took two years to ratify its membership.[811] The opposition was not against the agreement as such. Instead, the delay arose from the negotiation amongst domestic sugar interests, which wanted to ensure that adequate domestic safeguards were put into place, in light of the liberal sugar trade treaty. US Democratic Senator Frank Church, who was head of the Foreign

807 Gilbert, "Agreements: Obituary"; Smith, "Prospects," 318; Viton, *Sugar Agreements*, p. 230; Abbott, *Sugar*, p. 201.

808 Maizels, *Commodities*, pp. 132–3; ISO, ISC, Report on the Proceedings of the Second Session (May 17–18, 1978), ISC-Rep-2 (June 12, 1978), pp. 4–6, AVP, Box 8, Folder 10.

809 Abbott, *Sugar*, p. 201.

810 *Ibid.*; Maizels, *Commodities*, p. 133; Letter from "Michel" (Comité Européen des Fabricants de Sucre) to Albert Viton (FAO), July 12, 1978; Letter from G. Peroud (Confédération Internationale des Betteraviers Européens) to Albert Viton (FAO), July 13, 1978, AVP, Box 9, Folder 3.

811 Harris, "Policy Attitudes," 364.

Relations Committee, held up the process until Carter agreed to a price support system that would benefit beet growers in Church's state of Idaho. This domestic negotiation, against the backdrop of international law, looked to be a continuation of embedded liberalism's politics. But the effect of such a delay meant that the system of special stocks, which was included upon the US's insistence, was financially constrained until the US ratified the treaty.[812]

The death of ICAs

The 1977 ISA was the last sugar agreement to include economic provisions that purported to regulate the sugar market.[813] By 1980, many people were already losing confidence in the treaty's ability to stabilize sugar prices.[814] Many sugar diplomats considered the move from economic sugar agreements to toothless administrative sugar agreements to be the result of ISAs' failure to stabilize the price of sugar. Only now, however, can we appreciate that the end of sugar agreements with economic provisions was not only a result of the 1977 ISA's functionality.

The end of economic sugar treaties can best be explained as part of a general eroding faith in ICAs.[815] The collapse of the International Tin Agreement and the bankruptcy of the International Tin Council, along with its stabilization fund, in 1985, sounded the death knell of ICAs as an idea.[816] By the late 1980s, in light the dubious status of the Common Fund for Commodities, this lack of confidence broadened to include UNCTAD.[817] By the mid-1990s, experts would pronounce ICAs to be dead.[818]

Assuming that collapse of the Tin Agreement caused the demise of ICAs is too simplistic in light of the complex results of ICAs; it also ignores moments in the history of ICAs when they succeeded in

[812] Viton, *Sugar Agreements*, pp. 220–1.

[813] Subsequent sugar agreements can be described as administrative in nature, since they only focus on the sharing and dissemination of information.

[814] "The International Agreement: Address by William K. Miller, Executive Director, International Sugar Organization to the Sugar Club, New York, May 14, 1980," AVP, Box 9, Folder 10.

[815] Lowenfeld, "Book Review"; Rangarajan, "Commodity Conflict Revisited"; Gilbert, "Agreements: Obituary."

[816] Chimni, *Agreements*, pp. 197–215. [817] Yusuf, "Legal Framework," p. 63.

[818] Quill, "Failure"; Raffaelli, *Rise and Demise*; Gilbert, "Agreements: Obituary."

controlling prices. Rather, the collapse of the Tin Agreement in 1985 exemplified a moment in time when the *idea* of ICAs had lost political and intellectual popularity.[819]

The global collapse of commodity prices in 1980–2 that devastated the Third World, and an economic recession and high unemployment in many First World countries, destabilized embedded liberalism's hold on global policy-making. As a result, embedded liberalism was assaulted from the left by NIEO, and from the right by neoliberalism.[820] While much has been written about neoliberalism, it is worth outlining the institutional politics of how NIEO challenged embedded liberalism.

At UNCTAD II, the focus was on creating an integrated commodity policy and the need for a "general agreement on commodity arrangements."[821] Prebisch left open the possibility of negotiations to proceed on the basis of individual commodities, but suggested that this was not incompatible with laying down certain general principles for all ICAs. He believed that certain basic principles could be established to ensure that ICAs would stabilize fluctuating commodity prices.[822]

NIEO's language devised a clearer agenda.[823] After UNCTAD IV, Corea led the effort to operationalize the NIEO call and created the Integrated Programme for Commodities and the Common Fund for Commodities. International trade law and policy were now about ensuring that all ICAs were rationally organized by one institution for the purpose of price regulation, in order to benefit countries of the Third World.[824] UNCTAD's working premise now was that the global commodity market was primarily embedded in a global social context, and thus only a global institution would be able to regulate commodities – thereby moving away from embedded liberalism.

Until this point, ICAs were negotiated on a commodity-by-commodity basis by essentially independent bodies, with no clear common objective. The Integrated Programme for Commodities was the first time that one international organization attempted to bring

[819] Gilbert, "Agreements: Obituary."

[820] Neoliberalism was an emerging global political economic consensus, with a descriptive aversion against treating markets as institutions, normative penchant for deregulation, and inherent bias in favor of markets as the principal social forum.

[821] United Nations Conference on Trade and Development, *Proceedings*, pp. 34–8.

[822] Prebisch, *Global Strategy*, pp. 16–18.

[823] E.g. United Nations General Assembly, Programme for Action on the Establishment of a New International Economic Order, May 1, 1974, Res. 3202 (S-VI), sect. 1, para. 3(a)(iv).

[824] See Corea, *Taming*; Cuddy, "Theory and Practice."

all ICAs within a single institution, directed by a single fund. In the past, two commodities, sugar and wheat, were negotiated under the auspices of the League of Nations, and both agreements employed doctrines of rationalization. Nonetheless, each commodity agreement's respective institution was designed to operate mostly autonomously from the League. This was also not the first time that a fund was created to stabilize commodity prices. In partial response to UNCTAD II, the IMF created the Buffer Stock Facility.[825] This program, however, was not empowered to finance internationally controlled commodities and was put to little use.[826]

UNCTAD's new program also differed in form from the ITO Charter because it treated the regulation of international commodities as the norm, rather than the exception. The Integrated Programme for Commodities was intended to cover a wide range of commodities, in order to permit and encourage simultaneous negotiations, which would allow for an overall balancing of interests. Also, the Common Fund was intended to promote the timely conclusion of ICAs, since the question of financing would be prearranged.[827]

Western countries preferred to negotiate ICAs in a piecemeal fashion and had regularly opposed Prebisch's suggestion of integrating commodity policies.[828] According to some, OPEC's success in raising oil prices in 1973–4 provided evidence of the potential strength of commodity producers of the South in relation to the North.[829] Thus, the Integrated Programme for Commodities was also thought to be bold in its politics, since it allowed developing countries to negotiate as a bloc.

Despite its innovative institutional structure and radical politics, the Integrated Programme for Commodities was not a new idea. This was a well-known economic policy serving a new political program. As mentioned, during the final years of the Second World War, Keynes devised an economic recovery plan which included the creation of an international buffer stock scheme to regulate the price of primary commodities. He envisaged an international organization, albeit primarily driven by Anglo-American interests, to be created, along

[825] Horsefield (ed.), *International Monetary Fund*, vol. I, p. 609.
[826] Brown, *Primary Commodity Control*, p. 99.
[827] Maizels, "World Economy," pp. 101, 106. [828] Corea, *Taming*, pp. 44–5.
[829] Weiss *et al.* (eds.), *UN Voices*, pp. 225–32.

with the International Monetary Fund and the International Bank of Reconstruction and Development, which would stabilize commodity prices.[830] Nicholas Kaldor, the famed economist, would revisit Keynes's ideas and conclude that UNCTAD's Common Fund had the same effect as Keynes's proposal.[831]

When the Integrated Programme for Commodities was launched in 1976, six ICAs were already in operation – tin, coffee, cocoa, sugar, wheat, and olive oil.[832] Cocoa, tin, sugar, and wheat negotiations were thought by some to be nominally UN undertakings, because G77 or NIEO doctrine barely appeared in most commodity negotiations. With the exception of Prebisch's involvement in the 1968 International Sugar Agreement negotiations, the UNCTAD secretariat's main contribution during the negotiations was thought to be the provision of conference facilities.[833]

Different ICAs, informed by embedded liberalism, employed diverse forms for market regulation, all of which included the international regulation of commodity prices, through both international and domestic institutions. NIEO only focused on redistribution of wealth on an international scale, and did not address or make provision for domestic policies of redistribution. The fact that the Integrated Programme for Commodities was a plan to control international commodities, though UNCTAD held, controlled, and financed stock, did not sit too easily with national governments. Commodity producers, especially Latin American countries, expressed anxiety in regard to the Common Fund, because they feared that they would lose decision-making power over certain products, such as setting maximum and minimum prices, to a forum where countries without an interest in those products would participate. What is also telling is that major commodity producers, such as Brazil, Malaysia, Ivory Coast, Chile, and Colombia, did not lead in creating the Integrated Programme.[834]

National governments' fears over of the potential demise of ICAs and losing control of commodity trade to UNCTAD were not unfounded. Members of the UNCTAD Secretariat thought that a single agency, most likely the Common Fund, could regulate commodity price fluctuation. UNCTAD's original proposal placed very little emphasis on ICAs. According to Corea:

[830] John Maynard Keynes, "Letter to Sir Arnold Overton" (February 3, 1943); "Letter to Sir Arnold Overton" (February 12, 1943); "Letter to James Meade" (December 15, 1942), reprinted in Moggridge, (ed.), *Collected Writings*, vol. XXVI, pp. 261, 266, 268, 272.

[831] Kaldor, "Commodity Prices." [832] Corea, *Taming*, p. 141.

[833] Weiss, *Diplomacy*, pp. 104–5. [834] *Ibid.*, pp. 44–5.

in its original form, the thrust of the proposed Integrated Programme was clearly the establishment of international stocking arrangements rather than negotiation of a series of individual commodity agreements.[835]

The reasoning was that, "This would dispense with the frustrations that seemed inevitable in the negotiation of traditional commodity agreements."[836] In the end, UNCTAD did not submit this idea to the governments.[837] In fact, the Latin American countries would insist that the Common Fund would regulate commodity markets via individual ICAs.[838]

By now, industrialized countries were, for the most part, responsive to the idea of commodity regulation and ICAs. They reacted most vehemently against the idea of the Common Fund. Corea was the subject of these criticisms, and therefore it is worth quoting him at some length:

> The prospect of establishing a single institution with the authority and resources to intervene in commodity markets – possibly outside the framework of commodity agreements – was truly alarming among them [developed countries]. Their anxiety was all the greater in light of the prospect that the control of such an institution would not be in their hands, and that it would not be dependent on them for financing. To the developed countries the Common Fund was the most dangerous element of the Integrated Programme and the one to be resisted most fiercely.[839]

From all this, we can detect that national governments from both the North and South, to some degree, accepted ICAs, yet they were either cautious or opposed outright to the idea of UNCTAD gaining power over the regulation of commodities. The UNCTAD Secretariat positioned the Integrated Programme for Commodities and the Common Fund as an "all or nothing" component of NIEO,[840] thereby raising the stakes behind ICAs and interlinking the fate of the commodity policy with

[835] Corea, *Taming*, p. 34. [836] *Ibid.*

[837] *Ibid.*, pp. 33, 44–6. Oil producers were also cool about the idea of the Integrated Programme for Commodities and the Common Fund, since they were asked to provide a significant amount of the financing and because they were commodity importers, not exporters. The socialist countries of Eastern Europe responded favorably to the UNCTAD initiative, but did not champion the Common Fund. They were not very enthusiastic about buffer stocks, but made no objections. They preferred contractual arrangements and quota schemes over market operations by an intergovernmental agency. They were also cautious about joining an international financial institution.

[838] Toye and Toye, *UN*, p. 245. [839] Corea, *Taming*, p. 45.

[840] United Nations Conference on Trade and Development, *UNCTAD*, p. 64.

NIEO doctrines. Thomas Weiss, a former Senior Economic Affairs Officer in UNCTAD, would wonder, "If the past approach of UNCTAD had been more oriented toward individual commodities rather than global and confrontational, more might have been achieved and could still be achieved."[841]

Conclusion

The end of the last economic sugar agreement coincided with the global shifts in power. Many situate the end of UNCTAD as a Third World forum, and the end of "North–South dialogue" at the Conference on International Cooperation and Development held on October 21–22, 1981, in Cancún.[842] This conference made it clear that developed countries had regained power in determining global economic policy. This also marked a shift in developing countries' discourse. As Robert Cox quipped about this time, "The NIEO was killed by neoliberalism."[843] But so was embedded liberalism. The institutionally corollary was that UNCTAD and ICAs were killed by the GATT/WTO. Starting around 1979, UNCTAD started looking for a "different analytical base."[844] Soon after, UNCTAD went through a "crisis, retreat, and reinvention," and by the mid-1980s, as the Uruguay Round began, UNCTAD and many developing country leaders decided that developing countries should direct most of their trade law and policy energy into the GATT.[845]

Even those from the North and South who had not given up entirely on ICAs as an idea, started to look to the GATT, rather than UNCTAD, as the institutional milieu for ICAs.[846] There was also a shift from discussing ICAs in terms of debating appropriate economic mechanisms regulating prices, to suggesting that international commodity organizations should focus on administrative functions, such as research, consultation, and international cooperation[847] – which is the status of most ICAs today.

[841] Weiss, *Diplomacy*, p. 106.

[842] Weiss *et al.* (eds.), *UN Voices*, p. 258; Tomlinson, "Third World," 314; Toye and Toye, *UN*, pp. 272–4.

[843] Weiss *et al.* (eds.), *UN Voices*, p. 258. [844] *Ibid.*, p. 198.

[845] Taylor and Smith, *UNCTAD*, pp. 67–90; Kasahara and Gore (eds.), *Conventional Wisdom*, pp. 5–10.

[846] Mark and Weston, "Havana Charter," vol. I, p. 45; The South Centre, *Problems and Policies*.

[847] Gordon-Ashworth, *Commodity Control*, p. 286; McIntyre, "Summary and Conclusions," p. 423.

Within the League of Nations and ITO, ICAs were part of a broader economic agenda. After the end of the ITO, embedded liberalism's compromises unraveled and spun off into two different institutional forms. The GATT regulated the international trade of manufactured products and was thought to reflect primarily Northern interests. UNCTAD focused on the international trade of agricultural products and was thought to reflect primarily Southern interests. Since the 1902 Brussels Sugar Convention, countries always had different understandings regarding the purpose of trade and the function of multilateral trade institutions. What is remarkable is that the demise of the ITO marked a moment in modern trade history which is defined by inter-institutional conflict. Both state and institutional actors argued over different conceptions of trade, and over who claimed institutional legitimacy to define what international trade meant.[848]

By the 1970s, the intuitional landscape of international trade/economic law was functionally differentiated into different international institutions. The GATT was informed by embedded liberalism for the purpose of maintaining domestic and international stability in industry, whereas UNCTAD would be informed by embedded liberalism for the purpose of ensuring domestic and international stability in agriculture. The GATT had only one reference to agriculture and it was an exception to a rule – the GATT generally prohibited quantitative restrictions (quotas, import/export licenses, and the like) on the import and export of products, but allowed some exceptions for agricultural products.[849] These products could be restricted if they were used as part of a domestic price support system, which, according to the logic of embedded liberalism, many developed countries used to secure full employment.[850] Developed and developing countries would then use UNCTAD to negotiate their interests in the international regulation of trade in agricultural products, while using the GATT for manufactured products.

[848] I borrow and adapt this idea from Koskenniemi, "Politics," 10.

[849] GATT Art. XI.2(c).

[850] Ruggie "International Regimes," 397. See also GATT Article XVI(3), which allowed subsidization of primary products (which included agricultural products), but only to the extent that subsidies "be applied in a manner which results in that contracting party having more than an equitable share of world export trade in that product, account being taken of the shares of the contracting parties in such trade in the product during a previous representative period, and any special factors which may have affected or may be affecting such trade in the product."

Developing countries debated amongst each other and developed countries as to what the nature of UNCTAD's relationship with the GATT would be. Most developing countries established a sophisticated, two-pronged approach, using UNCTAD to generate trade policies conducive to development and to (continue to) enhance and improve ICAs, while at the same time participating in the GATT, in an effort to ensure access to developed countries' markets. ICAs, such as the sugar treaties, had some degree of independence from these other trade institutions, but they were also somewhat connected to them through doctrine and institutional affiliation.

UNCTAD would eventually lose power and prestige, and the GATT would be supplanted by the WTO. But in a curious parallel, the WTO would mirror NIEO's emphasis on the global over the national, and the move away from embedded liberalism. The advent of the WTO marked a moment when international trade law no longer became a system of negotiating the twin goals of domestic welfare and international cooperation within the context of different national economy systems. Instead, the WTO was informed by theories of legal harmonization, driven by a desire to ensure that the global market was structured by global rules.

PART V

Epilogue

we haven't discovered a way to harmoniously coexist with plastics, pesticides, etc. . . . While inter-human relationships are much easier to grasp, it's not humans but plants and microorganisms that actually let us survive; they are clearly the root of our lives but we keep forgetting this point . . . one would have to recognize that inter-human production and distribution systems depend greatly on plants.

Miyazaki, "*Princess Mononoke*"

9 Using the past to open up the future of trade law

Sugar began its life as a wild grass. Through harvesting, processing, refining, and trading, this biomass was transformed into a commodity. At times, sugar was a luxurious addition to savory dishes. Other times, it was a sweetener in everyday meals and drinks. Eventually, it became a factor of production in the confectionary, preserves, and beverage industries. The plant was turned into a commodity not through machinery, but through law, which created the rules regarding how sugar was produced, sold, and bought. Multilateral trade institutions set the conditions for (and, at times, determined) some of those laws, and regulated the plant's global production and distribution, and ensured that it was traded around the world.

Free trade was a central concept in the creation of these international institutions. Marx, like his British contemporaries, accepted free trade as a desirable goal.[851] To Marx, however, the doctrine of free trade could not explain why some countries were more adept at trading certain commodities over others:

> You believe, perhaps, gentlemen, that the production of coffee and sugar is the natural destiny of the West Indies. Two centuries ago, nature, which does not trouble herself about commerce, had planted neither sugar-cane nor coffee trees there. And it may be that in less than half a century you will find there neither coffee nor sugar, for the East Indies, by means of cheaper production, have already successfully combated this alleged natural destiny of the West Indies.

[851] To Marx, however, free trade was necessary because it is a revolutionary force that destroys conservative protectionist policies and "breaks up old nationalities and pushes the antagonism of the proletariat and the bourgeoisie to the extreme point." Marx, "Free Trade," p. 465.

It is notable that Marx used sugar and the West Indies as an example to make his point, which was the following:

> If the free-traders cannot understand how one nation can grow rich at the expense of another, we need not wonder, since these same gentlemen also refuse to understand how within one country one class can enrich itself at the expense of another.[852]

He thought it necessary to understand how some countries established comparative advantage and benefited from free trade while others did not. To Marx and some present-day scholars, "comparative advantage can be created as well as discovered."[853]

Historically, free trade has benefited some more than others, and has not created a harmonious international division of labor, as promised by popular theories of free trade. This implies that competing economic and political stakes are behind different free trade policies. The sugar treaties teach us that to organize international trade in a way that assumes that the market should be "free" from the state has little practical meaning; market actors cannot operate without certain legal structures, political decisions, and social relations. In international trade, the debate is better understood to be about negotiating the relationship between the (public, political) state and (private, economic) market, while the international institution's role – after political contest and compromise – is to demarcate those tenuous boundaries.

The sugar treaties and their ensuing organizations also tell us that the distinction between the domestic and the international is fluid in several ways. As a commodity agreement, each configured domestic, regional, and international markets differently. As a multilateral institution, each was informed by different notions of sovereignty, deriving power from and empowering states in a variety of ways. As a sugar union, each coordinated the relationship between the member states differently.

Despite these moving and porous lines, the historical account of international trade law and institutions through the story of sugar has had a set range of possibilities, through which people made their choices about and through law.[854] It has been a tension between different groups coalescing as agricultural interests versus those coalescing as industrial interests. The people and politics that make up these

[852] *Ibid.*, pp. 464, 464–5. [853] Unger, *Free Trade*, p. 36. [854] Marks, "False Contingency."

interests have always been multifaceted: international trade law has been built upon the inequality between agricultural producers and industrial consumers, small countries and large countries, workers on the land and owners of the land, former black slaves and remaining white bosses, colonial subjects and imperial overlords, and the Third World and First World.

Nevertheless, the assumption held by the architects of trade institutions has been, for the most part, that agriculture's principal role in the world is to serve industry. Trade law has been part of a larger development plan, whose end goal is to use the financial gains from agriculture to industrialize, whether it was the British West Indies, Cuba, or the Third World. The First World thought NIEO was radical because it was a call for a global institution to address the global redistribution of wealth. But NIEO was not radical in its plans to industrialize the Third World.

It remains very difficult to avoid framing international trade law as a contest between agriculture and industry, or, in today's terms, between developing and developed countries. Agriculture remains one of the most important and controversial aspects of current trade law and politics. Without providing a complete analysis of the WTO[855] (but with over a century's worth of trade history in mind), I can only offer some parting thoughts and fresh questions for the future in lieu of a conclusion. My focus is on what trade law has left out or placed into the background thus far.

First, agricultural workers' perspectives have not had a prominent role in the development and application of trade law – neither in ideational/doctrinal terms, nor in terms of direct worker participation – even though these workers' welfare is the most vulnerable to the capricious price of sugar. There was a brief moment when trade addressed questions of labor during the ITO's false start, but it was narrower than what some Third World delegates demanded and was primarily framed as an issue of avoiding unemployment or underemployment rather than worker welfare.[856] A more equitable trade law would have to reconcile with this disparity and involve agricultural workers more directly in the development of international trade law and practice.

[855] For an excellent account of the WTO, see Lang, *Trade Law*.

[856] Though one might still argue that Art. 7 of the ITO Charter kept open the possibility of substantive worker welfare laws and policies by referring to, albeit in very general terms, "fair labour standards" and the ILO.

Second, today's trade law jurists rarely look to the history of ICAs as part of the repertoire of possible institutional configurations for the future. One could imagine a plurilateral system in which different ICAs are structured in a variety of ways in order to serve different purposes and respond to different political, economic, and social conditions particular to each commodity. Many of the administrative, financial, and legal structures remain for the different ICAs, but they operate with very little power and purpose. Indeed, this may be the time to reinvigorate ICAs in totally new ways. Three treatises, Kabir-ur-Rahman Khan's *The Law and Organisation of International Commodity Agreements*, Ervin Ernst's *International Commodity Agreements*, and B. S. Chimni's *International Commodity Agreements: A Legal Study*, offer fertile places from which to develop new ideas.

Another way out of the deadlock is to no longer privilege the idea of industry, with its attendant values such as mechanical speed and economic growth, and instead use agriculture as an ideational starting point. While the distinction between agriculture and industry is becoming more blurred – with the increasing rate of patented seeds, chemical fertilizers, and large-scale mechanized monocrop farming – it is an opacity that makes agriculture look more like industry every day. After an age of industrialization, the questions that might open up the horizon of possibilities may very well be: How could we interpret and change trade law in a way that assumes that industry should serve or resemble agricultural practices? What does it mean to think about agricultural cultivation as an end in and of itself? In answering these questions, we may want to explore agricultural practices that consider values such as ecological resilience and biological diversity, in order to transform trade law for the future.

Sources and Bibliography

SOURCES

Archival sources

The Albert Viton Papers, Purdue University, West Lafayette, Indiana, USA (AVP)
Series 1: Sugar Related Documents

Archives of the League of Nations, Library of the United Nations, Geneva, Switzerland (LON)
Registry (R) *Series*
10 Economic and Financial
10A General
10D Economic

National government documents

Final Report of the Royal Commission Appointed to Inquire into the Depression of Trade and Industry, C. 4893 (1886)

Correspondence Relating to the Sugar Industry in the West Indies, C. 8359 (1897)

Report of the West India Royal Commission, C. 8655, 8656, 8657, 8669 (1898)

Correspondence Relating to the Sugar Bounties, C. 8780 (1898)

Correspondence Relating to the Conference at Brussels on the Question of Sugar Bounties, C. 8938 (1898)

US Senate Committee on Finance, *Proceedings of the Conference on the Question of Bounties, held at Brussels, June 7–25, 1898* (Blue Book Commercial No. 6, 1898)

Correspondence Relating to the Sugar Conference At Brussels 1901–1902, Cd 940 (1902)

Correspondence Relating to the Sugar Bounty Conference, Cd 1013 (1902)

Findings of the Permanent Commission established under Article VII of the Sugar Convention of March 5, 1902, and Report of the British Delegate, Cd 1632 (1903)

Further Findings of the Permanent Commission Established Under Article VII of the Sugar Convention of March 5, 1902 and Further Reports of the British Delegate, Cd 2094 (1904)

Further Findings of the Permanent Commission Established Under the Sugar Convention of March 5, 1902, Report of the British Delegate and Appeal of His Majesty's Government Against Certain of those Findings, Cd 2349 (1905)

International Sugar Commission Spring Session 1905, Report of British Delegate and Correspondence, Cd 2531 (1905)

Papers Relating to the Brussels Sugar Convention, Cd 3565 (1907)

Correspondence Respecting the Additional Act to the Brussels Sugar Convention of March 5, 1902, signed at Brussels, August 28, 1902, Cd 3780 (1907)

Correspondence Respecting the Adhesion of Russia to the Brussels Sugar Convention of March 5, 1902, Cd 3877 (1908)

Despatches to His Majesty's Minister at Brussels Respecting the Signature and Ratification of the International Sugar Union, Cd 6146 (1912)

Correspondence Relating to the Withdrawal of His Majesty's Government from the Brussels Sugar Convention, Cd 6325 (1912)

Correspondence Relating to the Withdrawal of His Majesty's Government from the Brussels Sugar Convention, Cd 6877 (1913)

International Trade Organization, Hearings Before the Committee on Finance, Part I, US Senate, 80th Congress, 1st Session (1947)

United States Department of State, *Suggested Charter for an International Trade Organization of the United Nations* (1947)

World Economic Interdependence and Trade in Commodities, Cd 6061 (1975)

International institutional documents

International Trade Organization

The Calling of an International Conference on Trade and Employment, ESC Res. 13(I), UN ESCOR, 1st Sess., UN Doc. E/22 (1946) 133

Report of the First Session of the Preparatory Committee of the United Nations Conference on Trade and Employment, E/PC/T/33, UN ESCOR (1946) [London Draft]

Report of the Drafting Committee of the Preparatory Committee of the United Nations Conference on Trade and Employment, E/PC/T/34, UN ESCOR (March 5, 1947) [New York Draft]

Interim Report of the Second Session of the Preparatory Committee of the United Nations Conference on Trade and Employment, E/PC/T/117 Rev.1, UN ESCOR (July 9, 1947)

Report of the Second Session of the Preparatory Committee of the United Nations Conference on Trade and Employment, E/PC/T/186, UN ESCOR (August 22, 1947) [Geneva Draft]

League of Nations

Conf. Sugar

E/Sugar/

UN Conference in Trade and Employment
TD/SUGAR
UN ESCOR, *United Nations Conference on Trade and Development*, UN Doc. E/Conf.2/23 (December 24, 1947)
UN ESCOR, *United Nations Conference on Trade and Development*, UN Doc. E/Conf.2/36 (February 4, 1948)

BIBLIOGRAPHY

n.a., "Sugar at the World Economic Conference" (1933) **25** *International Sugar Journal* 293
n.a., "Cuba: Loot the Place!" (August 21, 1933) *Time*
n.a., "Now or Never" (April 10, 1937) **127**:4885 *The Economist* 65
n.a., "Editor's Note" (1974) **4** *Journal of International Economics* 299
n.a., "Notes and Comments" (February 1975) **77**:914 *International Sugar Journal* 33
n.a. (March 7, 1975) **26** *Commodities Bulletin* (International Sugar Colloquium)
n.a., "Notes and Comments" (April 1975) **77**:916 *International Sugar Journal* 97
n.a., "Notes and Comments" (May 1975) **77**:917 *International Sugar Journal* 129
n.a., "Sugar in the Year 1976" (December 31, 1976) **1316** *Sugar Review* (Czarnikow) 217
n.a., "Notes and Comments" (January 1978) **78**:925 *International Sugar Journal* 1
Aaronson, Susan A., *Trade and the American Dream: A Social History of Postwar Trade Policy* (Lexington, Ky.: University Press of Kentucky, 1996)
Abbott, George C., *Sugar* (London: Routledge, 1990)
Abbott, Elizabeth, *Sugar: A Bittersweet History* (Toronto: Penguin Canada, 2008)
Abdelal, Rawi and John G. Ruggie, "Principles of Embedded Liberalism: Social Legitimacy and Global Capitalism," in David Moss and John Cisternino (eds.), *New Perspectives on Regulation* (Cambridge: The Tobin Project, 2009), p. 151
Aguilar, Luis E., *Cuba 1933: Prologue to Revolution* (Ithaca, NY: Cornell University Press, 1972)
Ahlfeld, Helmut (ed.), *Sugar: Essays to Mark the 125th Anniversary of F. O. Licht* (Ratzenburg: F. O. Licht, 1989)
Ala'i, Padideh, "Leopold and Morel: A Story of 'Free Trade' and 'Native Rights' in the Congo Free State" (2005) **37** *Studies in Transnational Legal Policy* 33
Albert, Bill and Adrian Graves, "Introduction," in Bill Albert and Adrian Graves (eds.), *Crisis and Change in the International Sugar Economy 1860–1914* (Norwich: ISC, 1984), p. 1
Alexandrowicz, Charles Henry, *World Economic Agencies: Law and Practice* (New York: Praeger, 1962)
Alvarez, José, *Cuba's Agricultural Sector* (Gainesville, Fla.: University of Florida, 2004)
Alvarez, José and Leo C. Polopolus, "The History of U.S. Sugar Protection" (EDIS Document SC 019) (Gainesville, Fla.: Department of Food and Resource

Economics, Florida Cooperative Extension Service, Institute of Food and Agricultural Sciences, University of Florida, 2008), online: http://edis.ifas.ufl.edu/SC019 (accessed May 19, 2014)

Alvarez, José E., *International Organizations as Law-makers* (Oxford: Oxford University Press, 2005)

Amery, L. S., *The Fundamental Fallacies of Free Trade: Four Addresses on the Logical Groundwork of the Free Trade Theory* (London: Love, 1908)

Amzalak, Moses Bensabat, "Le café et le sucre au point de vue international" (1951) **78** *Recueil des cours* 123

Ando, Nisuke, "Permanent Court of Arbitration," in Rüdiger Wolfrum (ed.), *The Max Planck Encyclopedia of Public International Law* (Oxford: Oxford University Press, 2008), online edition: www.mpepil.com (accessed May 19, 2014)

André, Alexandre, "La convention sucrière de Bruxelles du 5 Mars 1902 et sa Commission permanente" (1912) **19** *Revue générale de droit international public* 665

Anghie, Antony, "Colonialism and the Birth of International Institutions: Sovereignty, Economy, and the Mandate System of the League of Nations" (2002) **34** *NYU Journal of International Law and Politics* 513

Imperialism, Sovereignty and the Making of International Law (Cambridge: Cambridge University Press, 2005)

Anti-Bounty League, *Report of Proceedings at the Deputation of Members of Parliament Received by the Right Hon. A. J. Balfour, M.P. on Thursday, April 28, 1898, at the Foreign Office* (London: Anti-Bounty League, 1898)

Armstrong, David (ed.), *Routledge Handbook of International Law* (New York: Routledge, 2009)

Aufricht, Hans, *Guide to League of Nations Publications* (New York: Columbia University Press, 1951)

Ayala, César J., *American Sugar Kingdom: The Plantation Economy of the Spanish Caribbean, 1898–1934* (Chapel Hill, NC: University of North Carolina Press, 1999)

Baer, George, *International Organizations 1918–1945: A Guide to Research and Research Materials* (Wilmington, Del.: Scholarly Resources, 1981)

Baer, Wener, "Import Substitution and Industrialization in Latin America: Experiences and Interpretations" (1972) **7**:1 *Latin American Research Review* 95

Baker, Ray Standard (ed.), *Woodrow Wilson: Life and Letters*, 8 vols. (New York: Doubleday, Doran & Company, 1939), **vol. VIII**

Balfour, Arthur, "International Chamber of Commerce" (1927) **134** *Annals of the American Academy of Political and Social Science* 124

Baranyai, L. and J. C. Mills, *International Commodity Agreements* (Mexico: Centro de Estudios Monetarios Latinoamericanos, 1963)

Beachey, R. W., *The British West Indies Sugar Industry in the Late Nineteenth Century* (Oxford: Basil Blackwell, 1957)

Beckert, Jens, "The Great Transformation of Embeddedness: Karl Polanyi and the New Economic Sociology," MPIfG Discussion Paper 07/1 (Cologne: Max Planck Institute for the Study of Societies, 2007)

Beer, Max, *The League of Nations on Trial: A Journey to Geneva* (W. H. Johnston) (Boston, Mass.: Houghton Mifflin Company, 1933)

Beeton, Mayson Moss, *The Truth about the Foreign Sugar Bounties: The Case for Abolition* (London: Simpkin, Marshall, Hamilton, Kent, 1898)

The "Open-Door" for British Sugar Industries in British Markets. The Case for Action, Summarised in the Speeches Delivered at the Public Meeting Held at Cannon Street Hotel, January 9, 1899, and at the Public Meeting Held at Birmingham, December 12, 1898, with Introductory Review, The Brussels Conference - and After? (London: Anti-Bounty League, 1899)

Twenty Years of Sugar Bounties: The Moral of the "Policy of Inactio" as Pointed in Speeches Delivered in the Debate on the Indian Countervailing Duties Act in the House of Commons, June 15th, 1899 (London: Anti-Bounty League, 1899)

Bell, Duncan, *The Idea of Greater Britain: Empire and the Future of World Order, 1860–1900* (Princeton, NJ: Princeton University Press, 2007)

Bell, Duncan (ed.), *Victorian Visions of Global Order: Empire and International Relations in Nineteenth-Century Political Thought* (Cambridge: Cambridge University Press, 2007)

Bhagwati, Jagdish N. (ed.), *The New International Economic Order: The North–South Debate* (Cambridge, Mass.: Massachusetts Institute of Technology, 1977)

Bidwell, P. W., *A Commercial Policy of the United Nations* (New York: Carnegie Endowment for International Peace, 1945)

Bidwell, P.W. and W. Diebold, Jr., "The United States and International Trade Organization" (1949) **49** *International Conciliation* 187

Black, Clinton V., *The History of Jamaica*, 3rd edn. (London: Collins Clear Type Press, 1965)

Block, Fred, "Towards a New Understanding of Economic Modernity," in Christian Joerges, Bo Stråth, and Peter Wagner (eds.), *The Economy as Polity: The Political Constitution of Contemporary Capitalism* (London: UCL Press, 2005), p. 3

Boomgaard, Peter, "Treacherous Cane: The Java Sugar Industry between 1914 and 1940," in Bill Albert and Adrian Graves (eds.), *The World Sugar Economy in War and Depression 1914–40* (London: Routledge, 1988), p. 157

Boyden, Roland William (ed.), *The Economic Consequences of the League: The World Economic Conference* (London: Europa Publishing Company, 1927)

Braudel, Fernand, *Civilization and Capitalism 15th–18th Century. Vol. II: The Wheels of Commerce*, Siân Reynolds (trans.), (New York: Harper & Row, 1982)

Bronz, George, "The International Trade Organisation Charter" (1949) **62** *Harvard Law Review* 1089

Brown, Christopher P., *Primary Commodity Control* (Kuala Lumpur: Oxford University Press, 1975)

The Political and Social Economy of Commodity Control (London: Macmillan Press, 1980)

Brown, Jr., William A., *The United States and the Restoration of World Trade: An Analysis and Appraisal of the ITO Charter and the General Agreement on Tariffs and Trade* (Washington DC: Brookings Institution Press, 1950)

Bruhns, G., "Zur Geschichte der Firma F. O. Licht und der Zuckerstatistic," English Summary: "F. O. Licht and the Development of Sugar Statistics," in Helmut Ahlfeld (ed.), *Sugar: Essays to Mark the 125th Anniversary of F. O. Licht* (Ratzenburg: F. O. Licht, 1989), p. 1

Buğra, Ayşe and Kaan Agartan, *Reading Karl Polanyi for the Twenty-First Century: Market Economy as a Political Project* (Houndmills: Palgrave Macmillan, 2007)

Bulmer-Thomas, Victor, *The Economic History of Latin America Since Independence*, 2nd edn. (Cambridge: Cambridge University Press, 2003)

Burawoy, Michael, "For a Sociological Marxism: The Complementary Convergence of Antonio Gramsci and Karl Polanyi" (2003) **31** *Politics & Society* 193

Burger, Kees, Christopher L. Gilbert, and Hidde Smit, "Regulation of Commodity Markets in the Twentieth Century," in Erik Chrispeels (ed.), *International Commodity Organisations in Transition* (London: Cameron, 2002), p. 17

Burns, Alan, *History of the British West Indies*, rev. 2nd edn. (London: Allen and Unwin, 1965)

Cain, P. J., "J. A. Hobson, Cobdenism, and the Radical Theory of Economic Imperialism, 1898–1914" (1978) **31** *The Economic History Review* 565

Cale, Edward G. and Oscar Zaglits, "Intergovernmental Agreements Approach to the Problem of Agricultural Surpluses" (1949) **34** *Iowa Law Review* 230

Carr, Barry, "Identity, Class, and Nation: Black Immigrant Workers, Cuban Communism, and the Sugar Insurgency, 1925–1934" (1998) **78** *Hispanic American Historical Review* 83

Carrington, George, *Our West Indian Colonies: A Retrospect of the Past, a Survey of the Present, and a Plea for Justice in the Future. A Paper Read before The Royal Colonial Institute, March 8th, 1898* (London: Anti-Bounty League, 1898)

Cassel, Gustav, *Recent Monopolistic Tendencies in Industry and Trade: Being an Analysis of the Nature and Causes of the Poverty of Nations* (Geneva: League of Nations, 1927)

Castelot, E., "The Brussels Sugar Conference" (1902) **12** *The Economic Journal* 217

"High Prices of Sugar" (1905) **15** *The Economic Journal* 1041

Cauvin, Jacques, *The Birth of the Gods and the Origins of Agriculture*, Trevor Watkins (trans.), (Cambridge: Cambridge University Press, 2000 [1994])

Cayley, David, "Ideas: Markets and Society," 5 parts (Toronto: CBC Radio podcast, 2006)

Chadbourne, Thomas L., "The International Stabilization of Sugar" (1931) **21** *American Labor Legislation Review* 383

Chalmin, Phillippe G., "The Important Trends in Sugar Diplomacy before 1914," in Bill Albert and Adrian Graves (eds.), *Crisis and Change in the International Sugar Economy 1860–1914* (Norwich: ISC, 1984), p. 9

The Making of a Sugar Giant: Tate and Lyle, 1859–1989, Erica E. Long-Michalke (trans.), (Chur, NY: Harwood Academic Publishers, 1990)

Chamberlain, Joseph, *Imperial Union and Tariff Reform* (London: Grant Richards, 1903)

Chang, Ha-Joon, *Kicking Away the Ladder – Developmental Strategy in Historical Perspective* (London: Anthem Press, 2002).

Charnovitz, Steve, "The World Trade Organization and Law Enforcement" (2003) **37** *Journal of World Trade* 817

Charnovitz, Steve and John Wickham, "Non-governmental Organizations and the Original International Trade Regime" (1995) **29** *Journal of World Trade* 111

Chimni, B. S., *International Commodity Agreements: A Legal Study* (London: Croom Helm, 1987)

Chomsky, Aviva, "Barbados or Canada?: Race, Immigration, and Nation in Early-Twentieth-Century Cuba" (2000) **80** *Hispanic American Historical Review* 415

Chrispeels, Erik (ed.), *International Commodity Organisations in Transition* (London: Cameron May, 2002)

Clair, Jean (ed.), *The 1930s: The Making of the "New Man"* (Ottawa: National Gallery of Canada, 2008)

Clarence-Smith, William G., "The Sugar and Rum Industries in the Portuguese Empire 1850–1914," in Bill Albert and Adrian Graves (eds.), *Crisis and Change in the International Sugar Economy 1860–1914* (Norwich: ISC Press, 1984), p. 227

"The Global Consumption of Hot Beverages, *c.* 1500 to *c.* 1900," in Alexander Nützenadel and Frank Trentmann (eds.), *Food and Globalization: Consumption, Markets, and Politics in the Modern World* (Oxford: Berg, 2008), p. 37

Claude, Jr., Inis L., *Swords into Ploughshares: The Problems and Progress of International Organization*, 4th edn. (New York: Random House, 1971 [1956])

Clavin, Patricia, *Securing the World Economy: The Reinvention of the League of Nations, 1920–1946* (Oxford: Oxford University Press, 2013)

Clavin, Patricia, and Jens-Wilhelm Wessels, "Transnationalism and the League of Nations: Understanding the Work of its Economic and Financial Organisation" (2005) **14** *Contemporary European History* 465

Cohen, Julius Henry, "The Practice of Law as a Franchise" (1932) **66** *United States Law Review* 25

Cohen, Morris, "Property and Sovereignty" (1927) **13** *Cornell Law Quarterly* 8

"The Basis of Contract" (1933) **46** *Harvard Law Review* 553

Colijn, H., "The World Economic Conference of 1927" (1927) **134** *Annals of the American Academy of Political and Social Science* 140

Conrad, Joseph, *The Heart of Darkness* (London: Penguin Books, 2000 [1899])

Cook, Walter Wheeler, "Privileges of Labor Unions in the Struggle for Life" (1918) **27** *Yale Law Journal* 779

Cooke, E. Cozens, "The Sugar Convention and the West Indies" (1907) **17** *The Economic Journal* 315

"Sugar and the Tariff" (1907) **17** *The Economic Journal* 566

"The Amended Sugar Convention" (1908) **18** *The Economic Journal* 649

Corea, Gamani, *Taming Commodity Markets: The Integrated Programme and the Common Fund in UNCTAD* (Manchester: Manchester University Press, 1992)

Cox, Robert (ed.), *International Organisation. World Politics: Studies in Economic and Social Agencies* (London: Macmillan, 1969)

Craven, Matthew, Malgosia Fitzmaurice, and Maria Vogiatzi (eds.), *Time, History, and International Law* (Leiden: Martinus Nijhoff Publishers, 2007)

Crespo, Horacio, "Trade Regimes and the International Sugar Market, 1850–1980: Protectionism, Subsidies, and Regulation," in Steven Topik, Carlos Marichal, and Zephyr Frank (eds.), *From Silver to Cocaine: Latin American Commodity Chains and the Building of the World Economy 1500–2000* (Durham, SC: Duke University Press, 2006), p. 147

Cropper, James, *Relief of West Indian Distress: Shewing the Inefficiency of Protecting Duties on East-India Sugar and Pointing Other Modes of Certain Relief* (London: Ellerton & Henderson, 1823)

Crosby, Jr., Alfred W. *The Columbian Exchange: Biological and Cultural Consequences of 1492* (Westport, Conn.: Greenwood, 1972)

Cross, Malcolm and Gad Heuman (eds.), *Labour in the Caribbean: From Emancipation to Independence* (London: Macmillan Caribbean, 1988)

Cuddy, J. D. A., "Theory and Practice in NIEO Negotiations on Commodities," in Gerald K. Helleiner (ed.), *For Good or Evil: Economic Theory and North–South Negotiations* (Toronto: University of Toronto Press, 1982), p. 33

Curzon, Gerard, "The General Agreement on Tariffs and Trade: Pressures and Strategies for Task Expansion," in Robert Cox (ed.), *International Organisation: World Politics; Studies in Economic and Social Agencies* (London: Macmillan, 1969), p. 248

Cypher, James M. and James L. Dietz, *The Process of Economic Development*, 3rd edn. (London: Routledge, 2009)

Dale, Gareth, *Karl Polanyi* (Cambridge: Polity, 2010)

Dalton, John E., *Sugar: A Case Study of Government Control* (New York: McGraw Hill Book Company, 1937)

Dasgupta, Swati, "Jules Verne Re-discovered" (2005) **32** *India International Centre Quarterly* 87

David, Paul A., "Why Are Institutions 'Carriers of History'?: Path Dependence and the Evolution of Conventions and Institutions" (1994) **5** *Structural Change and Economic Dynamics* 205

Davis, Joseph S., "Experience Under Intergovernmental Commodity Agreements, 1902–45" (1946) **54** *Journal of Political Economy* 193

International Commodity Agreements: Hope, Illusion, or Menace? (New York: Committee on International Economic Policy and Carnegie Endowment for International Peace, 1947)

De Barros, Juanita, Audra Diptee, and David V. Trotman (eds.), *Beyond Fragmentation: Perspectives in Caribbean History* (Princeton, NJ: Markus Weiner Publishers, 2006)

de Peyerimhoff, Henri, "Rationalisation of Industry," in Roland William Boyden (ed.), *The Economic Consequences of the League: The World Economic Conference* (London: Europa Publishing Company, 1927), p. 129

de Rousiers, Paul, *Cartels and Trusts and Their Development* (Geneva: League of Nations, 1927)

Deerr, Noël, *Sugar and the Sugar Cane: An Elementary Treatise on the Agriculture of the Sugar Cane and on the Manufacture of Cane Sugar* (Altrincham: Norman Rodger, 1905)

The History of Sugar, 2 vols. (London: Chapman and Hall, 1950)

Dell, Sidney, "The Origins of UNCTAD," in Michael Zammit Cutajar (ed.), *UNCTAD and the North–South Dialogue: The First Twenty Years. Essays in memory of W. R. Malinowski* (Oxford: Pergamon Press, 1985), p. 10

Delson, Robert, "Sugar Production for the Nineteenth-century British Market: Rethinking the Roles of Brazil and the British West Indies," in Bill Albert and Adrian Graves (eds.), *Crisis and Change in the International Sugar Economy 1860–1914* (Norwich: ISC Press, 1984), p. 59

deWilde, John C., "Sugar: An International Problem," **11**:15 *Foreign Policy Reports* (September 27, 1933), 162

Dexter, Byron, *The Years of Opportunity: The League of Nations, 1920–1926* (New York: Viking Press, 1967)

Díaz Alejandro, Carlos F., "The Argentine State and Economic Growth: A Historical Review," in Gustav Rainis (ed.), *Government and Economic Development* (New Haven, Conn.: Yale University Press, 1971), p. 216

Diebold, Jr., William, *The End of the ITO* (Princeton, NJ: Princeton University Press, 1952)

Dominguez, Jorge I., *Cuba: Order and Revolution* (Cambridge, Mass.: Belknap Press, 1978)

Drage, Geoffrey, *The Imperial Organization of Trade* (London: Smith, Elder & Co., 1911)

Driesen, David M., "What Is Free Trade?: The Real Issue Lurking Behind the Trade and Environment Debate" (2000) **41** *Virginia Journal of International Law* 279

Duggan, Stephen Pierce (ed.), *The League of Nations: The Principle and the Practice* (Boston, Mass.: Atlantic Monthly Press, 1919)

Dunoff, Jeffrey, "Rethinking International Trade" (1998) **19** *University of Pennsylvania Journal of International Economic Law* 347

Dutt, Sagarika, *India in a Globalized World* (Manchester: Manchester University Press, 2006)

Dryden, Steve, *Trade Warriors: USTR and the American Crusade for Free Trade* (New York: Oxford University Press, 1995)

Dye, Alan, *Cuban Sugar in the Age of Mass Production: Technology and the Economics of the Sugar Central, 1899–1929* (Stanford, Calif.: Stanford University Press, 1998)

Dye, Alan and Richard Sicotte, "How Brinkmanship Saved Chadbourne: Credibility and the International Sugar Agreement of 1931" (2006) **43** *Explorations in Economic History* 223

Ebner, Alexander, "Transnational Markets and the Polanyi Problem," in Christian Joerges and Josef Falke (eds.), *Karl Polanyi: Globalisation and the Potential of Law in Transnational Markets* (Oxford: Hart, 2011), p. 19

Economic Committee, *The World Sugar Situation* (Geneva: League of Nations, 1929)

Economic and Financial Section, *Agenda of Conference* (Geneva: League of Nations, 1926)

Report on the Economic Work of the League (Geneva: League of Nations, 1927)

Report and Proceedings of the World Economic Conference, 2 vols. (Geneva: League of Nations, 1927)

Economic, Financial and Transit Department, *Industrialization and Foreign Trade* (Geneva: League of Nations, 1945)

Edminster, Lynn R., "International Trade and Postwar Construction" (1943) **33** *American Economic Review* 303

Endres, Anthony M. and Grant A. Fleming, *International Organizations and the Analysis of Economic Policy, 1919–1950* (Cambridge: Cambridge University Press, 2002)

Engle, Nathan H., "Cartels and Commodity Control Schemes," in Joseph B. Harrison, Linden A. Mander, and Nathan H. Engle (eds.), *If Men Want Peace: The Mandates of World Order* (New York: Macmillan for the Universities Committee on Post-war International Problems, 1946), p. 156

Eppstein, John, *Ten Years' Life of the League of Nations: A History of Origins of the League and its Development from A.D. 1919 to 1929* (London: Mayfair Press, 1929)

Ernst, Ervin, *International Commodity Agreements: The System of Controlling the International Commodity Market* (The Hague: Martinus Nijhoff, 1982)

Fakhri, Michael, "Law as the Interplay of Ideas, Institutions, and Interests: Using Polanyi (and Foucault) to Ask TWAIL Questions" (2008) **10** *International Community Law Review* 455

Fanshawe, Maurice and C. A. Macartney, *What the League Has Done 1920–1936*, 9th edn. (London: League of Nations Union, 1936)

Farrer, Lord Thomas, *Free Trade Versus Fair Trade*, C. H. Chomley (ed.), 4th edn., (London: Free Trade Union, 1904 [1881])

Faundez, Julio, "International Economic Law and Development: Before and After Neo-liberalism," in Julio Faundez and Celine Tan (eds.), *International Economic Law, Globalization, and Developing Countries* (Cheltenham: Edward Elgar, 2010), p. 10

Fawcett, J. E. S., "The Function of Law in International Commodity Agreements" (1970) **44** *British Yearbook of International Law* 157

Fernández-Armesto, Felipe, *Near a Thousand Tables: A History of Food* (Toronto: Key Porter, 2002)

Ferrara, Orestes, *Lessons of the War and the Peace Conference* (New York: Harper & Brothers, 1919)

Finlayson, Jock A. and Mark W. Zacher, "International Trade Institutions and North/South Dialogue" (1981) **36** *International Journal* 732

Foucault, Michel, *Security, Territory, Population: Lectures at the Collège de France 1977–1978* (New York: Picador, 2007)

Franck, Thomas, "Book Review of The Changing Structures of International Law by Wolfgang Friedmann," (1965) **40** *NYU Law Review* 398

"Minimum Standards of Public Policy and Order Applicable to Collective International Commodity Agreements" (1978) **160** *Recueil des Cours* 395

Frank, Glenn, "The League of Nations and Economic Nationalism," in Stephen Pierce Duggan (ed.), *The League of Nations: The Principle and the Practice* (Boston, Mass.: Atlantic Monthly Press, 1919), p. 184

Freeman, Harrop A., "International Administrative Law: A Functional Approach to Peace" (1948) **57** *Yale Law Journal* 976

Friedmann, Harriet and Philip McMichael, "Agriculture and the State System: The Rise and Fall of National Agricultures, 1870 to the Present" (1987) **29** *Sociologia Ruralis* 93

Fulton, James G. and Jacob J. Javits, *The International Trade Organisation: An Appraisal of the Havana Charter in Relation to the United States Foreign Policy, with a Definitive Study of its Provision U.S. Congress, House Committee on Foreign Affairs* (Washington DC: 80th Congress, 2nd Session, 1948)

Funes Monzote, Reinaldo, *From Rainforest to Cane Field in Cuba: An Environmental History Since 1492*, Alex Martin (trans.), (Chapel Hill, NC: University of North Carolina Press, 2008)

Gaisford, J. D. and W. A. Kerr (eds.), *Handbook on Trade Policy* (Cheltenham: Edward Elgar, 2007)

Gallagher, John and Ronald Robinson, "The Imperialism of Free Trade" (1953) **6** *The Economic History Review* 1

Gallagher, Peter, *The First Ten Years of the WTO: 1995–2005* (Cambridge: Cambridge University Press and World Trade Organization, 2005)

Galloway, Jock H., *The Sugar Cane Industry: An Historical Geography from its Origins to 1914* (Cambridge: Cambridge University Press, 1989)

Gardner, Richard N., *Sterling-Dollar Diplomacy: The Origins and the Prospects of Our International Economic Order* (New York: University of Columbia Press, 1980 [1956])

Gariepy, Richard N., "International Commodity Agreements" (1976) **25** *International Comparative Law Quarterly* 677

Garvin, J. L., *The Economic Foundations of Peace: Or, World-Partnership as the Truer Basis of the League of Nations* (London: Macmillan, 1919)

Gautie, Jules, Andreas Hermes, and H. A. F. Lindsay, *Agriculture and the World Crisis* (Geneva: League of Nations, 1927)

Geerligs, H. C. Prinsen, *The World's Cane Sugar Industry Past and Present* (Altrincham: Norman Rodger, 1912)

"Production of Cane Sugar," in *Sugar: Memoranda Prepared for the Economic Committee* (E/Sugar/23(I), 24(I), 25(I)) (Geneva: League of Nations, April 15, 1929), p. 4

Geerligs, H. C. Prinsen and R. J. Prinsen Geerligs, *Cane Sugar Production 1912–1937* (London: Norman Rodger, 1938)

Geerligs, H. C. Prinsen, F. O. Licht, and Gustav Mikusch, *Sugar: Memoranda Prepared for the Economic Committee* (E/Sugar/23(I), 24(I), 25(I)) (Geneva: League of Nations, April 15, 1929)

General Agreement on Tariffs and Trade, *The Developing Countries and the GATT: The New Chapter on Trade and Development* (Geneva: General Agreement on Tariffs and Trade, 1965)

George, Susan, "Alternative Finances: The World Trade Organisation We Could Have Had," *Le Monde Diplomatique* (January 24, 2007)

Gerig, Benjamin, *The Open Door and the Mandates System: A Study of Economic Equality Before and Since the Establishment of the Mandates System* (London: George Allen & Unwin Ltd, 1930)

Gilbert, Christopher L., "International Commodity Agreements: An Obituary Notice" (1996) **24** *World Development* 1

"International Commodity Agreements," in J. D. Gaisford and W. A. Kerr (eds.), *Handbook on Trade Policy* (Cheltenham: Edward Elgar, 2007), p. 470

Girgis, Maurice, *Industrialization and Trade Patterns in Egypt* (Tübingen: Mohr, 1977)

Goldberg, Charlotte K., "Prospects for an International Sugar Agreement Note" (1977) **9** *Law and Policy of International Business* 591

Goldstein, Judith and Joanne Gowa, "US National Power and the Post-war Trading Regime" (2002) **1** *World Trade Review* 153

Goodwin, Geoffrey and James Mayall (eds.), *A New International Commodity Regime* (London: Croom Helm, 1980)

Gordon-Ashworth, Fiona, *International Commodity Control: A Contemporary History and Appraisal* (London: St Martin's Press, 1984)

Goreux, Louis M., "Stabilization of Commodity Prices and Export Earnings: The Coffee and Sugar Agreements" (1978–9) **4** *International Trade Law Journal* 140

Grampp, William Dyer, *The Manchester School of Economics* (Stanford, Calif.: Stanford University Press, 1960)

Graz, Jean-Christophe, *Aux Sources de l'OMC La Charte de La Havane* (Geneva: Librarie Droz, 1999)

Greaves, H. R. G., *The League Committees and World Order: A Study of the Permanent Expert Committees of the League of Nations as an Instrument of International Government* (London: Oxford University Press, 1931)

Grew, Raymond, "Food and Global History," in Raymond Grew (ed.), *Food in Global History* (Boulder, Colo.: Westview Press, 1999), p. 1

Griffin, Charles S., "The Sugar Industry and Legislation in Europe" (1902) **17** *The Quarterly Journal of Economics* 1

Grossman, Eugene, *Methods of Economic Rapprochement* (Geneva: League of Nations, 1926)

Guerra, Ramiro, *Sugar and Society in the Caribbean: An Economic History of Cuban Agriculture*, Marjory M. Urquidi (trans.), (New Haven, Conn.: Yale University Press, 1964 [1927])

Guerra y Debén, José Antonio, "Recent Evolution of the Sugar Industry," in Ramiro Guerra, *Sugar and Society in the Caribbean: An Economic History of Cuban*

Agriculture, Marjory M. Urquidi (trans.), (New Haven, Conn.: Yale University Press, 1964 [1927]), p. 171

Haberler, Gottfried *et al.*, *Trends in International Trade: Report by a Panel of Experts* (Geneva: The Contracting Parties to the GATT, 1958)

Hagelberg, G. B., "International Sugar Agreements, 1864–1977" (1977) **109** *F. O. Licht's International Sugar Report* 5

Hagelberg, G. B. and A. C. Hannah, "The Quest for Order: A Review of International Sugar Agreements" (1994) **19** *Food Policy* 17

Hager, L. Michael, "Commodity Agreements and the Developing Countries: A Collective Bargaining Approach" (1973) **7** *The International Lawyer* 309

Hale, Robert, "Coercion and Distribution in a Supposedly Noncoercive State" (1923) **38** *Political Science Quarterly* 470

Hamilton, Alexander, *Reports of the Secretary of the Treasury on the Subject of Manufactures* (Washington DC: US Department of the Treasury, 1791)

Harris, Simon, "British Sugar Markets in an International Market," in Simon Harris and Ian Smith (eds.), *World Sugar Markets in a State of Flux* (London: Trade Policy Research Centre, 1973) p. 1

"U.S. and E.E.C. Policy Attitudes Compared Towards the 1977 International Sugar Agreement" (1980) **31**:3 *Journal of Agricultural Economics* 351

Harrison, Joseph B., Linden A. Mander, and Nathan H. Engle (eds.), *If Men Want Peace: The Mandates of World Order* (New York: Macmillan for the Universities Committee on Post-war International Problems, 1946)

Hart, Michael (ed.), *Also Present at the Creation: Dana Wilgress and the United Nations Conference on Trade and Employment at Havana* (Ottawa: Centre for Trade and Policy, 1995)

Hart, Richard, "Origin and development of the working class in the English-speaking Caribbean area 1897–1937," in Malcolm Cross and Gad Heuman (eds.), *Labour in the Caribbean: From Emancipation to Independence* (London: Macmillan Caribbean, 1988), p. 43

Hartantyo, Budi and Hidde P. Smit (eds.), *International Commodity Development Strategies* (Amsterdam: VU University Press, 1993)

Harvey, David, *A Brief History of Neoliberalism* (Oxford: Oxford University Press, 2005)

Haviland, William E., *International Commodity Agreements* (Montreal: Private Planning Association of Canada, 1963)

Heilperin, M. A., "Economic and Financial Issues," in Institute on World Organization, *World Organization: A Balance Sheet of the First Great Experiment* (Washington DC: American Council on Public Affairs, 1942)

Held, David and Mathias Koening-Archibugi (eds.), *Taming Globalization: Frontiers of Governance* (Cambridge: Polity Press, 2003)

Helg, Aline, "The Aftermath of Slavery in the Spanish-Speaking Caribbean," in Juanita De Barros, Audra Diptee, and David V. Trotman (eds.), *Beyond Fragmentation: Perspectives in Caribbean History* (Princeton, NJ: Markus Weiner Publishers, 2006), p. 141

Helleiner, Eric, "Reinterpreting Bretton Woods: International Development and the Neglected Origins of Embedded Liberalism" (2006) **37** *Development and Change* 943

Helleiner, Gerald K., *International Trade and Economic Development* (Harmondsworth, UK: Penguin Books, 1974)

Helleiner, Gerald K. (ed.), *For Good or Evil: Economic Theory and North–South Negotiations* (Toronto: University of Toronto Press, 1982)

Herbert, Frank, *Dune* (New York: Ace Books, 2005 [1965])

Hermes, Andreas, [no title], in Roland William Boyden (ed.), *The Economic Consequences of the League: The World Economic Conference* (London: Europa Publishing Company, 1927) p. 65

Herrmann, Roland, Kees Burger, and Hidde P. Smit, *International Commodity Policy: A Quantitative Analysis* (London: Routledge, 1993)

Hexner, Ervin, *International Cartels* (Chapel Hill, NC: University of North Carolina Press, 1945)

Hicks, Frederick C., *The New World Order: International Organization, International Law, International Cooperation* (Garden City, NY: Doubleday, Page, 1920)

Higman, B. W., "The Sugar Revolution" (2000) **53** *Economic History Review* 213

Hill, Martin, *The Economic and Financial Organization of the League of Nations: A Survey of Twenty-Five Years' Experience* (Washington DC: Carnegie Endowment for International Peace, 1946)

Hirsch, Julius, *National and International Monopolies from the Point of View of Labour, the Consuming Public and Rationalisation* (Geneva: League of Nations, 1926)

Hobsbawm, Eric, *The Age of Extremes: The Short Twentieth Century 1914–1991* (London: Abacus, 1994)

Hobson, J. A., *Imperialism: A Study* (London: James Nisbet & Co., Limited, 1902)

"The Approaching Abandonment of Free Trade" (1902) **71** *Fortnightly Review* 434

Holmes, Oliver Wendell, "Privilege, Malice, and Intent" (1894) **8** *Harvard Law Review* 1

Hornbeck, Stanley, "The Most Favored-Nation Clause" (1909) **3** *American Journal of International Law* 619

Horsefield, J. Keith (ed.), *The International Monetary Fund 1945–1965: Twenty Years of International Monetary Cooperation*, 3 vols. (Washington DC: International Monetary Fund, 1969)

Houston, David, *Memo on Rationalization in the United States* (Geneva: League of Nations, 1927)

Howard-Ellis, C., *The Origin, Structure and Workings of the League of Nations* (London: George Allen & Unwin, 1928)

Howe, Anthony, *Free Trade and Liberal England 1846–1946* (Oxford: Clarendon Press, 1997)

"Free trade and global order: the rise and fall of a Victorian vision," in Duncan Bell (ed.), *Victorian Visions of Global Order: Empire and International Relations in Nineteenth-century Political Thought* (Cambridge: Cambridge University Press, 2007), p. 26

Howse, Robert, "From Politics to Technocracy – and Back Again: The Fate of the Multilateral Trading Regime" (2002) **96** *American Journal of International Law* 94

Howson, Susan and Donald Moggridge (eds.), *The Wartime Diaries of Lionel Robbins and James Meade, 1943–45* (London: Macmillan, 1990)

Hudec, Robert, "The GATT Legal System: A Diplomat's Jurisprudence" (1970) **4** *Journal of World Trade* 615

Developing Countries in the GATT Legal System (London: Trade Policy Research Centre, 1987)

Enforcing International Trade Law: The Evolution of the Modern GATT Legal System (Salem, NH: Butterworth Legal Publishers, 1993)

Hudson, Manley O., *Progress in International Organization, by Manley O. Hudson … Published for the University of Idaho upon the Occasion of the Inauguration of the William Edgar Borah Foundation for the Outlawry of War* (Stanford: Stanford University Press, 1932)

Hyam, Ronald, *Britain's Imperial Century 1815–1914. A Study of Empire and Expansion*, 3rd edn. (Houndmills: Palgrave Macmillan, 2002)

Understanding the British Empire (Cambridge: Cambridge University Press, 2010)

Information Section, *The Monetary and Economic Conference (London, 1933). An Account of the Preparatory Work for the Conference and an Outline of the Previous Activities of the Economic and Financial Organisation of the League of Nations* (Geneva: Secretariat of the League of Nations, 1933)

Institute on World Organization, *World Organization: A Balance Sheet of the First Great Experiment* (Washington DC, American Council on Public Affairs 1942)

International Institute of Agriculture, *Agricultural Problems in their International Aspect* (Rome: International Institute of Agriculture, 1927)

International Labour Office, *Intergovernmental Commodity Control Agreements* (Montreal: International Labour Organization, 1943)

Irwin, Douglas A., Petros C. Mavroidis, and Alan O. Sykes, *The Genesis of the GATT* (Cambridge: Cambridge University Press, 2008)

Ismail, Faizel, "Rediscovering the Role of Developing Countries in GATT before the Doha Round" (2008) **1** *Law and Development Review* 50

Jackson, John H., *World Trade and the Law of GATT* (Indianapolis, Ind.: Bobbs-Merril, 1969)

Restructuring the GATT System (New York: Council on Foreign Relations Press, 1990)

The World Trading System: Law and Policy of International Economic Relations, 2nd edn. (Cambridge, Mass.: MIT Press, 1997)

Sovereignty, the WTO and Changing Fundamentals of International Law (Cambridge: Cambridge University Press, 2006)

Jacobsson, Per, "The Theoretical Solution," in Roland William Boyden (ed.), *The Economic Consequences of the League: The World Economic Conference* (London: Europa Publishing Company, 1927), p. 43

James, Clifford L., "International Control of Raw Sugar Supplies" (1931) **21** *American Economic Review* 481

Jenks, Leland Hamilton, *Our Cuban Colony: A Study in Sugar* (New York: Vanguard Press, [1928])

Jessup, Philip, "Confidential Memorandum on the Cuban Situation" [*c.* early 1933], quoted from Louis A. Pérez, Jr., *Cuba Under the Platt Amendment 1902–1934* (Pittsburgh, Pa.: University of Pittsburgh Press, 1986), p. 303

"Negotiating Reciprocity Treaties" (1933) **27** *American Journal of International Law* 738

Joerges, Christian, Bo Stråth, and Peter Wagner (eds.), *The Economy as Polity: The Political Constitution of Contemporary Capitalism* (London: UCL Press, 2005)

Joerges, Christian and Josef Falke (eds.), *Karl Polanyi: Globalisation and the Potential of Law in Transnational Markets* (Oxford: Hart, 2011)

Johnson, Richard, *The Case Against the Sugar Tax and Sugar Convention: Letters Communicated to the Press by Richard Johnson, J. P., President of the National Union of Mineral Water Manufacturers* (London: Barclay, 1903)

Johnston, Charles R., *Law and Policy on Intergovernmental Primary Commodity Agreements*, loose-leaf (Dobbs Ferry, NY: Oceana Publications, 1976)

"Developments in the Tokyo Round of the Multilateral Trade Negotiations" (1979) **73** *American Journal of International Law* 520

Kaldor, Nicholas, "The Role of Commodity Prices in Economic Recovery" (July 1983) **149** *Lloyds Bank Review* 21

Kapcia, Antoni, *Havana: The Making of Cuban Culture* (Oxford: Berg, 2005)

Kasahara, Shigehisa and Charles Gore (eds.), *Beyond Conventional Wisdom in Development Policy: An Intellectual History of UNCTAD 1964–2004* (Geneva: United Nations Conference on Trade and Development, 2004)

Kaufmann, Wilhelm, *Welt-Zuckerindustrie und Internationales und Koloniales Recht* (Berlin: Franz Siemenroth, 1904)

Kennedy, David, "On the Cartel Bogey," (1977) **1** *The Fletcher Forum* 232

"The Move to Institutions" (1987) **8** *Cardozo Law Review* 841

"The International Style in Postwar Law and Policy" (1994) **1** *Utah Law Review* 7

"International Law and the Nineteenth Century: History of an Illusion" (1997) **17** *Quinnipiac Law Review* 99

"The Politics of the Invisible College: International Governance and the Politics of Expertise" (2001) **5** *European Human Rights Law Review* 463

"The 'Rule of Law', Political Choices, and Development Common Sense," in David Trubek & Alvaro Santos (eds.), *The New Law and Economic Development: A Critical Appraisal* (Cambridge: Cambridge University Press, 2006), p. 95

Keynes, John Maynard, *The Economic Consequences of Peace* (New York: Harcourt, Brace, and Howe, 1920)

"Pros and Cons of Tariffs," *The Listener* (November 30, 1932), reprinted in Donald Moggridge (ed.), *The Collected Writings of John Maynard Keynes*, 30 vols. (London: Macmillan, 1971), vol. **XXI**, p. 204

"The World Economic Conference 1933," *The New Statesmen and Nation* (December 24, 1932), reprinted in Donald Moggridge (ed.), *The Collected Writings of John Maynard Keynes*, 30 vols. (London: Macmillan, 1971), vol. **XXI**, p. 210

"The International Control of Raw Materials" (1942), in Donald Moggridge, (ed.), *The Collected Writings of John Maynard Keynes*, 30 vols. (London: Macmillan, 1971), vol. **XXVII**, p. 112

Khan, Kabir-ur-Rahman, "The International Sugar Agreement 1977: Market Regulator and Instrument of International Policy" (1978) **3** *Food Policy* 104

The Law and Organisation of International Commodity Agreements (The Hague: Martinus Nijhoff, 1982)

Kindleberger, Charles P., *The World in Depression 1929–1939*, rev. edn. (Berkeley, Calif.: University of California Press, 1973 [1986])

Kingsbury, Benedict, Nico Krisch, and Richard B. Stewart, "The Emergence of Global Administrative Law" (2005) **68** *Law and Contemporary Problems* 15

Klabbers, Jan, *An Introduction to International Institutional Law*, 2nd edn. (Cambridge: Cambridge University Press, 2009)

Klabbers, Jan and René Lefeber (eds.), *Essays on the Law of Treaties: A Collection of Essays in Honour of Bert Vierdag* (The Hague: Martinus Nijhoff Publishers, 1998)

Klein, Kenneth, "International Commodity Agreements" (1976) **6** *Georgia Journal of International & Comparative Law* 275

Knorr, Klaus, "Market Instability and United States Policy" (1945) **62** *Journal of Political Economy* 375

"The Problem of International Cartels and Intergovernmental Commodity Agreements" (1946) **55** *Yale Law Journal* 1097

Koch, F. E., "Cartels as Instruments of International Economic Organization: Public and Private Legal Aspects of International Cartels" (1945) **8** *Modern Law Review* 130

Koskenniemi, Martti, *The Gentle Civilizer of Nations: The Rise and Fall of International Law 1870–1960* (Cambridge: Cambridge University Press, 2001)

"The Legacy of the Nineteenth Century," in David Armstrong (ed.), *Routledge Handbook of International Law* (New York: Routledge, 2009), p. 141

"The Politics of International Law – 20 Years Later" (2009) **20** *European Journal of International Law* 7

Krueger, Anne O., *The Benefits and Costs of Import Substitution in India: A Microeconomic Study* (Minneapolis, Minn.: University of Minnesota Press, 1975)

Krueger, Anne O. (ed.), *The WTO as an International Organization* (Chicago, Ill.: University of Chicago Press, 1998)

Krugman, Paul R., Maurice Obstfeld and Marc J. Melitz, *International Economics: Theory & Policy*, 9th edn. (Boston, Mass.: Addison Wesley, 2012)

Krumme, Robert D., "International Commodity Agreements: Purpose, Policy, and Procedure" (1962–3) **31** *George Washington Law Review* 784

Lammers, Clemens, "The Cartel Question at the World Economic Conference," Karl Scholz (trans.), (1927) **134** *Annals of the American Academy of Political and Social Science* 145

Lang, Andrew, "Reconstructing Embedded Liberalism: John Gerard Ruggie and Constructivist Approaches to the Study of the International Trade Regime" (2006) **9** *Journal of International Economic Law* 81

World Trade Law After Neoliberalism: Reimagining the Global Economic Order (Oxford: Oxford University Press, 2011)

Lapeyrade, Pierre-Antoine Joseph, *La Question des Sucres* (doctoral thesis, Université de Bordeaux, Faculté de Droit, 1901)

Law, Alton, *International Commodity Agreements: Setting, Performance, and Prospects* (Lexington, Mass: Lexington Books, 1975)

League of Nations, *International Financial Conference, Brussels 1920: Proceedings of the Conference*, 3 vols. (London: League of Nations, 1920)

Ten Years of World Cooperation (Geneva: Secretariat of the League of Nations, 1930)

Journal of the Monetary and Economic Conference (London: World Monetary and Economic Conference, League of Nations, June 28, June 29, and July 20, 1933)

International Sugar Conference (Geneva: League of Nations, 1937)

Towards a Better Economic World (Geneva: Information Section, 1939)

Commercial Policy in the Interwar Period: International Proposals and National Policies (Geneva: League of Nations, 1942)

World Economic Conference, Geneva, May 1927, Final Report (Geneva: League of Nations, 1927)

Levermore, Charles H., *The First Yearbook of the League of Nations: What the League of Nations Accomplished in One Year* (Brooklyn, NY: Brooklyn Daily Eagle, 1921)

Lewis, Stephen R., *Pakistan: Industrialization and Trade Policies* (London: Oxford University Press for the Development Centre of the Organisation for Economic Co-operation and Development, 1970)

Lewis, W. Arthur, *Economic Survey 1919–1939* (London: George Allen and Unwin, 1949)

"The Export Stimulus," in W. Arthur Lewis (ed.), *Tropical Development 1880–1913* (London: George Allen & Unwin Ltd, 1970) p. 13

List, Friedrich, *The National System of Political Economy*, Sampson S. Lloyd (trans.), (London: Longmans Green, 1885)

Lobban, Michael, "English Approaches to International Law in the Nineteenth Century," in Matthew Craven, Malgosia Fitzmaurice, and Maria Vogiatzi (eds.), *Time, History, and International Law* (Leiden: Martinus Nijhoff, 2007), p. 65

Lobdell, Richard A., "British officials and the West Indian peasantry, 1842–1938," in Malcolm Cross and Gad Heuman (eds.), *Labour in the Caribbean: From Emancipation to Independence* (London: Macmillan Caribbean, 1988), p. 65

Look Lai, Walton, *Indentured Labor, Caribbean Sugar: Chinese and Indian Migrants to the British West Indies, 1838–1918* (Baltimore, Md.: Johns Hopkins University Press, 1993)

Lough, Thomas "The Brussels Sugar Convention" (1903) **83** *The Contemporary Review* 75

Lowenfeld, Andreas F., "International Commodity Controls – Some Lessons from the Coffee Agreement" (1967) **61** *American Journal of International Law* 785

"Book Review of Law and Policy of Intergovernmental Primary Commodity Agreements by Charles B. Johnston" (1979) **73** *American Journal of International Law* 309

Lugard, Lord Frederick, *The Dual Mandate in British Tropical Africa*, 5th edn. (London: Frank Cass, 1965 [1922])

Lyons, F. S. L., *Internationalism in Europe 1815–1914* (Leyden: A. W. Sythoff, 1963)

MacGregor, D. H., *International Cartels* (Geneva: League of Nations, 1927)

Mahler, Vincent A., "The Political Economy of North–South Commodity Bargaining: The Case of the International Sugar Agreement" (1984) **38** *International Organizations* 709

Maizels, Alfred, *Industrial Growth and World Trade: An Empirical Study of Trends in Production, Consumption and Trade in Manufactures from 1899 to 1959 with a Discussion of Probable Future Trends* (Cambridge: Cambridge University Press, 1963)

"Reforming the World Economy," in Michael Zammit Cutajar (ed.), *UNCTAD and the North–South Dialogue: The First Twenty Years. Essays in Memory of W. R. Malinowski* (Oxford: Pergamon Press, 1985), p. 101

Commodities in Crisis: The Commodity Crisis of the 1980s and the Political Economy of International Commodity Prices (Oxford: Clarendon Press, 1992)

"Economic Dependence on Commodities," in John Toye (ed.), *Trade and Development: Directions for the 21st Century* (Cheltenham: Edward Elgar and United Nations, 2003), p. 169

Malinvaud, Maurice, *Les Primes Sucres* (doctoral thesis, Université de Rennes, Faculté de Droit, 1901)

Mander, Linden A., *Foundations of Modern World Society* (Stanford, Calif.: Stanford University Press, 1941)

Mangone, Gerard J., *A Short History of International Organization* (New York: McGraw-Hill Book Company, 1954)

Mark, Janette and Ann Weston, "The Havana Charter Experience: Lessons for Developing Countries," in John Whalley (ed.), *Developing Countries and the Global Trading System*, **2** vols. (London: Macmillan, 1989), vol. I, p. 45

Marks, Susan, "False Contingency" (2010) **62** *Current Legal Problems* 1

Markwell, Donald, *John Maynard Keynes and International Relations* (Oxford: Oxford University Press, 2006)

Martineau, George, *The Statistical Aspect of the Question of Sugar* (London: Royal Statistical Society, 1899)

"The Brussels Sugar Convention" (1904) **14** *The Economic Journal* 34

Marx, Karl, "Speech on the Question of Free Trade," in Karl Marx and Friedrich Engels, *Collected Works. Volume VI: 1845–48* (New York: International Publishers, 1976), p. 450

Mason, Edward S., *Controlling World Trade: Cartels and Commodity Agreements* (New York: McGraw Book Company, 1946)

Matikkala, Mira, *Empire and Imperial Ambition: Liberty, Englishness and Anti-imperialism in Late-Victorian Britain* (London: I. B. Tauris, 2011)

Mazower, Mark, *No Enchanted Palace: The End of Empire and the Ideological Origins of the United Nations* (Princeton, NJ: Princeton University Press, 2009)

Mazoyer, Marcel and Laurence Roudart, *A History of World Agriculture: From the Neolithic Age to the Current Crisis*, James H. Membrez (trans.), (New York: Monthly Review Press, 2006)

McAvoy, Muriel, *Sugar Baron: Manuel Rionda and the Fortunes of Pre-Castro Cuba* (Gainesville: University Press of Florida, 2003)

McClure, Wallace M., *World Prosperity Through the Economic Work of the League of Nations* (New York: MacMillan Company, 1933)

McGillivray, Gillian, "'Dear President Machado': *Colono* Nationalism During Cuba's Turbulent 1920s and 1930s" (2003) **37** *Journal of Caribbean History* 70

Blazing Cane: Sugar Communities, Class and State Formation in Cuba, 1868–1959 (Durham, NC: Duke University Press, 2009)

McIntyre, Sir Alister, "Summary and Conclusions by the Moderator," in Budi Hartantyo and Hidde P. Smit (eds.), *International Commodity Development Strategies* (Amsterdam: VU University Press, 1993), p. 423

McLeod, Marc C., "Undesirable Aliens: Race, Ethnicity, and Nationalism in the Comparison of Haitian and British West Indian Immigrant Workers in Cuba, 1912–1939" (1998) **31** *Journal of Social History* 599

McMahon, Joseph A., "The Uruguay Round and Agriculture: Chartering a New Direction?" (1995) **29** *International Lawyer* 411

McNicol, David L., *Commodity Agreements and Price Stabilization* (Lexington, Mass.: Lexington Books, 1978)

Mermin, Samuel, "Sugar: A Rugged Collectivist" (1936–7) **31** *Illinois Law Review* 320

Mill, John Stuart, *Principles of Political Economy* (London, 1848)

Miller, David Hunter, *The Drafting of the Covenant*, 2 vols. (New York: G. P. Putnam's Sons, 1928)

Mintz, Sidney W., *Sweetness and Power: The Place of Sugar in Modern History* (New York: Penguin Books, 1985)

Miyazaki, Hayao, "The Making of Princess Mononoke," Series 2, Segment 1, Ghibli Blog, online: http://ghiblicon.blogspot.com/2008/11/making-of-princess-mononoke-series-two.html (accessed May 31, 2014)[taken from amateur subtitled translation from the Japanese to English]

Moggridge, Donald (ed.), *The Collected Writings of John Maynard Keynes*, 30 vols. (London: Macmillan, 1971)

Montesquieu, Charles Louis, *De L'Esprit des Lois*, Robert Derathé (ed.), 2 vols. (Paris: Garnier Frères, 1973)

The Spirit of the Law, Anne N. Cohler (trans.), Basia Carolyn Miller and Harold Samuel Stone (eds.) (Cambridge: Cambridge University Press, 1989 [1748])

Moreno Fraginals, Manuel R., "Caribbean Plantations and the European Sugar Beet Industry," in Helmut Ahlfeld (ed.), *Sugar: Essays to Mark the 125th Anniversary of F. O. Licht* (Ratzenburg: F. O. Licht, 1989), p. 1

Moura Filho, Heitor, "Pioneering Multilateralism: the Sugar Agreements 1864–1914" (2007) MPRA Paper No. 5208, online: http://mpra.ub.uni-muenchen.de/5208 (accessed May 26, 2014)

Moya Pons, Frank, *History of the Caribbean: Plantations, Trade and War in the Atlantic World* (Markus Wiener Publishers, 2007)

Murphy, Craig N., *International Organization and Industrial Change: Global Governance Since 1850* (Oxford: Oxford University Press, 1994)

Myers, D. P., *Manual of Collections of Treaties and of Collections Relating to Treaties* (Cambridge: Cambridge University Press, 1922)

Nappi, Carmine, *Commodity Market Controls: A Historical Review* (Lexington, Mass.: Lexington Books, 1979)

Newberry, David M. G. and Joseph E. Stiglitz, *The Theory of Commodity Price Stabilization* (Oxford: Oxford University Press, 1981)

North-South Institute, *Commodity Trade: Test Case for a New Economic Order* (Ottawa: North-South Institute, 1978)

Notz, William F., "International Private Agreements in the Form of Cartels, Syndicates, and Other Combinations" (1920) **28** *Journal of Political Economy* 658

Nützenadel, Alexander and Frank Trentmann, "Mapping Food and Globalization," in Alexander Nützenadel and Frank Trentmann (eds.), *Food and Globalization: Consumption Markets and Politics in the Modern World* (Oxford: Berg, 2008), p. 1

Odell, John and Barry Eichengreen, "The United States, the ITO, and the WTO: Exit Options, Agent Slack, and Presidential Leadership," in Anne O. Krueger (ed.), *The WTO as an International Organization* (Chicago, Ill.: University of Chicago Press, 1998), p. 181

Ohlin, Bertil, *The Course and Phases of the World Economic Depression: Report Presented to the Assembly of the League of Nations*, rev. edn. (Geneva: League of Nations, 1931)

Oppenheim, L. F. L., *International Law: A Treatise. Vol. I: Peace*, 1st edn. (New York: Longman, Greens and Co., 1905)

International Law: A Treatise. Vol I: Peace, 2nd edn. (New York: Longman, Greens and Co., 1912)

The League of Nations and Its Problems – Three Lectures (London: Longmans, 1919)

Orford, Anne, "The Past as Law or History? The Relevance of Imperialism for Modern International Law," in Mark Toufayan, Emmanuelle Tourme-Jouannet, and Hélène Ruiz Fabri (eds.), *International Law and New Approaches to the Third World: Between Repetition and Renewal* (Paris: Société de Législation Comparée, 2012), p. 97

Ortiz, Fernando, *Cuban Counterpoint: Tobacco and Sugar*, Harriet de Onís (trans.), (New York: A. A. Knopf, 1947)

Oualid, William, *Social Effects of International Industrial Agreements: The Protection of Workers and Consumers* (Geneva: League of Nations, 1926)

Pahuja, Sundhya, *Decolonising International Law: Development, Economic Growth and the Politics of Universality* (Cambridge: Cambridge University Press, 2011)

Pearson, H. S., "Scientific Management and Cartels," in *Two Memoranda Presented to the World Economic Conference, May 1927* (Geneva: International Management Institute, 1927)

Pemberton, Jo-Anne, "New Worlds for Old: The League of Nations and the Age of Electricity" (2002) **28** *Review of International Studies* 311

Penrose, E. F., *Economic Planning for the Peace* (Princeton, NJ: Princeton University Press, 1953)

Pérez, Jr., Louis A., *Cuba Under the Platt Amendment 1902–1934* (Pittsburgh, Penn.: University of Pittsburgh Press, 1986)

Cuba: Between Reform and Revolution, 2nd edn. (New York: Oxford University Press, 1995)

Cuba and the United States: Ties of Singular Intimacy, 3rd edn. (Athens, Ga.: University of Georgia Press, 2003)

Pigman, G. A., "Hegemony and Trade Liberalization Policy: Britain and the Brussels Sugar Convention of 1902" (1997) **23** *Review of International Studies* 185

Pitts, Jennifer, "Boundaries of Victorian International Law," in Duncan Bell (ed.), *Victorian Visions of Global Order: Empire and International Relations in Nineteenth-century Political Thought* (Cambridge: Cambridge University Press, 2007), p. 67

Poggi, Muriel, "The German Sugar Beet Industry" (1930) **6** *Economic Geography* 81

Polanyi, Karl, *The Great Transformation: The Political and Economic Origins of Our Times* (Boston, Mass.: Beacon Press, 2001 [1944])

"The Economy as Instituted Process," in Karl Polanyi, Conrad M. Arensberg, and Harry W. Pearson (eds.), *Trade and Market in the Early Empires* (New York: The Free Press, 1957), p. 243

Politis, Nicolas, "L'organisation de l'Union internationale des sucres" (1904) **2** *Revue de science et de législation financières* 1

Pollan, Michael, *The Omnivore's Dilemma: A Natural History of Four Meals* (London: Penguin Books, 2006)

Pollitt, Brian, "The Cuban Sugar Economy in the 1930s," in Bill Albert and Adrian Graves (eds.), *The World Sugar Economy in War and Depression 1914–40* (London: Routledge, 1988), p. 97

Pomeranz, Kenneth and Steven Topic, *The World that Trade Created. Society, Culture, and the World Economy: 1400 to the Present*, 2nd edn. (Armonk, NY: M. E. Sharpe, 2006)

Porter, Bernard, *Critics of Empire: British Radicals and the Imperial Challenge* (London: I. B. Tauris, 2008 [1968])

Pound, Roscoe, "Liberty of Contract" (1909) **18** *Yale Law Journal* 454

Power, Sir John, "Comments" (1927) **6** *Journal of the Royal Institute of International Affairs* 363

Pradier-Fodéré, P., "Le Congrès de droit international Sud-Américain et les traités de Montevideo" (1889) **21** *Revue de droit international et de législation comparée* 217

Prashad, Vijay, *The Darker Nations: A People's History of the Third World* (New York: New Press, 2007)

Prebisch, Raúl, *The Economic Development of Latin America and its Principal Problems* (Lake Success, NY: United Nations – Economic Commission of Latin America, 1950)

Towards a New Trade Policy for Development (New York: United Nations, 1964)
Towards a Global Strategy of Development: Report by the Secretary-General of the United Nations Conference on Trade and Development to the Second Session of the Conference (New York: United Nations, 1968)
Preparatory Commission of Experts, *Monetary and Economic Conference: Draft Annotated Agenda* (Geneva: League of Nations, 1933)
Preparatory Committee for the International Conference, *Report on the First Session of the Committee (held at Geneva from April 26th to May 1st, 1926)* (Geneva: League of Nations, 1926)
Questel, Peter J., *An Appeal on Behalf of the British West Indies as Affected by the Late Proposed Reduction of Duty on Foreign Sugar* (London: Smith, Elder & Co., 1841)
Quill, Edward, "The Failure of International Commodity Agreements: Forms, Functions, and Implications" (1994) **22** *Denver Journal of International Law and Policy* 503
Raffaelli, Marcelo, *Rise and Demise of Commodity Agreements* (Cambridge: Woodhead Publishing Limited, 1995)
Rainis, Gustav (ed.), *Government and Economic Development* (New Haven, Conn.: Yale University Press, 1971)
Rajagopal, Balakrishnan, *International Law from Below: Development, Social Movements and Third World Resistance* (Cambridge: Cambridge University Press, 2003)
Rangarajan, L. N., *Commodity Conflict: The Political Economy of International Commodity Negotiations* (Ithaca, NY: Cornell University Press, 1978)
"Commodity Conflict Revisited: From Nairobi to Belgrade" (1983) **5** *Third World Quarterly* 586
Rasulov, Akbar, "'The Nameless Rapture of the Struggle': Towards a Marxist Class-theoretic Approach to International Law" (2008) **18** *Finnish Yearbook of International Law* 243
Reinalda, Bob, *Routledge History of International Organizations: From 1815 to the Present Day* (New York: Routledge, 2009)
Reinsch, Paul S., "International Administrative Law and National Sovereignty" (1909) **3** *American Journal of International Law* 1
Public International Unions, 1st edn. (Boston, Mass.: Ginn and Company, 1911)
Reynolds, Paul D., *International Commodity Agreements and the Common Fund: A Legal and Financial Analysis* (New York: Praeger, 1978)
Rhodes, Sir Campbell W., [no title], in Roland William Boyden (ed.), *The Economic Consequences of the League: The World Economic Conference* (London: Europa Publishing Company, 1927), p. 74
Ricardo, David, *On the Principles of Economy and Taxation* (London: John Murray, 1817)
Richardson, Ben, *Sugar: Refined Power in a Global Regime* (Basingstoke: Palgrave MacMillan, 2009)
Richardson, Bonham C., *Igniting the Caribbean's Past: Fire in British West Indian History* (Chapel Hill, NC: University of North Carolina Press, 2004)

Rittich, Kerry, *Recharacterizing Restructuring: Law, Distribution, and Gender in Market Reform* (The Hague: Kluwer Law International, 2002)

Robertson, Charles L., "The Creation of UNCTAD," in Robert Cox (ed.), *International Organisation. World Politics: Studies in Economic and Social Agencies* (London: Macmillan, 1969)

Roll, Eric, *The Combined Food Board: A Study in Wartime International Planning* (Stanford, Calif.: Stanford University Press, 1956)

Rowe, J. W. F., *Studies in the Artificial Control of Raw Material Supplies* (London: Royal Economic Society, 1930 [Memorandum No. 23])

Markets and Men: A Study of Artificial Control Schemes in Some Primary Industries (Cambridge: Cambridge University Press, 1936)

"Sugar," in John Maynard Keynes, J. W. F. Rowe *et al.*, *Stocks of Commodities* (London: Royal Economic Society, 1937 [Memorandum No. 69])

Primary Commodities in International Trade (Cambridge: Cambridge University Press, 1965)

Ruggie, John, "International Regimes, Transactions, and Change: Embedded Liberalism in the Postwar Economic Order" (1982) **36** *International Organizations* 379

"At Home Abroad, Abroad at Home: International Liberalization and Domestic Stability in the New World Economy" (1994) **24** *Millennium* 507

"Taking Embedded Liberalism Global: The Corporate Connection," in David Held and Mathias Koening-Archibugi (eds.), *Taming Globalization: Frontiers of Governance* (Cambridge: Polity Press, 2003), p. 93

Runciman, W. Leslie, "The World Economic Conference at Geneva" (1927) **37** *Economic Journal* 465

Russell, Bertrand, "A Need for Political Scepticism" [1923], in Bertrand Russell, *Sceptical Essays* (London: Routledge, 2004 [1928]), p. 108

Said, Edward, *Culture and Imperialism* (New York: Vintage Books, 1993)

Salter, Arthur and Arthur Porritt (eds.), *The Causes of War: Economic, Industrial, Racial, Religious, Scientific, and Political* (New York: The Macmillan Company, 1932)

Salter, J. Arthur, *Allied Shipping Control: An Experiment in International Administration* (Oxford: Clarendon Press, 1921)

"Contributions of the League of Nations to the Recovery of Europe" (1927) **134** *Annals of the American Academy of Political and Social Science* 132

"The Economic Conference: Prospects and Practical Results" (1927) **6** *Journal of the Royal Institute of International Affairs* 350

"The League's Contribution," in Roland William Boyden (ed.), *The Economic Consequences of the League: The World Economic Conference* (London: Europa Publishing Company, 1927), p. 1

"The Economic Causes of War," in Arthur Salter and Arthur Porritt (eds.), *The Causes of War: Economic, Industrial, Racial, Religious, Scientific, and Political* (New York: The Macmillan Company, 1932)

World Trade and its Future (Philadelphia, Penn.: University of Pennsylvania Press, 1936)

Memoirs of a Public Servant (London: Faber and Faber, 1961)
Sands, Philippe, "Book Review of The Law and Organisation of International Commodity Agreements by Kabir-ur-Rahman Khan" (1986) **57** *British Yearbook of International Law* 386
Sauvant, Karl P., *The Group of 77: Evolution, Structure, Organization* (New York: Oceana Publications, 1981)
Sauvant, Karl P. and Hajo Hasenpflug (eds.), *The New International Economic Order: Confrontation or Cooperation Between North and South?* (Boulder, Colo.: Westview Press, 1977)
Sayre, Francis B., *Experiments in International Administration* (New York: Harpers, 1919)
Schüller, R., [no title], in Roland William Boyden (ed.), *The Economic Consequences of the League: The World Economic Conference* (London: Europa Publishing Company, 1927)
Scott, George, *The Rise and Fall of the League of Nations* (London: Hutchinson, 1973)
Scott, James, "Developing Countries in the ITO and GATT Negotiations" (2009) Brooks World Poverty Institute Working Paper 95, online: www.bwpi.manchester.ac.uk/medialibrary/publications/working_papers/bwpi-wp-9509.pdf (accessed May 26, 2014)
Semmel, Bernard, *The Rise of Free Trade Imperialism: Classical Political Economy and the Empire of Free Trade and Imperialism 1750–1850* (Cambridge: Cambridge University Press, 1970)
Shaw, D. John, *World Food Security: A History Since 1945* (Basingstoke: Palgrave Macmillan, 2007)
Shelley, Mary, *Frankenstein* (Lakewood, Colo.: Millipede Press Book, 2007 [1831])
Shephard, C. Y., "The Sugar Industry of the British West Indies and British Guiana with Special Reference to Trinidad" (1929) **5** *Economic Geography* 149
Shepheard, Wallwyn P. B., "The Most-favoured-nation Article" (1902) **5** *Journal of the Society of Comparative Legislation* 132
Silverstrini, Blanca G., "New National Spaces in the Spanish Caribbean," in Juanita De Barros, Audra Diptee, and David V. Trotman (eds.), *Beyond Fragmentation: Perspectives in Caribbean History* (Princeton, NJ: Markus Weiner Publishers, 2006), p. 231
Singer, Hans W., "The Distribution of Gains between Investing and Borrowing Countries" (1950) **40** *American Economic Review* 473
Singer, Joseph William, "Legal Realism Now" (1988) **76** *California Law Review* 465
Slaughter, Anne-Marie, *A New World Order* (Princeton, NJ: Princeton University Press, 2004)
Smart, William, *The Sugar Bounties: The Case for and against Government Interference* (Edinburgh and London: William Blackwood and Sons, 1887)
Smith, Ian, "Commonwealth Sugar Exporters and the European Community," in Simon Harris and Ian Smith (eds.), *World Sugar Markets in a State of Flux* (London: Trade Policy Research Centre, 1973), p. 49

"Structure and Policy Changes in World Sugar" (1977) **11** *Journal of World Trade Law* 228

"Prospects of a New International Sugar Agreement" (1983) **17** *Journal of World Trade Law* 308

Smith, Robert, *The United States and Cuba: Business and Diplomacy, 1916–1960* (New Haven, Conn.: College and University Press, 1960)

Smuts, Jan, *The League of Nations: A Practical Suggestion* (London: Hodder and Stoughton, 1918)

The South Centre, *International Commodity Problems and Policies: The Key Issues for Developing Countries* (Geneva: The South Centre, 1996)

Spitzer, H. M., "Rationalization and Cartels," in *Two Memoranda Presented to the World Economic Conference, May 1927* (Geneva: International Management Institute, 1927)

Staples, Amy L. S., *The Birth of Development: How the World Bank, Food and Agriculture Organization, and World Health Organization Have Changed the World, 1945–1965* (Kent, O.: Kent State University Press, 2006)

Steffek, Jens, *Embedded Liberalism and its Critics: Justifying Global Governance in the American Century* (New York: Palgrave Macmillan, 2006)

Steil, Benn, *The Battle of Bretton Woods: John Maynard Keynes, Harry Dexter White, and the Making of a New World Order* (Princeton, NJ: Princeton University Press, 2013)

Stein, Robert Louis, *The French Sugar Business in the Eighteenth Century* (Baton Rouge, La.: Louisiana State University Press, 1988)

Stocking, George W. and Myron W. Watkins, *Cartels in Action: Case Studies in International Business Diplomacy* (New York: Twentieth Century Fund, 1947)

Stubbs, William C., "Sugar" (1904) **5** Publications of the American Economic Association, 3rd ser., *Papers and Proceedings of the Sixteenth Annual Meeting* 79

Swerling, Boris C., *International Control of Sugar, 1918–41* (Stanford, Calif.: Stanford University Press, 1949)

"Control of an Export Industry: Cuban Sugar" (1951) **33** *Journal of Farm Economics* 346

"The International Sugar Agreement of 1953" (1954) **44** *American Economic Review* 837

Sykes, Alan O., "The Questionable Case for Subsidies Regulation: A Comparative Perspective" (2010) **2** *Journal of Legal Analysis* 473

Sylvest, Casper, "International Law in Nineteenth-century Britain" (2004) **75** *British Yearbook of International Law* 9

Symposium, "International Commodity Agreements" (1963) **28** *Law & Contemporary Problems* 271–415

"International Trade After the Cold War: Revisiting Allies' Idealistic Vision of the Post-World War II International Economic Order" (1993–4) **14**:2 *Northern Illinois University Law Review*

"The League of Nations and the Construction of the Periphery" (2011) **24**:4 *European Journal of International Law* 797–922

Tarullo, Daniel K., "Logic, Myth, and the International Economic Order" (1985) **26** *Harvard International Law Journal* 533

Taussig, F. W., "The End of Sugar Bounties" (1903) **18** *Quarterly Journal of Economics* 103

Taylor, Benjamin, "Sugar and the Convention" (1902) **71** *The Fortnightly Review* 636

"The Brussels Sugar Convention" (1909) **190** *The North American Review* 347

Taylor, Ian and Karen Smith, *United Nations Conference on Trade and Development (UNCTAD)* (Abingdon: Routledge, 2007)

Taylor, Miles, "Imperium et libertas? Rethinking the radical critique of imperialism during the nineteenth century" (1991) **19** *Journal of Imperial and Commonwealth History* 1

Timoshenko, Vladimir P. and Boris Swerling, *The World's Sugar: Progress and Policy* (Stanford, Calif.: Stanford University Press, 1957)

Tomlinson, B. R., "What Was the Third World?" (2003) **38** *Journal of Contemporary History* 307

Topik, Steven, Carlos Marichal, and Zephyr Frank (eds.), *From Silver to Cocaine: Latin American Commodity Chains and the Building of the World Economy 1500–2000* (Durham, SC: Duke University Press, 2006)

Toufayan, Mark, Emmanuelle Tourme-Jouannet, and Hélène Ruiz Fabri (eds.), *International Law and New Approaches to the Third World: Between Repetition and Renewal* (Paris: Société de Législation Comparée, 2012)

Toussaint-Samat, Meguelonn, *History of Food*, Anthea Bell (trans.), (Cambridge, Mass.: Blackwell, 1994)

Toye, John (ed.), *Trade and Development: Directions for the 21st Century* (Cheltenham: Edward Elgar and United Nations, 2003)

Toye, John and Richard Toye, *The UN and Global Political Economy* (Bloomington, Ind.: Indiana University Press, 2004)

Toye, Richard, "Developing Multilateralism: The Havana Charter and the Fight for the International Trade Organization, 1947–1948" (2003) 25 *International History Review* 253

Toynbee, Arnold, *The Industrial Revolution* (Boston, Mass.: Beacon Press, 1962 [1884])

Trentmann, Frank, "Coping with Shortage: The Problem of Food Security and Global Visions of Coordination, c. 1890s–1950," in Frank Trentmann and Flemming Just (eds.), *Food and Conflict in Europe in the Age of the Two World Wars* (New York: Palgrave Macmillan, 2006)

Free Trade Nation: Commerce, Consumption, and Civil Society in Modern Britain (Oxford: Oxford University Press, 2008)

Trentmann, Frank (ed.), *The Oxford Handbook of the History of Consumption* (Oxford: Oxford University Press, 2012)

Trubek, David and Alvaro Santos (eds.), *The New Law and Economic Development: A Critical Appraisal* (Cambridge: Cambridge University Press, 2006)

Tsou, Stanley S. and John D. Black, "International Commodity Arrangements" (1944) **58** *Quarterly Journal of Economics* 521
Unger, Roberto Mangabeira, *Free Trade Reimagined: The World Division of Labor and the Method of Economics* (Princeton, NJ: Princeton University Press, 2007)
United Nations Conference on Trade and Development, *Proceedings of the United Nations Conference on Trade and Development, Second Session*, vol. I (New York: United Nations, 1968)
The History of UNCTAD 1964–1984 (New York: United Nations, 1985)
United Nations Economic and Social Council, *Official Records: First Year* (London: United Nations, 1946)
United States Department of State, *Proposals for Expansion of World Trade and Employment* (Washington DC: Department of State, 1945)
Press Release, "Joint Statement by the United States and the United Kingdom" (December 6, 1945) **13** *Department of State Bulletin* 912
Press Release, "Trade Negotiation Proposed" (December 13, 1945) **13** *Department of State Bulletin* 970
Havana Charter for an International Trade Organization; Including a Guide to the Study of the Charter (Washington DC: Department of State, 1948)
Press Releases, "Future Administration of GATT" (December 6 and 18, 1950) **23** *Department of State Bulletin* 977
Vaccaro, Pamela, *Beyond the Ice Cream Cone: The Whole Scoop on Food at the 1904 World's Fair* (St. Louis, Mo.: Enid Press, 2004)
Verne, Jules, *Vingt mille lieues sous les mers* (Paris: Hetzel, 1870)
L'Île mystérieuse (Paris: Hetzel, 1874)
Viner, Jacob, *Dumping: A Problem in International Trade* (Chicago, Ill.: University of Chicago, 1923)
Memorandum on Dumping (Geneva: League of Nations, 1923)
"National Monopolies of Raw Materials," in Arthur Salter and Arthur Porritt (eds.), *The Causes of War: Economic, Industrial, Racial, Religious, Scientific, and Political* (New York: The Macmillan Company, 1932), p. 185
"Conflicts of Principle in Drafting a Trade Charter" (1947) **25** *Foreign Affairs* 612
Visser, L.-E., "La clause de 'la national la plus favorisé' dans les traits de commerce (deuxième article)" (1902) **4** *Revue de droit international et de législation comparée* 159
Viton, Albert, *The International Sugar Agreements: Promise and Reality* (West LaFayette, Ind.: Purdue University Press, 2004)
von Graevenitz, Fritz Georg, "Changing Visions of the World Sugar Market in the Great Depression" (2008) **15** *European Review of History* 727
Walker, Herman, "The International Law of Commodity Agreements" (1963) **28** *Law and Contemporary Problems* 392
Wallace, Benjamin Bruce and Lynn Ramsay Edminster, *International Control of Raw Materials* (Washington DC: Brookings Institution, 1930)
Walters, F. P., *A History of the League of Nations* (London: Oxford University Press, 1952)

Weber, Max, *Roman Agrarian History: The Political Economy of Ancient Rome*, Richard Frank (trans.), (Claremont, Calif.: Regina Books, 2010 [1891])

Webster C. K., and S. Herbert, *The League of Nations in Theory and Practice* (London: Allen & Unwin, 1933)

Weiler, Joseph H. H., "The Rule of Lawyers and the Ethos of Diplomats: Reflections on the Internal and External Legitimacy of WTO Dispute Settlement" (2001) **35** *Journal of World Trade* 191

Weiss, Friedl, "From Havana to Marrakesh: Treaty Making for Trade," in Jan Klabbers and René Lefeber (eds.), *Essays on the Law of Treaties: A Collection of Essays in Honour of Bert Vierdag* (The Hague: Martinus Nijhoff Publishers, 1998), p. 155

Weiss, Thomas G., *Multilateral Development in Diplomacy in UNCTAD: The Lessons of Group Negotiations, 1964–84* (London: Macmillan, 1986)

Weiss, Thomas G. *et al.* (eds.), *UN Voices: The Struggle for Development and Social Justice* (Bloomington, Ind.: Indiana University Press, 2005)

Welby, Lord *et al.* (eds.), *Report of the Proceedings of the International Free Trade Congress, London, August, 1908* (London: Unwin Bros. and Cobden Club, 1908)

Westlake, John, *International Law. Part I: Peace*, 1st edn. (Cambridge: Cambridge University Press, 1904)

International Law. Part II: Peace, 2nd edn. (Cambridge: Cambridge University Press, 1910)

Whalley, John (ed.), *Developing Countries and the Global Trading System*, 2 vols. (London: Macmillan, 1989)

Wiedenfeld, Kurt, *Cartels and Combines* (Geneva: League of Nations, 1927)

Wilcox, Clair, *A Charter for World Trade* (New York: Arno Press, 1949)

Wilgress, Edward Dana, *A New Attempt at Internationalism: The International Trade Conferences and the Charter a Study of Means and Ends* (doctoral thesis, University of Geneva, 1949)

Wilk, Kurt, "International Affairs: The International Sugar Régime" (1939) **33** *American Political Science Review* 860

Wilkinson, Rorden and James Scott, "Developing Country Participation in the GATT: A Reassessment" (2008) **7**:3 *World Trade Review* 473

Wilson, Florence, *The Origins of the League Covenant: Documentary History of its Drafting* (London: Leonard and Virginia Woolf at The Hogarth Press, 1928)

Wolf, Eric R., *Europe and the People Without History* (Berkeley, Calif.: University of California Press, 1982 [1997])

Wolfe, Robert and Matthew Mendelsohn, "Embedded Liberalism in the Global Era: Would Citizens Support a Grand New Compromise?" (2004) **59** *International Journal* 261

Wolfrum, Rüdiger, "International Administrative Unions," in Rüdiger Wolfrum (ed.), *The Max Planck Encyclopedia of Public International Law* (Oxford: Oxford University Press, 2008), online edition: www.mpepil.com

Wood, Ellen Meiksins, "The Separation of the Economic and Political in Capitalism" (1981) **127** *New Left Review* 66

Woolf, Leonard S., *International Government* (New York: Brentano's, 1916)
World Trade Organization, *Guide to GATT Law and Practice: Analytical Index*, 6th edn. (Geneva: World Trade Organization, 1995)
Wright, Philip G., *Sugar in Relation to the Tariff* (New York: McGraw Hill Book Company, 1924)
Wynia, Gary W., "Opening Late-industrializing Economies: Lessons from Argentina and Australia (1990) **23** *Policy Sciences* 185
Yusuf, Abdulqawi A., "The Legal Framework for Stable, Remunerative and Equitable Commodity Prices in International Trade," in Detlev Christian Dicke and Ernst-Ulrich Petersmann (eds.), *Foreign Trade in the Present and a New International Economic Order* (Fribourg: University Press, 1988), p. 63
Zammit Cutajar, Michael (ed.), *UNCTAD and the North–South Dialogue: The First Twenty Years. Essays in memory of W. R. Malinowski* (Oxford: Pergamon Press, 1985)
Zebel, Sydney H., "Fair Trade: An English Reaction to the Breakdown of the Cobden Treaty System" (1940) **12** *The Journal of Modern History* 161
Zeiler, Thomas W., *Free Trade, Free World: The Advent of GATT* (Chapel Hill, NC: University of North Carolina Press, 1999)
Zimmern, Alfred, *The League of Nations and the Rule of Law 1918–1935*, 2nd edn. (London: Macmillan, 1939)
Zumbansen, Peer, "Defining the Space of Transnational Law: Legal Theory, Global Governance and Legal Pluralism" (2012) **21** *Transnational Law & Contemporary Problems* 305

Index

CAMBRIDGE STUDIES IN INTERNATIONAL AND COMPARATIVE LAW

Books in the series

Sugar and the Making of International Trade Law
Michael Fakhri

Strategically-created Treaty Conflicts and the Politics of International Law
Surabhi Ranganathan

Investment Treaty Arbitration as Public International Law: Procedural Aspects and Implications
Eric De Brabandere

The New Entrants Problem in International Fisheries Law
Andrew Serdy

Substantive Protection under Investment Treaties: A Legal and Economic Analysis
Jonathan Bonnitcha

Popular Governance of Post-Conflict Reconstruction: The Role of International Law
Matthew Saul

Evolution of International Environmental Regimes: The Case of Climate Change
Simone Schiele

Judges, Law and War: The Judicial Development of International Humanitarian Law
Shane Darcy

Religious Offence and Human Rights: The Implications of Defamation of Religions
Lorenz Langer

Forum Shopping in International Adjudication: The Role of Preliminary Objections
Luiz Eduardo Ribeiro Salles

International Law and the Arctic
Michael Byers

Cooperation in the Law of Transboundary Water Resources
Christina Leb

Underwater Cultural Heritage and International Law
Sarah Dromgoole

State Responsibility: The General Part
James Crawford

The Origins of International Investment Law
Kate Miles

The Crime of Aggression under the Rome Statute of the International Criminal Court
Carrie McDougall

Crimes against Peace and International Law
Kirsten Sellars

The Non-legal in International Law
Fleur Johns

Armed Conflict and Displacement: The Protection of Refugees and Displaced Persons under International Humanitarian Law
Mélanie Jacques

Foreign Investment and the Environment in International Law
Jorge Viñuales

The Human Rights Treaty Obligations of Peacekeepers
Kjetil Larsen

Cyberwarfare and the Laws of War
Heather Harrison Dinniss

The Right to Reparation in International Law for Victims of Armed Conflict
Christine Evans

Global Public Interest in International Investment Law
Andreas Kulick

State Immunity in International Law
Xiaodong Yang

Reparations and Victim Support in the International Criminal Court
Conor McCarthy

Reducing Genocide to Law: Definition, Meaning, and the Ultimate Crime
Payam Akhavan

Decolonizing International Law: Development, Economic Growth and the Politics of Universality
Sundhya Pahuja

Complicity and the Law of State Responsibility
Helmut Philipp Aust

State Control over Private Military and Security Companies in Armed Conflict
Hannah Tonkin

"Fair and Equitable Treatment" in International Investment Law
Roland Kläger

The UN and Human Rights: Who Guards the Guardians?
Guglielmo Verdirame

Sovereign Defaults before International Courts and Tribunals
Michael Waibel

Making the Law of the Sea: A Study in the Development of International Law
James Harrison

Science and the Precautionary Principle in International Courts and Tribunals: Expert Evidence, Burden of Proof and Finality
Caroline E. Foster

Transition from Illegal Regimes in International Law
Yaël Ronen

Access to Asylum: International Refugee Law and the Globalisation of Migration Control
Thomas Gammeltoft-Hansen

Trading Fish, Saving Fish: The Interaction between Regimes in International Law
Margaret Young

The Individual in the International Legal System: Continuity and Change in International Law
Kate Parlett

The Participation of States in International Organisations: The Role of Human Rights and Democracy
Alison Duxbury

"Armed Attack" and Article 51 of the UN Charter: Evolutions in Customary Law and Practice
Tom Ruys

Science and Risk Regulation in International Law
Jacqueline Peel

Theatre of the Rule of Law: Transnational Legal Intervention in Theory and Practice
Stephen Humphreys

The Public International Law Theory of Hans Kelsen: Believing in Universal Law
Jochen von Bernstorff

Vicarious Liability in Tort: A Comparative Perspective
Paula Giliker

Legal Personality in International Law
Roland Portmann

Legitimacy and Legality in International Law: An Interactional Account
Jutta Brunnée and Stephen J. Toope

The Concept of Non-International Armed Conflict in International Humanitarian Law
Anthony Cullen

The Challenge of Child Labour in International Law
Franziska Humbert

Shipping Interdiction and the Law of the Sea
Douglas Guilfoyle

International Courts and Environmental Protection
Tim Stephens

Legal Principles in WTO Disputes
Andrew D. Mitchell

War Crimes in Internal Armed Conflicts
Eve La Haye

Humanitarian Occupation
Gregory H. Fox

The International Law of Environmental Impact Assessment: Process, Substance and Integration
Neil Craik

The Law and Practice of International Territorial Administration: Versailles to Iraq and Beyond
Carsten Stahn

Cultural Products and the World Trade Organization
Tania Voon

United Nations Sanctions and the Rule of Law
Jeremy Farrall

National Law in WTO Law: Effectiveness and Good Governance in the World Trading System
Sharif Bhuiyan

The Threat of Force in International Law
Nikolas Stürchler

Indigenous Rights and United Nations Standards
Alexandra Xanthaki

International Refugee Law and Socio-Economic Rights
Michelle Foster

The Protection of Cultural Property in Armed Conflict
Roger O'Keefe

Interpretation and Revision of International Boundary Decisions
Kaiyan Homi Kaikobad

Multinationals and Corporate Social Responsibility: Limitations and Opportunities in International Law
Jennifer A. Zerk

Judiciaries within Europe: A Comparative Review
John Bell

Law in Times of Crisis: Emergency Powers in Theory and Practice
Oren Gross and Fionnuala Ní Aoláin

Vessel-Source Marine Pollution: The Law and Politics of International Regulation
Alan Tan

Enforcing Obligations Erga Omnes in International Law
Christian J. Tams

Non-Governmental Organisations in International Law
Anna-Karin Lindblom

Democracy, Minorities and International Law
Steven Wheatley

Prosecuting International Crimes: Selectivity and the International Law Regime
Robert Cryer

Compensation for Personal Injury in English, German and Italian Law: A Comparative Outline
Basil Markesinis, Michael Coester, Guido Alpa, and Augustus Ullstein

Dispute Settlement in the UN Convention on the Law of the Sea
Natalie Klein

The International Protection of Internally Displaced Persons
Catherine Phuong

Imperialism, Sovereignty and the Making of International Law
Antony Anghie

Necessity, Proportionality and the Use of Force by States
Judith Gardam

International Legal Argument in the Permanent Court of International Justice: The Rise of the International Judiciary
Ole Spiermann

Great Powers and Outlaw States: Unequal Sovereigns in the International Legal Order
Gerry Simpson

Local Remedies in International Law
C. F. Amerasinghe

Reading Humanitarian Intervention: Human Rights and the Use of Force in International Law
Anne Orford

Conflict of Norms in Public International Law: How WTO Law Relates to Other Rules of International Law
Joost Pauwelyn

Transboundary Damage in International Law
Hanqin Xue

European Criminal Procedures
Edited by Mireille Delmas-Marty and John Spencer

The Accountability of Armed Opposition Groups in International Law
Liesbeth Zegveld

Sharing Transboundary Resources: International Law and Optimal Resource Use
Eyal Benvenisti

International Human Rights and Humanitarian Law
René Provost

Remedies Against International Organisations
Karel Wellens

Diversity and Self-determination in International Law
Karen Knop

The Law of Internal Armed Conflict
Lindsay Moir

International Commercial Arbitration and African States: Practice, Participation and Institutional Development
Amazu A. Asouzu

The Enforceability of Promises in European Contract Law
James Gordley

International Law in Antiquity
David J. Bederman

Money Laundering: A New International Law Enforcement Model
Guy Stessens

Good Faith in European Contract Law
Reinhard Zimmermann and Simon Whittaker

On Civil Procedure
J. A. Jolowicz

Trusts: A Comparative Study
Maurizio Lupoi

The Right to Property in Commonwealth Constitutions
Tom Allen

International Organizations before National Courts
August Reinisch

The Changing International Law of High Seas Fisheries
Francisco Orrego Vicuña

Trade and the Environment: A Comparative Study of EC and US Law
Damien Geradin

Unjust Enrichment: A Study of Private Law and Public Values
Hanoch Dagan

Religious Liberty and International Law in Europe
Malcolm D. Evans

Ethics and Authority in International Law
Alfred P. Rubin

Sovereignty Over Natural Resources: Balancing Rights and Duties
Nico Schrijver

The Polar Regions and the Development of International Law
Donald R. Rothwell

Fragmentation and the International Relations of Micro-states: Self-determination and Statehood
Jorri Duursma

Principles of the Institutional Law of International Organizations
C. F. Amerasinghe